D0309155

The Service Economy

The Service Economy

A GEOGRAPHICAL APPROACH

SVEN ILLERIS
Roskilde University, Denmark

JOHN WILEY & SONS

Chichester · New York · Brisbane · Toronto · Singapore

Other Wiley Editorial Offices

John Wiley & Sons, Inc., 605 Third Avenue,
New York, NY 10158-0012, USA

Jacaranda Wiley Ltd, 33 Park Road, Milton,
Queensland 4064, Australia

John Wiley & Sons (Canada) Ltd, 22 Worcester Road,
Rexdale, Ontario M9W 1L1, Canada

John Wiley & Sons (SEA) Pte Ltd, 37 Jalan Pemimpin #05-04,
Block B, Union Industrial Building, Singapore 2057

Library of Congress Cataloging-in-Publication Data

Illeris, Sven.
    The service economy: a geographical approach / Sven Illeris.
        p.   cm.
    Includes bibliographical references and index.
    ISBN 0-471-96618-5 (alk. paper)
    1. Service industries.   I. Title.
  HD9980.5.I5   1996
338.4–dc20   96-5962
                                                      CIP

British Library Cataloguing in Publication Data

A catalogue record for this book is available from the British Library

ISBN 0 471 96618 5

Typeset in 10/12pt Times by MHL Typesetting Ltd, Coventry
Printed and bound in Great Britain by
This book is printed on acid-free paper responsibly manufactured from sustainable
forestation, for which at least two trees are planted for each one used for paper production.

Contents

Preface

The study of service activities, almost non-existent 20 years ago, has made great progress over the last 10 years. It is now time to attempt to synthesize at least some of the many studies that have been carried out, to present the knowledge which we think we have about services, and to add some original contributions to the study of the many questions that we need to understand better. That is the purpose of this book.

When, in the 1950s, I studied geography at the University of Copenhagen, this discipline was strongly orientated towards empirical research, but theoretically weak. For me, it was a kind of revelation when I discovered that the Estonian geographer Edgar Kant, as a refugee working at the neighbouring University of Lund in Sweden, had brought with him the theoretical understanding of the otherwise forgotten German geographer Walter Christaller, dealing with the location of service activities. Like others in the 1960s, I worked on central place theory, but gradually this subject was exhausted, and the research interest in service activities died out.

However, my work on regional problems in the Danish central government administration brought me back to the location of service activities several times, first in connection with the 1970 Local Government Reform, later in connection with the regional planning preparations starting up in the second half of the 1970s.

In the 1980s, international research interest in service activities and their location revived. This was due to the increasing share of services in total employment and production, in many countries approaching 70 per cent. In addition, there was a dawning understanding that some service activities played a much more important role both in total economic development and in regional development than was previously thought.

On the strength of my former activities, I was prepared to take up the thread. As a result of my work with the FAST team (Forecasting and Assessment in Science and Technology) of the Commission of the European Communities, I wrote a survey on *Services and Regions in Europe* (Illeris 1989e). (A Danish version, focusing on the role of services in local government economic development policies, was published by the Local Governments' Research Institute in Copenhagen in 1987.)

The present book is also a survey, but with the wider scope of discussing the geography and economics of service activities within the perspective of an emerging service society. It is primarily based on research published from 1987 to 1995, but of course, older 'classics' are taken into consideration, too. The book takes into account literature in English, French, German, Dutch, and the

Scandinavian languages, and thus aims at making the important research progress in other languages known to the English-reading public.

The book's primary target group is academics and graduate students working on services, but I have attempted to write it in such a style that anyone with a basic knowledge of social and economic concepts should be able to read it.

It has been fascinating to work in this field, not only because of the pioneering character of service studies, but also because it is an area of fruitful cooperation: cooperation between disciplines; cooperation between different schools which have avoided the sterile entrenchment that characterized the social sciences in the 1970s (without hiding that there are differences of opinion); and cooperation between researchers from different countries—in Western Europe partly organized in the research network RESER (Réseau Services et Espace) of which I am a member.

Most of the writing has taken place in Lyons, where the Centre d'Echange et d'Information sur les Activités de Service (CEDES) of the French National Centre for Scientific Research hosted me for seven months, and where Joël Bonamy, André Barcet and Yves Manenti discussed my drafts and gave me much inspiration. I am also indebted to the Danish Social Science Research Council which contributed financially to this stay, and to the Department of Geography and International Development Studies at the Roskilde University which is my home base. Finally, my thanks are due to Jon Sundbo at our interdisciplinary Centre of Service Studies at Roskilde University, as well as to Peter Sjøholt at the Norwegian School of Economics in Bergen, who have both commented on earlier drafts. Roger Leys improved my English. Of course, the responsibility for all weaknesses is mine alone.

Sven Illeris

Part I

WHAT IS IT ALL ABOUT?

1 Introduction

This introductory chapter serves three purposes. First, the premise of the book will be documented, namely that service activities are rapidly becoming the most important economic activities in the Western world. Second, it will be explained more precisely what this book is about and what has been left out. And third, an outline of the book and its main questions is presented.

Table 1.1 and Figure 1.1 show employment in the service sector (for definition, see Chapter 3), as per cent of total employment, in a number of countries in the period 1890–1990.

Table 1.1 and Figure 1.1 show a steady growth in the service share of total employment over the last century, in economically developed countries. In the most 'tertiarized' economy, the United States, the share is now well over 70 per cent.

Another way to illustrate the development of service activities is to look at the employment in service occupations—the jobs of individuals irrespective of what organization and sector they are working in. The best time series of data is from the United States, shown in Table 1.2.

The recent development in service occupations is shown in Table 1.3 for a number of countries. Service occupations, too, employ a regularly increasing share of the total labour force. Most of the recent growth has happened in professional and technical occupations.

As regards the 'production' of services, their share of total GDP must be considered an extremely crude statistic, since it is not possible to measure the output of many service activities meaningfully—see discussion in Chapter 5. However, Table 1.4 shows the share of the service sector in the GDP at current prices in the EU countries, the United States and Japan 1960–90, while Figure 1.2 shows the 1948–85 development in the United States at constant (1982) prices.

Table 1.1. Employment in the service sector 1890–1992 in five countries. *Sources:* To 1980: M. Ott (1987), The Growing Share of Services in the US Economy: Degeneration or Evolution? *Review*, Federal Reserve Bank of St Louis, June/July, 5–22. From 1980: OECD: Labour Force Statistics.

			\% of total employment				
	1890	1950	1960	1970	1980	1980	1992
France	27	25.9	39.5	47.2	55.5	55.4	65.8
Germany	25	36.4	32.2	42.8	52.7	51.0	58.5
Japan	13	33.7	41.8	47.4	54.7	54.2	59.0
United Kingdom	31	45.4	48.5	53.6	61.1	59.7	71.3
United States	30	54.7	57.1	62.3	67.1	65.9	72.5

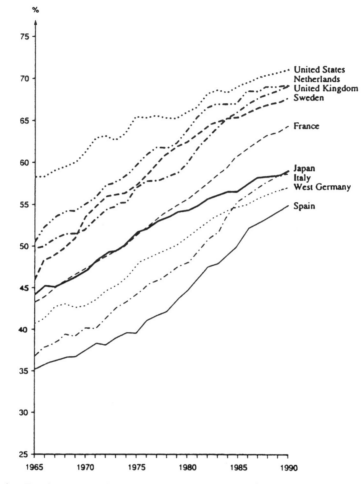

Figure 1.1.   Employment in the service sector, as per cent of total employment 1965–1990. *Source*: Reproduced with permission from J. Gadrey (1992a) *L'Economie des Services*, Paris: La Découverte.

Table 1.2.   Employment in service occupations, USA 1900–1980. *Source:* M. Ott (1987)

	% of total employment
1900	26.7
1910	30.9
1920	32.9
1930	39.2
1940	42.8
1950	47.1
1960	56.3
1970	60.4
1980	65.9

Table 1.3. Employment in service occupations, six countries since 1983. *Source:* ILO, *Yearbook of Labour Statistics 1993.*

		% of total employment		
Belgium	1983	61.0	1990	63.4
Denmark	1984	62.9	1991	65.1
Japan	1983	53.6	1992	58.2
Sweden	1986	65.8	1992	69.6
United States	1983	68.1	1991	71.1
W. Germany	1984	59.6	1991	63.5

Table 1.4. Value added in services in the EU, USA and Japan 1960–1990. *Source:* F. Prosche (1993), *Vers une Europe post-industrielle?* Reproduced by permission of Economica, Paris.

Country	Services (% total value added)		
	1960	1980	1990
Belgium	52.6	63.8	68.1
W. Germany	41.0	55.5	59.2
France	50.4	62.0	68.0
Italy	46.4	55.2	63.8
Luxemburg	41.2	58.7	61.0[a]
Netherlands	46.7	63.7	64.2
Denmark	46.9	70.2	71.7
Ireland	52.4	55.4	57.8[a]
United Kingdom	53.8	61.5	69.2
Greece	56.9	56.5	62.1
Spain	45.2	54.3	61.0
Portugal	42.1	49.5	55.7[a]
EC	47.7	58.5	64.4
USA	57.9	63.8	68.8[b]
Japan	42.7	54.4	55.7

[a] 1989
[b] 1987

With the above-mentioned reservations, Table 1.4 and Figure 1.2 indicate that the share of service 'production' in the total GDP tends to increase, though much more in current than in constant prices (since service prices increase more than goods prices, see discussion in Chapter 4). The share is now about 70 per cent in several countries.

The share of service activities in the total economy, however measured, is highest in the 'richest' countries, those with the highest GDP per capita, and increases over time as does GDP per capita. This is illustrated by Figure 1.3, in which employment shares for a large number of countries have been plotted against the same countries' GDP per capita. With the exception of the East European countries, the correlation is clear, though not very narrow—at the same level of GDP per capita, countries may have rather different service shares, as will be

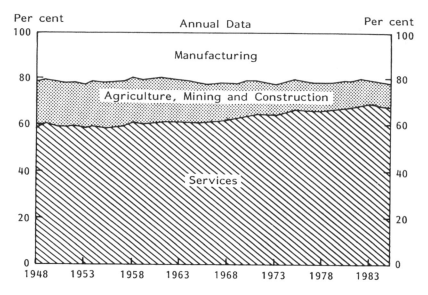

Figure 1.2. Distribution of real GNP (in 1982 dollars) in the United States 1948–1985. *Source:* M. Ott (1987)

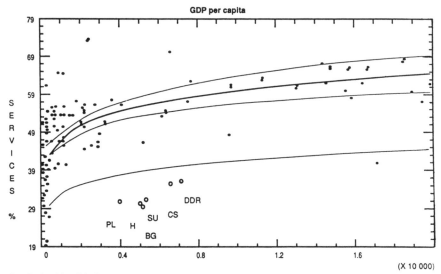

SU : Soviet Union; CS : Czechoslovakia; H : Hungary; PL : Poland; BG : Bulgaria; DDR : Eastern Germany, (GDR before the unification of Germany).

Figure 1.3. Share of service sector and level of GDP per capita. *Source:* OECD, Paris (1991), *Services in Central and Eastern European Countries*. Reproduced by permission of the OECD

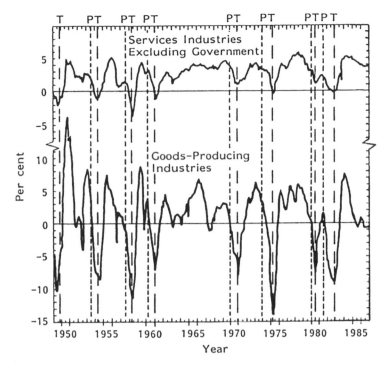

Figure 1.4. Growth rate in employment in the services industries and goods-producing industries, USA 1948–1986. Growth rates are annual rates based on the ratio of the current month's employment to the average level of employment during the previous 12 months, by using seasonally adjusted data. Vertical lines are business cycle peaks (P) and troughs (T). *Source:* Quinn (1988). Reprinted with permission from *Technology in Services: Policies for Growth, Trade and Employment.* Copyright © 1988 by the National Academy of Sciences. Courtesy of the National Academy Press, Washington, DC

discussed in Chapter 12. And, of course, it says nothing about what is cause and what is effect. Anyhow, the reservations concerning the GDP must be kept in mind. Furthermore, per definition, activities carried out in households ('the informal economy') are excluded—and these activities are substantial, as discussed in Chapter 4.

A particular characteristic of the development of service employment over time is that it is less sensitive to business cycle fluctuations than other types of employment. This is illustrated for the United States in 1948–86 in Figure 1.4. (This figure excludes public services which are even less sensitive to fluctuations.)

In *The Economist* of 20 May 1995, it is shown that service output also declined less than industrial output in the recession of the early 1990s.

There are several reasons behind this relative insensitivity to business cycle fluctuations. Some, but not all, services serve relatively basic needs that are rather inelastic. In particular, they are inelastic in the short run, because they cannot be stored, as discussed in Chapter 2. In some countries, service wages are less rigid than those of goods producers, and employers may cut wages rather than fire personnel in bad times. Some service sectors have served as refuges during recessions (e.g. retailing). Finally, public services are relatively stable (not included in the figure).

To summarize: the share of service activities in the total economy has increased rapidly in all economically developed countries and is now close to two thirds, whether measured in terms of sectoral or occupational employment or sectoral GDP (though in terms of GDP at constant prices, the share has increased only slightly). The reasons for the growth will be discussed in Chapters 4 and 6.

WHAT THIS BOOK IS ABOUT

As stated in the preface, the purpose of this book is to survey at least a part of the many studies which over the last decade or two have been carried out on services, and to discuss them. However, it is hardly possible for one scholar to cover all aspects of service research. Out of the general need for better understanding of the services, some more detailed questions and approaches have been carved out for discussion, while others have been excluded.

The choice of what has been included is a rather pragmatic one. Some questions have—to a certain degree by chance—been studied by groups of researchers in a more or less integrated way, other questions by other groups of researchers. I have included a number of questions on which there is a more or less coherent research tradition, but the delimitation can hardly be said to be theoretically founded.

My point of departure has been that of a geographer. Where are the service activities, why are they there, what are their geographical implications? But the book is not confined to these questions. Since research on services is so young a study, geographers involved in it have felt that they could not take a more general theory on service activities as their starting point. They had to work together with other social scientists on the creation of a general understanding, including the role of services in the transformation of our societies into a 'service society'. Hence, this book devotes many pages to non-geographical questions. It may be expressed this way: in the universe of not-understood phenomena, service activities form one continent, only slightly explored from different angles. The approach made by geographers to some degree overlaps approaches made by regional economists and macroeconomists. Other approaches have been made by microeconomists, management researchers and sociologists. However, the overlapping of the former explorations makes it natural to discuss their results together, with less reference to the latter approaches.

Early service research focused on services to households. Since the mid-1980s, however, attention has shifted towards producer services and their role in transforming economic activities. While by no means ignoring the problems of household services, this book—primarily based on recent research—will give a certain priority to producer services.

The book focuses primarily on questions which concern all or many services. This means that the substantial, but rather specialized research on such subsectors as retailing, transport, finance, public services, and tourism has not been considered.

The discussion is confined to the economically developed part of the world: Western and Eastern Europe, North America, Japan, Australia, and New Zealand. For most of these areas, the shorter term 'the Western world' is usually applied, while East-Central Europe has been given separate treatment in Chapter 12. The Third World can hardly be called an emerging service society, and the research on services there has followed other directions, see for instance Riddle (1986). Of course, some Third World countries are rapidly developing, with a corresponding importance in respect to service activities, e.g. Singapore and Taiwan (Selya 1994).

AN OUTLINE OF THE BOOK AND ITS MAIN QUESTIONS

In the remainder of Part I, the basic concepts are discussed. Chapter 2 is devoted to discussions of the nature of service activities and their role in economic development. It is stressed that services are extremely heterogeneous and hence, wherever possible, different categories of services should be distinguished. Classification systems are presented and discussed in Chapter 3.

In Part II, the development of services is discussed, mainly from an economic point of view. How have production and employment changed, how can they be measured meaningfully, what are the consequences in terms of labour force qualifications? Chapter 4 presents data on the development of the main classes of services, and discusses changes in services produced for households. Research on this sector has encountered major problems connected with the concepts of productivity and effectiveness, which are discussed in Chapter 5. Chapter 6 deals with the development of services produced for firms. Among other questions, it is discussed whether the apparent growth of the producer service sector is a statistical illusion, due to externalization of service activities which previously were produced internally in the user firms. Finally, Chapter 7 focuses on the consequences of service development for changes in skills and labour market conditions.

Part III takes up the geographical aspects of service activities. Where do they locate, and why? What are the consequences for regional economic development? Most of this part focuses on the inter-urban question—in what cities and towns? Chapter 8 discusses recent changes in service location and summarizes a number of recent case studies which investigate the areas they serve. In Chapter 9, the factors of location are discussed, such as the need to locate close to customers or to sources of information inputs, the changes which improvements in transport and telecommunications bring about in this need for proximity, and the dependence of some service activities on the possibilities of recruiting skilled personnel. In Chapter 10, the influence of service activities on regional economic development is discussed, and regional policies based on services are suggested. And in Chapter 11, the detailed location of service activities inside cities is described, and intra-urban factors of location discussed.

Part IV widens the geographical approach to an international one. In Chapter 12, the differences between service development in different economically developed countries are discussed. Special attention is given to the particular processes taking place in East-Central Europe. In Chapter 13, the volume and forms of international trade in services are described, and barriers to international trade are discussed.

There is no overall summary of the book, but each chapter is provided with a brief summary of its main findings, and Part V attempts to draw together conclusions in two ways: Chapter 14 offers a broad perspective on the now emerging economy in which service activities play a crucial role, and which is therefore labelled a 'service society'. And in Chapter 15, some findings which were unexpected in terms of current 'conventional wisdom' are emphasized, and needs for further research are discussed.

As an appendix, three case studies of business services are presented which illustrate many of the discussions of the book: engineering consultants, computer services, and management consultants.

2 The Nature and Role of Services

The purpose of this chapter is twofold. First, the nature and definition of services are discussed. This discussion is difficult, but at the same time fruitful, since it has led to an improved understanding of the nature of service activities, and to the need to reconsider basic economic concepts. Second, it is discussed whether services can be said to create wealth, and how services influence economic development.

THE MEANINGS OF THE WORD 'SERVICES'

The noun 'service' (from Latin servus = slave) is used with several different meanings. The *Oxford English Dictionary* mentions 38 meanings, but only 4 are relevant for this book:

1   The broadest sense seems to be: help, benefit, advantage, use. This includes physical objects, for instance food. Gershuny and Miles (1983) often use the word in this way: 'in a sense, the *final* products of the economic system are *all* services'. However, this seems to be a rather unusual application of the word, and an unpractical one, given the other meanings also ascribed to the word.
2   A service may more often mean a *product* (a commodity, an output or outcome) *of an immaterial nature*, for instance a consultation, a sale, a journey, a withdrawal of money from one's bank account, a concert, research. As will be discussed later in this chapter, it is essential to stress that service products are different from goods (material products). When the national accounts mention services, it is in this sense (including the use of dwellings which is understood as a service product).

   A service—in this sense—may be the result of work, of a service activity, which is the fourth sense of the word 'service', to which we return later. But it may also come about only with the help of a physical tool or infrastructure.
3   A *tool* which helps create a service product may also be called a service. Thus, telephone booths and bus stop shelters are 'services', as are cash dispensing machines helping me to draw money from my bank account. The most important service product produced exclusively with the help of a physical tool is the use of dwellings, but these tools—houses—are rarely called services.
4   The work which produces service products is called a service or *service activity*. Waiters, drivers, bank staff, doctors and other professionals perform service activities. Service activities may be carried out as paid work in firms or public institutions (the formal economy), or alternatively as unpaid service work in households, voluntary associations and so on (the informal economy).

Work in the formal economy may be classified according to the main output of the firm, establishment or institution in which it takes place: if the main outputs are service products, then the employment is registered as taking place in a service sector or industry (irrespective of the tasks which the different employees individually carry out). On the other hand, work may be classified into occupations, according to the tasks of each individual. Thus, inside the manufacturing sector, there are a number of people having service occupations, such as engineers, drivers and secretaries. Unfortunately, statistical information about occupations is scarce.

This book will mainly focus on service activities (also called tertiary activities), but this will often make it necessary to discuss service products, too.

THE DEFINITION AND BASIC NATURE OF SERVICE ACTIVITIES

The traditional definition, on which official statistics are based, is a residual one: *service (or tertiary) activities are those which do not produce or modify physical goods*. Their products are immaterial and cannot be stored, transported, or owned—as *The Economist* says, you can sell them and buy them, but you cannot drop them on your feet.

This definition has come under heavy attack in recent years, though Dale (1994) stresses that for consumers, it is of real importance whether after a purchase they have a good that can be stored and may be sold again, or not. Theoretically, this means that typical services have no exchange value, only a use value, and many authors emphasize that services satisfy needs (Grönroos 1990).

However, it is unsatisfactory that activities which in developed countries form much more than half of the total economy can only be defined in a negative way, as a residual.

One line of criticism stresses the fact that service activities cover an extremely wide range. Total or average figures for the whole tertiary sector may for this reason tell very little, the image of such a large and heterogeneous sector must be more detailed if we are to discuss the problems in a meaningful way. There is an urgent need for subdivisions, a question which is discussed in Chapter 3. Some critics even argue that the concept of 'service activities' is useless because of this variation (e.g. Castells 1989).

Another line of criticism tries to reach a more positive and more substantial definition, which implies that it is meaningful to keep 'services' as one class of activities.

Most positive definitions of service activities characterize them as *relations between service producers and service users*. Among these attempts, Hill's definition (1977) has gradually been recognized as the most satisfactory one, though heavy to read. It is basically a definition of service products but mentions the activities that create them: *a service may be defined as a change in the condition of a person, or of a good belonging to some economic unit, which is*

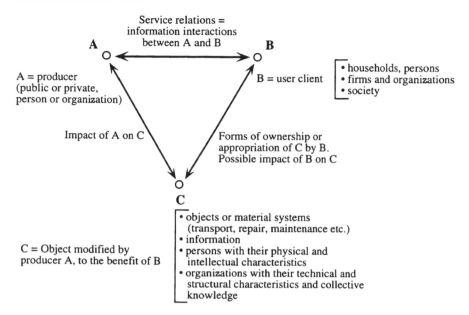

Figure 2.1. Service producers, service users, service objects, and the relations between them. *Source:* Reproduced and translated with permission from J. Gadrey (1992a) *L'Economie des Services*, Paris: La Découverte.

brought about as the result of the activity of some other economic unit, with the prior agreement of the former person or economic unit.

Another definition in this line has been suggested by Mayère (1988) who says that a change in the condition of a person or a thing cannot always be observed: service activities are actions which concern a person, a thing, or information, and which require that a relation of exchange is established with the user.

Some examples of typical service activities may illustrate these definitions. Thus, teaching will change the condition of students—they will know or understand more—as the result of the activity of their teacher. Medical treatment will change the health condition of the patient, as the result of the activity of the doctor. Trade will change the ownership condition of a good belonging formerly to the seller, afterwards to the buyer, as a result of their trading activity.

Gadrey (1992a) illustrates the definition graphically in Figure 2.1: the service activity is an activity through which the service producer A changes the condition of an object (thing, information or personal characteristic) C belonging to the service user B, on the latter's request. There are many types of As, Bs and Cs as well as many types of relations, as will be discussed in this chapter and the following one.

IMPORTANT CHARACTERISTICS OF SERVICE ACTIVITIES, AND THEIR IMPLICATIONS

The most important characteristics of service activities should be stressed, even if they are not explicitly included in Hill's definition. Some of these characteristics have been recognized for a long time. But recent French research has shown that the derived consequences of these characteristics are much more fundamental than anybody had realized a decade ago, and make revisions of basic economic thinking necessary (Barcet 1987, 1991; Bressand & Nicolaïdis 1988; de Bandt 1994b, 1995).

First, in the typical service relation, the producer and the user are both more or less involved in the 'change of condition', and hence must be present at the same time and place, face to face (the 'uno actu principle')—a fact with many geographical consequences, though contemporary telecommunications may modify it, see Chapter 9. This integrated process is very different from the production, storage, transport and selling of material goods, a process with many isolated steps, and in which the consumer's role is totally independent of production.

Second, in typical service activities, the user participates in the production. In French, a practical word has been coined for service production with user participation—'servuction': the patient has to tell the doctor about the symptoms, the student must actively absorb the teaching. If the concert listener falls asleep, the music does not change his/her condition. The clients of a management consultant firm must—as discussed by Tordoir (1993), and see the Appendix—combine specific knowledge about their needs, conditions and applications with the general knowledge of the consultant. All this means that typical service products are unique, there are never two identical relations. It also means that neither party can know in advance exactly what the service product will be. (Some authors talk of an 'information asymmetry'—the user will know less in advance about the service product than the producer—but even the producer cannot be very certain about the relation either.)

Third, the relation character of service activities means that they are typically labour-intensive, with limited possibilities for economies of scale, and that their quality depends heavily on the qualifications of the labour involved. As a consequence, it is difficult to apply the concept of 'labour' without characterizing its qualifications. And it is difficult to increase labour productivity in the traditional sense, as discussed further in Chapter 5.

Fourth, a service product as 'a change of condition' is fundamentally different from a material product, a good. In many cases, it cannot be clearly delimited—for instance in the case of teaching. This means that it makes little sense to measure the product, and hence that the basic economic concepts of GDP and productivity are difficult to apply. (It is often said that the service product is 'ephemeral' or perishable—it is produced and consumed simultaneously. But this is not necessarily the case if Hill's definition is applied: the change of condition may be very durable, as in the case of teaching.) However, the distinction between the immediate 'output' and the long-term 'effect' is often difficult to make. This question, as well as the GDP and productivity problems, will be discussed in Chapter 5.

Fifth, the change in the condition of the person or thing is usually irreversible—one may think of a surgical operation, as mentioned by Gadrey (1994b).

These characteristics of typical services mean that the basic economic concept of 'market' is not really applicable (de Bandt 1994b, 1995). There are no well-defined products about which supply and demand can meet and for which a standard price can emerge. Both parties must engage in relations in a state of uncertainty, and some degree of mutual trust is required. Of course, the parties will try to reduce the uncertainty, for instance by agreement on the use of certain methods in accounting, or the use of staff with certain qualifications, or the use of material support—e.g. hotel rooms—with certain specifications, see Barcet and Bonamy (1994a). States also protect customers in some of these opaque markets, for instance by requiring authorized service providers to have specific qualifications (physicians, lawyers). A typical 'sale' of a service is not defined as a shift in ownership, but as an agreement to work in order to bring about a change in the condition. The price-building of services has not been sufficiently studied, but often tends to reflect the input costs (number of man-hours). It seems, however, that customers increasingly try to assess in each case what the service products are worth for them (a use-value or utility) and are willing to pay accordingly (de Bandt 1995).

While neo-classical and Keynesian economics, as reflected in current national account systems, have an implicit notion that services are just like goods—only immaterial—Hill and his followers (e.g. Gadrey & de Bandt 1994) argue that services form a logically different category, for the above-mentioned reasons. That is also why they maintain service activities as one class of activities, however heterogeneous it is, and in spite of the many exceptions which will be discussed below.

OTHER CHARACTERISTICS OF SERVICE ACTIVITIES

Apart from the characteristics of service activities and service products already listed, there are others which are less connected with their fundamental nature, but still important for their economic and geographical consequences.

Thus service activities employ a high percentage of women, and many in part-time jobs (except the capital-intensive transport sector).

Most persons engaged in service occupations perform non-manual ('white-collar') work and in many European countries are employed on relatively stable terms (salaried staff). Exceptions are the manual work and employment on wage terms in transport occupations (including internal transport within firms), repair occupations, cleaning and so forth. Especially in the US, there are a large number of unskilled workers in service activities employed on very insecure terms, the 'bad jobs' to be discussed in more detail in Chapter 7.

The household consumption of services has a high income elasticity: if measured at a certain point in time, rich people consume relatively more services than poor people (Engel's law, 1857). It is more debatable whether service consumption increases over time with increasing incomes, a question which will be discussed in Chapter 4. And as mentioned in Chapter 1, some services are rather insensitive to business cycle fluctuations.

The relatively low capital intensity of most service activities means that it is comparatively easy to start new firms (low entry barriers). Consequently, most new firms created are in the service sectors (not least in Eastern Europe)—though manufacturing entrepreneurs often get the most attention. In most private service sectors, there are many very small firms, and large corporations, e.g. in accounting and management consultancy, tend to organize themselves in ways that leave many decisions to the operative staff. There are, however, sectors with predominantly large corporations and traditions of strict hierarchical organization, e.g. banks, transport companies and retail chains.

Service activities use few natural resources and little energy. They cause little pollution, compared to agriculture and manufacturing. But again, there are exceptions, e.g. transport and in some cases tourism.

The participation of users in service relations and the need for trust between service producers and users make it difficult for service producers to monopolize expertise. Their knowledge easily acquires the character of a 'public good', at the free disposal of everybody. Legislation on copyright is difficult to enforce.

Innovation in service activities has not been studied sufficiently, but seems to have characteristics different from innovation in the production of goods. According to Barras (1990), technological innovation often shows a 'reverse life-cycle', starting as supply-driven process innovations and ending as demand-driven product innovations. At any rate, the interaction with service users is extremely fruitful as regards innovation (de Jong 1990).

EXCEPTIONS

I have used the term 'typical services', because there are exceptions to almost all the statements above. Even though Hill's definition covers a wide array of activities, he has to add an amendment, namely the 'pure public services' which serve society in general, while no particular end user of relations can be distinguished: general government, police, defence. The two latter sectors do not even necessarily carry out activities: their primary purpose is to prevent undesirable changes (for instance crime).

A number of service products are fairly well defined, they can be delimited and measured, the user does not participate in the production, they are more standardized, there is more of a market and more price competition, even if they cannot be stored and even though the producer and the user still have to meet. This is the case with regular travel by public transport systems (a railway trip from London to Birmingham), retail trade with standard goods, fast food eating places, and similar activities.

Another group of exceptions is formed by information services which may be embodied in media that can be stored, for instance books, journals, tapes, discs and films. This means that the relation between producer and user is less direct, that they do not meet, that many copies are identical, and that there is a market—though it still depends partly on the user what changes occur in his or her condition.

Some service activities, in particular transport and telecommunications, but also information and financial service activities using computer technology, are highly capital-intensive and show increases in productivity.

Neither the notion of relations nor Hill's definition apply to the self-services, which have become widespread—as discussed in Chapter 4—but which in most respects have the same characteristics as services performed for and with others.

BORDERLINE CASES BETWEEN SECONDARY AND TERTIARY ACTIVITIES

As already mentioned, a number of service activities do not show all the characteristics of 'typical' services. In some cases, it is really questionable whether activities should be classified as tertiary or secondary.

Public utilities (supply of water and energy) are considered secondary sector industries in official European statistics, but tertiary activities in America. Considering that the products delivered are of a physical nature (though in the case of electricity not really tangible), and that there is no character of relation in their production, the strongest argument points towards their inclusion in the secondary sector.

While many firms produce both services and goods, there are a few cases where *it is debatable which is the most important.* Restaurants are traditionally classified as service activities, though some customers primarily buy prepared meals and only secondarily buy the use of the premises and the serving of the meals (especially in fast food eating places). Butchers' shops were earlier classified as secondary sector firms (in the International Standard Industrial Classification, see Chapter 3), but are now classified as retail trade.

Repair activities have also been reclassified from the secondary to the tertiary sector. Indeed, the production and repair of goods may very often be similar activities and carried out by the same firms and workers. But otherwise, repair activities have many of the characteristics of services, and they correspond very well to Hill's definition of 'changing the condition of a good belonging to some economic unit'.

Leasing and letting activities are classified as services. But from a user's point of view, the difference between buying a machine from a manufacturing firm and hiring it from a leasing firm is often marginal, and the choice is made on the basis of financial and fiscal conditions which may change overnight.

A few goods-producing activities of an *artistic character* are classified as services (e.g. sculptors). The value of the product does not depend on its sheer physical qualities, but on its information content (expression, symbols). The same goes for the production of industrial prototypes.

Information transmission service activities using mass media form the most important borderline case, as already mentioned. Of course, information transmission was originally oral and had all the characteristics of service activities. With hieroglyphs and cuneiform writing, the first storage media were invented, and with Gutenberg, the mass media. Ownership became possible (though there are ownership problems in connection with data transmission). International statistical classifications today—even after the latest revisions—classify some information production as manufacturing (publishing and printing of books and journals), while the productions of other media (films, records, tapes, TV, etc.) are classified as service activities. This is completely illogical; if I buy a literary product in book form, it is classified as a good, if I buy the same work as a CD-ROM, it is a service! If the decisive criterion is the existence of a discrete product—as suggested by Sayer and Walker (1992)—all mass media must be called goods. If, on the other hand, one stresses that their value almost exclusively depends on their information content, and that this information is able to change the condition of the user (reader, listener, spectator), the activities that produce mass media must be considered service activities.

THE DISTINCTION BETWEEN GOODS AND SERVICES GETS BLURRED

The existence of borderline cases is not the only problem with the definition of services. Another problem, which is rapidly increasing, is that many products include both goods and service components. The distinction gets blurred.

This statement does not relate to the intermediate inputs required to produce a good or a service. Some service inputs have always been necessary to produce goods (administration, book-keeping, etc.). In recent years, the amount of service inputs has increased, and they now typically constitute 75 or 80 per cent of the costs of a good, as discussed in Chapter 6.

However, a rapidly increasing phenomenon is that the product which is sold comprises both goods and service elements. It has always been the case in restaurants, as already mentioned. But now, many such packages are marketed: cars sold with after-sales service, computer packages of hardware and software, turn-key factories or institutions are exported, including the training of their personnel. (Of course, some packages may include only services, such as packaged tourist trips with travel, hotel accommodation, sight-seeing, and so on.) Usually, it is possible to distinguish between a core product (for instance the air transport from one city to another) and peripheral services (such as booking, baggage registration, serving of meals or drinks, offer of newspapers, etc.).

The recognition that many service products do not function (have no use value) without the support of material goods, and vice versa, has led several authors to talk of a goods–services continuum (which does not exclude the above-mentioned view, that service products are radically different from goods). Thus Barcet (1987) distinguishes five possibilities:

1   Pure goods, which have a use value independent of any services, e.g. food.
2   Mixed goods, which only have use value if some service products are also used. Example: machine—instructions how to use it.
3   Goods–service complexes, where both components are mutually dependent, e.g. hardware–software packages.
4   Services depending on goods support. Thus trade strongly depends on having goods to trade (in consumption statistics, the purchase of goods is classified under consumption of goods, not under consumption of services).
5   Pure services, e.g. a management consultation.

This approach stresses the complementarity between goods and services, while other authors have stressed the possible substitution between buying a service (e.g. transport) and buying a good (e.g. a car). See the discussion in Chapter 4.

DO SERVICES CREATE WEALTH?

Different authors mean different things by the concept of 'wealth', and consequently answer the question as to whether services create wealth differently. As pointed out by Nusbaumer (1987), Andersen (1988), and Barcet (1987), different concepts of wealth have led to different answers as regards the role of services in the creation of wealth. The opinion of Adam Smith and Karl Marx was that services are not productive. Behind the Marxist notion is a concept of wealth as human labour, accumulated in products that can be appropriated. As discussed above, typical services are relations, and do not result in such products.

In this book, I shall assume that services create wealth if and when they contribute to the satisfaction of human needs. I shall not go deeper into the history of service theories, which has been excellently presented by Delaunay and Gadrey (1987) and further discussed by Maciejewicz and Monkiewicz (1989), Miskinis (1990) and de Bandt (1995).

The Smith-Marxian opinion corresponds to the deep-rooted popular notion that such people as wholesalers, bureaucrats and speculators are parasites. One often hears even highly educated people say that 'We cannot live by taking in each others' laundry'—or as the saying goes in Denmark: 'We cannot live by shaving one another'. (Which is not wrong, but the same is true of all economic activities: we cannot live by making, for instance chairs, for one another. The division of labour starts by my shaving you, and you making chairs for me.) Today, the Smith-Marxian notion is not very useful: we would not have our contemporary wealthy society if we did not have services, as argued below. The notion that services are not productive must be abandoned (Sayer & Walker 1992).

On the other hand, the neo-classical point of view is not satisfactory either. This may be illustrated by an example from town planning: it is—sensibly—attempted to plan cities in such a way that the volume of traffic is minimized. In other words, we do not accept that even if transport can be sold on a market, and is taken into account as a contribution to the GDP, it creates wealth.

De Bandt (1995) maintains that the services which in Chapter 3 are called 'pure public' (police, government, art, etc.) are non-productive. They do not create economic wealth and have never been sold on a market, but are always financed by taxes, voluntary contributions or Maecenases. But he does not offer operational criteria for the delimitation of these (few) activities.

There is still a need for theoretically well-based criteria which make it possible to distinguish between economic activities that create wealth and those which do not create wealth. It seems that the question primarily, but not exclusively, concerns services.

THE ROLE OF SERVICES IN ECONOMIC GROWTH

The last question of this chapter is the more dynamic one of the role of service activities in economic growth. Are services motors or laggards?

This question, too, is far from clear. Different authors obviously use different criteria when they try to answer it. For some, the real question is where the highest growth rates in productivity are to be found (however problematic the productivity concept is, as discussed in Chapter 5). For others, what activities in the production chain create most value added? Or what activities are the most innovative ones? Or what types of exports increase most? While still others ask who depends on whom in the growth process? The answers which different authors offer vary considerably. The four most important positions are as follows.

The first answer is that *the role of services is a passive or dependent one*—called by Gadrey (1992a) the neo-industrial answer: the service sector is a laggard, while the motors of economic growth are to be found in manufacturing industries. Argued on the basis of the non-productive character of service activities, there is usually no clear distinction between the static and the dynamic aspects of this answer.

It is the traditional Marxist position, which led the East European regimes to neglect their service sectors—possibly one of the basic causes of their economic decline in the 1970s and 80s (Shelp 1981)—a problem which will be discussed in Chapter 12. The position is now represented by Cohen and Zysman (1987). It is also the answer of some authors of the Keynesian school (Petit 1986). It is the more general version of the 'non-basic' label of services in the regional economic base model (to be discussed in Chapter 10). Keynesians would point out that service activities may fulfil a sponge function during recessions, soaking up some unemployment without contributing to economic growth (Gadrey 1987).

The second answer is that *service activities cause a 'cost-disease' which eventually will stop economic growth*. The mechanism is as follows: productivity increases are tiny or non-existent in (most) service activities, whereas wages and salaries increase more or less at the same rate as in other sectors. As the share of service activities in the total economy gradually increases, productivity increases and hence economic growth in the total economy gets smaller and smaller, until the growth finally suffocates in increasing costs and prices. This point of view was developed by the neo-classical economist Baumol (1967) and later slightly modified by Baumol, Blackman and Wolff (1985).

However, it may be pointed out, first that the productivity measurements on which Baumol relies are extremely questionable (see Chapter 5); and second that the roles of sectors cannot be understood in isolation from one another, as Baumol does.

The latter point of view is emphasized by the third position: *it is through the use of services that productivity increases and innovations are created in the user sectors and thus in the total economic system.* In other words, though productivity increases are registered for instance in the manufacturing sector and cannot be measured in the service sector, they arise from the relations between service producers and service users. Services make systems function, they are 'affectors' (to use a biological concept, see Nusbaumer 1987). As a result, the price of a good includes an increasing share of costs of service inputs, as mentioned above. Business services are most important in this respect, see discussion in Chapter 6. But even some household services, e.g. education, contribute more indirectly to productivity increases elsewhere. This answer is given by many authors, including for example Andersen (1988, 1991), Barcet (1988), Bonamy (1988), Browne (1986), Castells (1989), de Bandt (1995), Delaunay and Gadrey (1987), Giarini and Stahel (1989), Gruhler (1990), Illeris (1989a), Marshall and Wood (1992, 1995), Martinelli (1991a), Olivry (1986), Quinn and Doorley (1988), Selstad and Hagen (1991), Stanback and Noyelle (1990), Strassmann (1985), and Tordoir (1991).

Thus countries in which these services are best developed—in particular the US—gain a competitive advantage over other countries (Noyelle 1991). The GATS negotiations showed that governments, especially in the Third World, gradually became aware of the necessity of these types of services, even though they had to import many of them (Barcet & Bonamy 1990). It may be noted that these service activities are largely the same ones that are now considered directly or indirectly basic in a regional context, see Chapter 10.

One should be aware that this answer to the question of the influence of service activities on economic growth comes very close to answering the different, but connected, question of 'why do service activities grow?'. However, there is no circular reasoning: the market mechanism inherently puts pressure on firms to increase their competitiveness and productivity, in order to do so the firms demand services, and as a result the total economy grows.

It is clear that from this point of view some service activities, which serve households without improving the qualifications of workers, are not seen as contributing to economic growth.

The fourth answer claims that *service activities may be independent motors of economic growth* (the 'post-industrial' position according to Gadrey 1992a): if service products satisfy a need, in particular if there is a demand with a high income elasticity, such services create new economic circuits with new production and employment. This is the argument of Bell (1973), and is the perspective behind the technological search for new, innovative service products, as studied for instance by the FAST II programme of the EC (Ruyssen 1987a) and by Miles (1993). So far, however, the amount of new services has been rather limited; and they must show a high productivity to avoid the above-mentioned 'cost-disease'—which on the other hand limits their capability of creating employment.

CONCLUSION

In this chapter, the nature and role of services are discussed. The word 'services' is primarily used in the sense of *service products* or *service activities*. The traditional definition of service activities is: economic activities which do not produce or modify physical goods. Many authors have suggested positive definitions. Most of them characterize services as relations between service producers and service users. An example is Hill's definition: a service is a change in the condition of a person, or of a thing belonging to some economic unit, which is brought about as the result of the activity of some other economic unit, with the prior agreement of the former person or economic unit.

Important characteristics of typical service activities are that:

1   Users participate in the production, and hence must meet producers.
2   Service activities are labour-intensive and depend on the skills of the personnel.
3   There is no well-defined 'product' that can be measured, and services are unique each time. Hence the concepts of GDP and productivity are difficult to apply. This also means that supply and demand must meet in a state of uncertainty about the outcome of the service relation, and that service markets are opaque.

Services vary considerably, and there are many exceptions to the typical services. Furthermore, there are borderline cases between secondary and tertiary activities, and between goods and services—for instance mass media. Nevertheless, I find it fruitful to apply the concepts of 'service activities' and 'service products'. More important than formal definitions, however, is the insight into the nature of economic activities and their geographical implications which the discussion on the nature and definitions may create.

It is debated whether services create wealth. The answer depends on what is meant by wealth. It is argued that the Marxian position, that wealth is labour accumulated in products, and that services are not productive, is unsatisfactory. But so is the neo-classical position that wealth is utility, and that all goods and services that can be sold have a utility. Criteria which make it possible to distinguish between wealth-creating and non-wealth-creating activities are needed.

Another discussion is whether service activities contribute to economic development. Again, different schools have proposed different answers. Those who consider service activities non-productive answer that their role is passive, they depend on the production of goods. A second answer is that, because they result in no or low productivity increases, service activities will eventually stop economic growth. A third answer is that producer services and many household services, either directly or indirectly, are crucial for productivity increases in other sectors, and hence for economic development. But some service activities depend on growth elsewhere in the economic system. A fourth answer is that new service products may be invented which satisfy needs, are demanded, and create new production and employment. These activities contribute to economic development.

3 Classification of Service Activities

Service activities are extremely heterogeneous. Whenever possible, they should be subdivided into more homogeneous classes, in order that statements about them may be more meaningful. Service analysts have, over the last decade or two, felt the need for classifications which were relevant for their studies, and a considerable number of classifications have been suggested. In this chapter, only those which have gained wide acceptance will be discussed.

Activities may be registered according to sector (or industry), or according to occupation. Some of the classifications may be applied to both dimensions, while others are applicable to only one of them.

It should be mentioned that a third dimension is the type of buildings or premises in which the activities take place: offices, shops, warehouses, institutions (hospitals, schools, etc.), transport terminals (e.g. airports) and so on. For physical planning, this dimension is important, and many 'office studies' were carried out in the 1970s, but later research has rather focused on the activity types. In this chapter, the classification of buildings will not be discussed.

OFFICIAL STATISTICAL CLASSIFICATIONS

Statistical data are primarily reported according to classifications by sector, based on the nature of the main products of the firms or establishments. International classifications have been established by the UN (The International Standard Industrial Classification, or ISIC) and the EU (Nomenclature des Activités dans les Communautés Européennes, or NACE)—with some mutual coordination. These are the definitions used for instance in the statistical tables and figures of this book. National classifications more or less follow the international ones.

Traditionally, these classifications have been very unsatisfactory as regards service activities. Thus, the currently used ISIC68 and the, in this respect, similar NACE classification only have four service classes:

6   Trade, hotels and restaurants
7   Transport and communications
8   Financial and business services
9   Other services

The recently revised 'NACE rev 1', which is now being introduced, shows some improvements. In the tertiary sector, its main classes are:

G   Trade, repair of automobiles and domestic articles

H   Hotels and restaurants
I   Transport and communications
J   Financial activities
K   Real estate, leasing and business services
L   Public administration
M   Education
N   Health and social services
O   Waste treatment, associations, recreative, cultural and sport activities, personal
    services
P   Domestic services
Q   Diplomacy, international organizations

There is also a UN International Standard Classification of Occupations (ISCO), but only a few countries publish data according to it. The main service classes are:

0/1   Professional, technical and related workers
2   Administrative and managerial workers
3   Clerical and related workers
4   Sales workers
5   Service workers

OTHER SECTORAL CLASSIFICATIONS

A widely used classification, also in this book, is according to user sectors, namely into *producer services* and *household services* (or 'intermediate services' and 'consumer services', respectively, though households also buy services which are not strictly for final consumption, as will be discussed in Chapter 4). Notice that the term 'producer services' is used about *all* service industries which primarily sell to enterprises and public institutions (including e.g. cleaning services), while 'business services' is used below about the narrower class of professional, information, or intellectual services to producers.

The problem with this classification is that a number of sectors are 'both-and', as shown by Table 3.1 which displays a pattern typical of West European countries. Table 3.1 shows that trade, hotels and restaurants, real estate activities and 'other household services' primarily sell to households. The latter are also the main customers of public services. Transport and insurance share their turnover more or less evenly between producers and final consumers, and this is the case of hotels and banks too (not shown in the table). These sectors constitute a mixed class. When firms use them, it is mainly in connection with the distribution of products, which leads de Bandt (1995) to call them 'accompanying services', while in Marxist terminology they belong to the sphere of circulation (see below). Wholesale trade, communications and producer services primarily serve firms and public institutions.

Another kind of services, which serve neither producers nor households directly, and which often are singled out from the producer/household services dichotomy,

Table 3.1. Users of marketed services (except finance), France 1984. *Source:* Fontaine (1987).

	Households (%)	Firms and public institutions (%)	Exports (%)
Trade	76	18	2
Hotels, restaurants	85	15	
Transport	16	61	23
Telecommunications	28	71	1
Real estate, leasing	87	13	
Insurance	56	40	4
Producer services	9	70	
Other household services	86	14	
Total	56	36	6

are services which regulate, defend and serve the total society, namely the 'pure public services' of general government, justice, police, fire protection and defence. Some manifestations of religion, art (sculpture in public places), and pure science may also be included under this category.

Another widely used classification is according to ownership: into *private services* and *public services*. However interesting this distinction is from a political point of view, its weak side is that the borderline changes from country to country and from one period to another.

A not quite identical distinction is according to the method of finance: into *marketed* and *non-marketed services*. Notice that some public services are marketed—railways in most West European countries—while some privately owned welfare services are largely government-financed. In France, health is classified as a marketed service.

Sayer and Walker (1992) distinguish the following fundamental elements of economic activity: labour inputs; production (which may be material or labour services); circulation; and consumption (collective or personal). From a service classification point of view, their most interesting class is circulation, which serves to bring products from production to consumption, and payments in the opposite direction, combined with background flows of information and changes in ownership. Circulation comprises trade and leasing, transport, financial activities and marketing. Marshall and Wood (1995) stress, however, that the financial sector not only supports circulation, but also generates gains for productive capital and thus, like other producer services, belongs to the 'indirect labour' of production.

Combining the user sector and ownership criteria in a rather pragmatic way, Browning and Singelmann in 1975 made a classification into four groups which captures some of the most important variations and which has been widely used:

1   Distributive services: transport and communications, wholesale and retail trade.
2   Producer services: finance, insurance, business services.
3   Social services (called reproductive by Martinelli, 1991a): health, welfare

services, education, postal services, government.
4 Personal services: domestic and personal services, hotels and restaurants, repairs, entertainment.

From a geographical point of view, the fundamental distinction is between activities which can sell to customers irrespective of distance, '*basic activities*', and on the other hand, activities which can sell only to customers within a limited area and hence are restricted in their development by their purchasing power, '*non-basic activities*'. This distinction is discussed in Chapter 10, and the underlying need for proximity in Chapter 9. Service activities were formerly classified as non-basic, but now some are clearly basic, while others in indirect ways contribute to an area's basic sector.

Another specialized classification is applied by Baumol (1967) who, in order to study the development of productivity, divided activities into *stagnating* ones with little or no growth in labour productivity, and on the other hand *progressive* activities with high growth in labour productivity. Service industries were, with some exceptions such as telecommunications, in the former category. Baumol, Blackman and Wolff in 1988 added a third category of 'asymptotically stagnating' sectors, mixed ones like TV production, in which the stagnating elements gradually will dominate. This problem will be discussed in Chapter 5.

OTHER OCCUPATIONAL CLASSIFICATIONS

From Chapter 2 it may be recalled that service activities are often performed internally in user firms of all kinds. Hence, many persons in the secondary sector have tertiary occupations. It may also be recalled that whereas most service occupations are non-manual ('white-collar', salaried), some are manual ('blue-collar', wage-earning) occupations.

A set of classifications focuses on the character, object, and qualification demands of service work. It thus seems appropriate to discuss these classifications in connection with occupations, though they often are applied to service industries, too. As a starting point, Gottmann (1961) may be mentioned. In an analysis of metropolitan economic activities, he split off from the traditional tertiary sector a *quaternary* one, which was defined in terms of managerial and artistic occupations, government, education, research and brokerage of all kinds. As we would say today, typically urban, information-treating occupations with high qualification requirements and high growth rates.

Gottmann (1961) and Machlup (1962) may be seen as the forerunners of the later definition of *information activities*, presented in the widely quoted Porat report (1977). In this, the object of activities ('what is handled') is the criterion. Porat included not only information-handling service occupations, but also the physical production of information equipment, TV sets, computer hardware, and so on. His report was a point of departure for an information research tradition which partly overlaps the service research tradition.

Hill's definition of service products and activities (1977, discussed in Chapter 2) also focused on the object: he distinguished between changes in the conditions of (a) persons and (b) things, and added a third class of pure public services with no identifiable object. This line of thought has been followed up by several authors (Illeris 1985; Barcet 1986; Bonamy & Mayère 1987; Delaunay & Gadrey 1987), who more or less independently of each other classified service activities on the basis of their object: things, information, persons, plus the pure public services. This classification according to object is used by Gadrey (1992a) in Figure 2.1.

More often than not, the object-based classes have been cross-classified with another work-based distinction, namely between individual and standardized activities. As mentioned in Chapter 2, it is typical for service products—as opposed to goods—that they are different each time. But there are exceptions, standardized services. In this way one arrives at the following classes, which have been used to study not only skill and productivity issues, but also geographical problems:

A   Goods-related services (man–thing relations)
A1 Individual production: cleaning, hotels and restaurants, repair, renting
A2 Standardized production (distribution): goods transport, retail and wholesale trade
B   Information services (man–symbol relations)
B1 Individual production (quaternary): management, consultants, research, culture, strategic bank
B2 Standardized production: back offices, routine administration, tele-communication
C   Person-related services (man–man relations)
C1 Individual production: education, health, childcare, sports, bodycare
C2 Standardized production: transport of persons
D   Pure public services: general government, police, defence, justice, fire-protection.

The information category here is narrower than in Porat's terminology: not only is the production and distribution of information hardware excluded, but education is viewed primarily as a person-related activity, in which social and psychological aspects are important, not as a sheer transfer of information. However, it might be argued that higher and adult education is more information-related than schools for children.

It should be stressed that many firms and sectors include work from several of the above-mentioned occupational classes. Retail and wholesale trades, for instance, not only distribute goods, the ownership of which changes: they produce and disseminate information, arrange payment, keep books—all these activities being information-related.

Generally, thing-related and person-related activities (A and C), as well as individual information services (B1) require proximity between the service producer and the service user or the thing whose condition is changed. But sometimes they may be transported to each other at low cost—small things may be sent to a repair workshop. As discussed in Chapter 9, among individual information services, it is not necessarily the most sophisticated ones that depend most on proximity between service producers and users. They often do require face-to-face meetings, but because of their high price they can better 'carry' high travelling costs than less sophisticated, frequently used individual services. Standardized information services (B2) are today liable to be transmitted via telecommunications.

In individual service production (A1, B1, C1), it is only to a limited degree possible to increase productivity, and since wages tend to follow wage increases in other activities, prices tend to increase. As discussed in Chapter 4, there is therefore a pressure to transfer these activities to unpaid (informal) work, or to reduce them through maintenance-free or throw-away products (A1). If none of these solutions is possible, and if demand is increasing, we witness steep increases in employment (B1 and C1). In standardized services, on the other hand (A2, B2, C2), productivity increases are normally possible, and employment tends to be constant or declining. Such rationalizations often require economies of scale which make it difficult to maintain service activities in sparsely populated areas and off-peak periods.

It should be stressed that many activities are borderline cases, and they may change over time. Retailing, for instance, was earlier a much more individualized activity. It is now classified according to its prevailing standardized self-service character, which it acquired in North America in the 1940s and 50s, in Northwestern Europe in the 1960s, and in Southern Europe only in recent decades. But a more expensive, individualized segment always remained, and in North America this is now reconquering part of the market.

Recently, an occupation-based classification of activities, based on similar criteria, has become influential, in particular in connection with employment, qualification, productivity, conditions of work and international trade problems; namely the one suggested by Reich (1991). The author does not distinguish between service and non-service activities, the former are found in all classes:

1   *Routine production.* Low-skill jobs exposed to international competition and automation. Declining employment. Primarily found in manufacturing, also in back offices.
2   *In-person services.* Low-skill jobs, handling persons face to face, or things. Not exposed to international competition or automation. Growing employment.
3   *Symbolic-analytic services.* High-skill jobs, individually handling information (problem-identifying, problem-solving, strategic-brokering). Not exposed to automation, but in most cases Western opportunities in international competition. Growing employment.

The remaining jobs in agriculture and public services are not included in the classification.

The classification according to object may of course also be cross-classified with the producer/mixed/household-dimension, as it has been done by Selstad and Hagen (1991) and Miles (1993).

CONCLUSION

Since services are extremely heterogeneous, they should be subdivided into more homogeneous classes whenever possible. In this chapter, the following classifications are discussed: official classifications based on output; classifications based on user sector, on ownership, on way of finance, and on geographical markets; furthermore, on skill demands, on object, and on degree of standardization.

It must be recognized that no classification will be the only, preferred one, but that many of them will be used for different purposes (as in this book). This fact reflects the many-sided characteristics of service activities and of the societies in which they are carried out.

Part II

THE DEVELOPMENT OF SERVICES

4 Development of Household Services

The purpose of this chapter is to present the main lines of research on the development of household (or consumer) services. Until the 1970s, this was more or less the only kind of service research—in fact, household services were by far the most important ones until then. Research on the development of producer (or intermediate) services, which has become very important since the 1980s but has followed separate paths, will be presented in Chapter 6.

The changing volume and characteristics of household service activities in developed countries will be described, and the causes behind this development discussed. The discussion will be structured according to the different phases of research. Government policies directed towards household services will also be discussed.

Most types of services, according to the classifications of Chapter 3, are produced for household use. Household services are, however, specially important among public services and person-related services. Employment in household service activities is, especially in the United States, dominated by low-skill jobs. Household services are generally sold or delivered over short distances, and except for tourist services hardly ever traded internationally. Internationalization, e.g. in retailing or fast food, has happened through the setting up of branch or franchised establishments in each country.

THE VOLUME OF HOUSEHOLD SERVICES

Given the difficulties in measuring the production of many service activities, as discussed in Chapter 2, employment figures have been chosen to illustrate the development of the activities. Table 4.1 shows the percentage of total employment to be found in service sectors in 10 selected OECD countries during 1970–90, according to the ISIC classification (see Chapter 3). This classification does not distinguish between household and producer services. Trade and transport serve both households and firms, business services primarily serve firms, while the last category, dominated by educational and health services which in most countries are public, primarily serves households.

In Figure 4.1, the composition of employment in the last decade is shown for five countries. Using more detailed data, the following sectors have been distinguished: primary and secondary; producer services; mixed services (transport and communications, financial services, etc.); private and public household services; and pure public services (government, military and police forces, etc.). It has not

Table 4.1. Civilian service employment by subsectors, 10 countries 1970–1990. *Source:* Godbout (1993).

	United States	Canada	Australia	Japan	France	Germany	Italy	Netherlands	Sweden	United Kingdom
Wholesale and retail trade, restaurants and hotels:										
1970	20.3	20.4	22.8	21.0	15.4	14.7	(²)	(²)	14.5	16.4
1975	21.8	21.9	22.9	22.8	15.6	(²)	⁴18.0	17.6	14.5	18.3
1980	21.5	22.5	23.8	23.8	16.0	15.4	18.6	17.8	13.8	19.3
1985	22.2	23.3	23.3	24.1	16.5	16.2	21.3	17.4	13.8	20.3
1990	22.1	24.0	24.9	24.1	17.3	16.3	³21.5	17.8	14.4	³19.5
Transportation and communication:										
1970	6.0	7.7	7.6	6.5	5.9	5.7	(²)	(²)	6.9	6.7
1975	5.9	7.6	7.8	6.4	6.1	(²)	⁴5.6	5.8	6.7	6.4
1980	5.7	7.3	7.3	6.4	6.2	5.9	5.6	5.9	7.0	6.3
1985	5.4	6.7	7.7	6.0	6.5	5.9	5.3	6.2	7.0	6.0
1990	5.3	6.5	6.8	6.1	6.4	5.8	³5.6	6.2	7.0	³5.9
Finance, insurance, real estate, and business services:										
1970	6.8	7.1	7.1	4.3	5.3	4.2	(²)	(²)	5.0	5.0
1975	7.5	8.1	7.3	5.2	6.3	(²)	⁴2.1	6.5	5.3	6.6
1980	8.4	9.5	8.2	5.8	7.5	5.8	2.6	7.9	6.7	7.3
1985	10.3	10.1	9.9	6.9	8.2	7.2	3.5	9.2	7.5	9.7
1990	11.3	11.6	11.5	8.4	10.0	7.9	³4.1	10.4	8.7	³11.7
Community, social, and personal services:⁵										
1970	28.0	26.3	17.5	15.1	20.7	17.5	(²)	(²)	26.8	23.8
1975	30.1	27.0	21.4	17.0	23.0	(²)	⁴19.7	30.1	30.4	25.6
1980	30.4	26.7	23.1	18.2	25.7	23.9	20.9	32.5	34.5	26.8
1985	31.0	29.4	25.4	19.4	29.2	25.2	25.2	34.6	36.8	29.6
1990	32.2	29.1	25.8	20.1	30.2	26.7	³27.0	34.5	37.0	³30.2

¹ Included in industry. ² Not available. ³ 1989. ⁴ 1977. ⁵ Includes public administration, education, health, and recreation services.

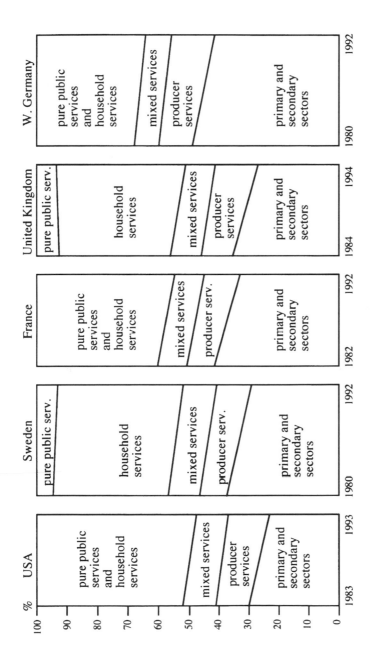

Figure 4.1. Employment in household and producer and other services, five countries early 1980s–early 1990s. *Sources:* Beyers (1994), national statistical yearbooks.

been possible to obtain totally comparable data for all countries; in particular, 'producer services' in Germany include some activities which in the other countries are registered as 'household services'.

Table 4.1 and Figure 4.1 show that the general growth trend in service employment of recent decades, mentioned in Chapter 1, is due primarily to growth in household services (including education, health, and other social services) and in business services. The growth rates of social services, however, slowed down in the late 1980s—because of cut-backs in public budgets. Employment in trade has only grown moderately in this period, and the share of such mixed services as transport and communications in total employment has not increased at all. The share of pure public services was different in the two countries where data were available. The difference was partly due to differential military cut-backs since 1990.

This description is extremely crude, of course. There are important differences within the subsectors, and also between countries, as it will be discussed in more detail in Chapter 12.

EXPLANATIONS OF THE GROWTH OF HOUSEHOLD SERVICES

THE 'THREE-SECTOR THEORY'

The question of why service activities—and in particular household services—grow at higher rates than the economy as a whole has been answered by different authors in various ways. It was the economic crisis of the 1930s that first provoked an interest in the question, and an early answer was suggested by Fisher (1935). He based his explanation on the observation that the richer households are, the bigger is the share of service products in their total consumption. In other words, service consumption shows a high income elasticity. This tendency is known as 'Engel's law' and was first shown by the Saxon statistician Engel in 1857.

Fisher's argument was that this law must also be valid over time. Poor societies can, by and large, only afford to consume the absolute necessities for survival (especially food), produced by the primary sector. When they grow richer, they cannot consume much more food per capita, but they can expand their consumption of clothes and other manufactured products. At a still later and richer stage, the consumption of secondary sector products will also approach a ceiling, but a growing consumption of culture, travel, entertainment, education, health and other tertiary sector products is possible. Employment in the different sectors will develop according to the demand of the sector's products. This notion is known as the 'three-sector theory' of economic development. It has been accused of lacking a causal explanation. But it has an obvious background in the Maslowian 'pyramid of human needs'.

Clark (1940) connected the three-sector theory with the development of labour productivity in the different sectors. A condition of economic progress would be a shift from the primary sector to the secondary and tertiary sectors in which he thought that productivity would be higher.

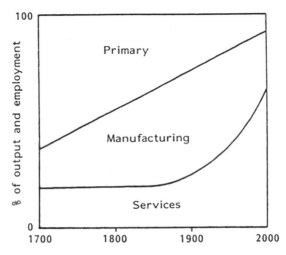

Figure 4.2. The Fourastié three-sector model. *Source:* Reproduced with permission from J. Gershuny and I. Miles (1983), *The New Service Economy: The Transformation of Employment in Industrial Societies.* London: Frances Pinter.

Fourastié (1949) gave the three-sector theory a more convincing shape, showing that the tertiary sector was characterized by lower growth in productivity than the other sectors (this will be further discussed in Chapter 5). In this way, a population's needs for primary and secondary products can be satisfied by the work of a decreasing share of the total labour force, and the remaining labour force can engage in the production of services. The distribution of employment over the three sectors' changes is illustrated by Figure 4.2.

In a radically changed environment, after the post-war decades of rapid economic growth, sociologists such as Bell (1973) and Touraine (1967) presented visions of a 'post-industrial society' which may be seen as further developments of Fourastié's ideas. Bell describes—without digging deeper into the societal processes—a society with increasing consumption of leisure services, tourism, education and health services. He did observe a number of phenomena that would modify this picture, but he did not consider them important.

The factors influencing the development of the three sectors, according to Fisher, Fourastié and the 'post-industrialists', have been summarized by Gruhler (1990) in Table 4.2.

SELF-SERVICE IN HOUSEHOLDS

A few years later, Skolka (1976), Gershuny (1978) and Gershuny and Miles (1983) presented a second and fundamentally different answer to the question of the development of services. These authors are primarily concerned with household services, and explicitly distinguish these from producer services. They argue that we are not heading for the kind of service society which Bell described, but rather

Table 4.2. Causal criteria of the three-sector model, according to several authors. *Source:* Translated and reproduced with permission from W. Gruhler (1990), *Dienstleistungs-bestimmter Strukturwandel in deutschen Industrieunternehmen*. Köln: Deutscher Instituts-Verlag.

	Demand		Supply
Influences	Needs, income elasticity	Technical progress	Constraints on productivity through dominance of one factor production
Sector	(Fisher)	(Fourastié)	(Wolfe)
Primary	Satisfaction of basic needs. Income elasticity of demand < 0.5	Medium– high	Nature: Dominance of the factor agricultural land
Secondary	Satisfaction of non-vital needs by uniform commodities. Income elasticity of demand 0.5–1	High	Technology: Dominance of the factor capital
Tertiary	Satisfaction of needs by luxury commodities. Income elasticity of demand > 1.	Low or none	Mental capacity: Dominance of the factor labour.

for a self-service society in which the consumers increasingly produce the service products themselves inside the households, using purchased goods, in order to fulfil the same final needs. For instance, we wash our clothes in purchased washing machines instead of bringing them to a laundry. We drive our purchased car instead of using public transport. We look at and listen to our purchased TV, hi-fi and video equipment instead of going to concerts or cinemas. And we maintain our belongings as 'do-it-yourself' work with purchased tools instead of calling in professionals.

Thus, the production of services is shifted from paid work in the formal economy to unpaid work in the informal economy. But households then have to buy goods from the formal economy and demand infrastructure (roads), as well as to buy services which have an intermediate character, since they are only conditions for the final consumption (e.g. complicated car repairs). Instead of Fourastié's simple model of the changing proportion between sectors, Gershuny and Miles present the model of sector development shown in Figure 4.3.

The causes of these processes are, according to Gershuny and Skolka, to be found in the tendency of service products to increase in price, relative to goods. And this tendency, again, is due to the *lower productivity growth in service activities than in the production of goods*, combined with the tendency of wages to develop in a parallel way in the two sectors.

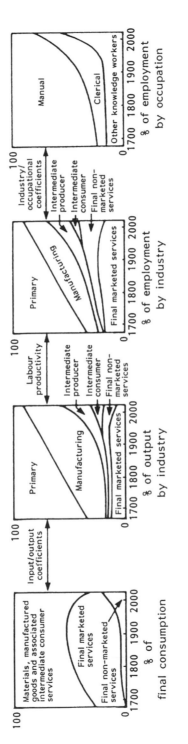

Figure 4.3. Gershuny's model. *Source:* Reproduced with permission from J. Gershuny and I. Miles (1983), *The New Service Economy: The Transformation of Employment in Industrial Societies.* London: Frances Pinter.

A supplementary reason why services produced in the informal sector tend to be cheaper than those produced in the formal sector, is to be found in taxation. If the consumer has the choice between buying and producing a service, which requires one hour's work, he or she will have to work much more than an hour in the formal economy to earn the money to buy the service, because both the income and the service are taxed. The higher the income tax and VAT rates, the larger is the advantage of production in the informal economy—according to calculations by the Danish Ministry of Finance (Finansministeriet 1992), the consumer may have to work up to five hours to pay for one hour's service.

Finally, it should be mentioned that productivity in 'do-it-yourself' work may be quite high, compared to professional work. Not only have many amateur tools and household machines been developed, but in the household, activities can also be done whenever it is convenient, while in the formal economy, firms and institutions often have periods with unused capacity.

Gershuny and Skolka argue that Engel's law cannot be applied to a development over time, however valid it might be to a cross-section at a particular moment. They also stress that many services are produced and consumed inside households in economically less developed countries—previously in Europe, now in the Third World. However, this activity is by definition excluded from GDP and employment figures.

Gershuny's British data show that the share of services in total household consumption did not increase from 1954 to 1974. Indeed, if measured by volume instead of in current monetary terms, household consumption of services—which get more expensive over time, compared to goods—rather tends to decrease.

In Gershuny's opinion (1986), there are household services in the formal economy which escape the general trend because of rapidly increasing demand, for instance tourism and leisure services. He has also predicted innovations in service production. If such innovations allow rapid increases in productivity and hence price reductions, they might lead to increased consumption of services. But so far, few innovations have appeared in the production of household services. One example is the services offered over the French Minitel system, but so few people are needed to produce them that the employment effect has been negligible.

The mechanism described by Gershuny operates both in the private and the public (tax-financed) sectors of the formal economy, and it offers an explanation of the financial crises of governments which has attracted little attention: because it is difficult to obtain productivity increases in the production of public services similar to those obtained in the rest of the economy, while wages and salaries follow those paid elsewhere, public expenditure tends to increase even at constant levels of service production. In other words: over time, the population has to pay higher taxes, only to get an unchanged amount of services.

Gershuny and Skolka had to be pessimistic as regards the possibilities of increased employment through increased formal sector production of household services. Thus, their position is similar to that represented by Baumol (1967) and Kaldor (1966)—economists who, as mentioned in Chapter 2, fear that the 'cost disease' of the service sector (due to low growth of productivity) and de-industrialization are fundamental mechanisms which limit economic growth in highly developed societies.

It may be argued that the term 'cost disease' is unfortunate, since it implies that it could be cured. But as discussed in Chapter 5, there are fundamental reasons why productivity cannot grow fast in the production—whether private or public—of household services.

DO HOUSEHOLDS BUY MORE SERVICES, AFTER ALL?

Gershuny and Skolka have argued their case brilliantly, and have drawn the highly relevant substitution between the formal and the informal sector, usually ignored by economists, into the discussion. But almost all their propositions have been challenged. In particular, the French economist Gadrey (1986a) and the American sociologist Silver (1987) have developed alternative ideas, without returning to Bell's point of view which now appears rather superficial. There is thus a third answer to our initial question: Yes, households do demand more services. Table 4.3 attempts to summarize Gadrey's and Silver's criticism of Gershuny and Skolka, and the arguments behind their answer.

The point of departure for Gadrey and Silver lies in the fundamental changes taking place in the composition and time budgets of Western households: above all the increasing activity rates of women in paid work, and hence the strong reduction of time available for 'self-service' in the households (even if men compensate a little by doing more household work than before). At the same time, the social networks of the informal economy—the mutual help between relatives and neighbours—have probably been weakened.

Table 4.3. Propositions about the production of household services

Gershuny and Skolka	Gadrey and Silver
Increasing share of service production within households, e.g. laundry, hairdressing, entertainment	Increasing share of service production in the formal economy, e.g. childcare, care of the elderly
Services increase in price relative to goods	Agreement
Service share of private consumption decreasing in constant prices, e.g. Scandinavia	Service share of private consumption stable in constant prices, e.g. most Western countries
Stagnation in service production in the formal economy, e.g. public services	Growth in service production in the formal economy, e.g. tourism, bodycare
Competition between service production in formal and informal economy	Complementarity between service production in formal and informal economy
Zero-sum game, decided by costs	Increasing need for services due to societal developments
Amateur tools, 'do-it-yourself'	Specialist knowledge, e.g. bank adviser

The increasing activity rates of women are accompanied by a rapid externalization of care work from households to the formal economy. This is particularly true of childcare, but also of care of the elderly and handicapped persons. In most West European countries, these tasks have been taken up by the public sector, and are at least partly financed by taxes. In his analysis of private consumption, Gershuny completely ignored this type of consumption.

But the growing paid work of married women is not the only change in the traditional household type of husband-with-paid-work + housewife + children. There is a growth in other household types. In Denmark, couples with children formed 25 per cent of all families in 1980, but only 18 per cent in 1994. Smaller households for various reasons demand more services from the formal economy, according to Gadrey and Silver:

1   There are single parents with children, who have a very tight time-budget and no time for 'self-service'.
2   There is an increasing number of childless households who are quite well-to-do and can afford to buy even expensive services from the formal economy.
3   There is an increasing number of elderly households who are unable to do much 'self-servicing'.

Gadrey (1988c, 1992a) has emphasized, furthermore, that the balance between service production in the formal and the informal economy is not only a zero-sum game, in which households weigh purchases against self-production on the basis of economic criteria. There are service products which require such specialized skills that households are unable to produce them (e.g. most medical assistance). Any transport planner knows that private cars and public transport compete not only on the basis of costs, but also on comfort, independence of fixed timetables and status. And many activities, such as meals, have social and symbolic functions which are ignored by Gershuny's narrow economic 'buy or make' calculations. Skolka (1989) may have expressed it better when suggesting that households make small, often intuitive, cost–benefit analyses of their possibilities, into which not only monetary factors enter.

An important aspect, in Gadrey's eyes, is that both the functioning of the households themselves and the society in which they exist are becoming more and more complicated, and that more and more technical, legal, economic and other types of knowledge are necessary—much of which must be acquired externally. This aspect, which is in the foreground of producer service research, is also relevant for the development of household services. For banking services, this is illustrated by Figure 4.4.

Gadrey also stresses that there is not always competition between services and goods to help fulfil the same needs, but in some cases a complementarity: cars and insurance demonstrate such a case. In particular, in the production of person-related services (care, health, education) machines may be helpful tools, but normally they can only support, not substitute for, the personal production of services, as shown for instance in experiments with computer-based education.

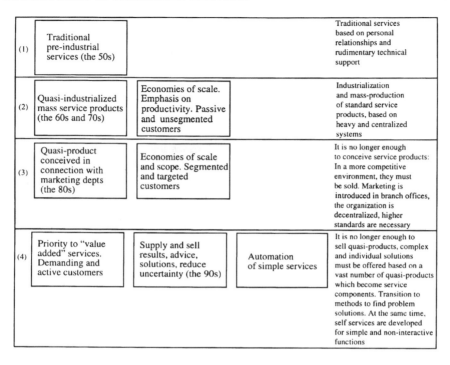

(1)	Traditional pre-industrial services (the 50s)			Traditional services based on personal relationships and rudimentary technical support
(2)	Quasi-industrialized mass service products (the 60s and 70s)	Economies of scale. Emphasis on productivity. Passive and unsegmented customers		Industrialization and mass-production of standard service products, based on heavy and centralized systems
(3)	Quasi-product conceived in connection with marketing depts (the 80s)	Economies of scale and scope. Segmented and targeted customers		It is no longer enough to conceive service products: In a more competitive environment, they must be sold. Marketing is introduced in branch offices, the organization is decentralized, higher standards are necessary
(4)	Priority to "value added" services. Demanding and active customers	Supply and sell results, advice, solutions, reduce uncertainty (the 90s)	Automation of simple services	It is no longer enough to sell quasi-products, complex and individual solutions must be offered based on a vast number of quasi-products which become service components. Transition to methods to find problem solutions. At the same time, self services are developed for simple and non-interactive functions

Figure 4.4.   Four phases in changing banking services to households. *Source:* Reproduced and translated with permission from J. Gadrey (1992a) *L'Economie des Services*, Paris: La Découverte.

In information- and goods-related services, productivity growth is possible in some cases. The simple banking services mentioned in Figure 4.4 constitute an example. However, new machines do not necessarily induce us to reduce costs, but may also be used to increase standards. Thus, the average Dane washed 360 kilograms of clothes annually in 1945, but when washing machines had become widespread, 860 kilograms in 1982 (Cronberg 1987).

Expressed in very general terms, the Gershuny–Skolka theory is accused of belonging to a 'Fordist' economy, based on standardized production and easy substitution between various goods and services, and is assumed to have little relevance in a complicated 'post-Fordist' society characterized by diversification and the search for quality and flexibility (Barcet 1987; Dale 1994).

The debate has clearly been influenced by the personal values of the participants. Gershuny and Skolka have been accused of representing an isolated, individualistic life-style. On the other hand, Skolka (1989) observes that self-servicing promotes equality: now all social classes use more or less the same time for housework. It may also be argued that 'do-it-yourself' reduces alienation.

WHERE ARE WE NOW?

Recent empirical studies have produced knowledge which makes it possible to assess the ideas referred to. As regards the basic question, whether the service purchases of households form an increasing share of final consumption or not, it is obvious that Gershuny and Skolka made a severe error in their first publications when they ignored the largely tax-financed public services. Even if there are problems connected with the measurement of public services, there can be no doubt that they have increased so much in recent decades that the net result has been an externalization of tasks from households to the formal economy. Households do buy more services, some of them via the taxes they pay to finance public services.

But on the other side, there is no doubt that the mechanisms which Gershuny and Skolka describe do exist. There is much evidence showing that service prices as a whole do increase faster than the prices of goods (Finansministeriet 1992; Elfring 1988; Ecalle 1989; Gadrey 1992a). Whether the price increases are caused by low productivity growth or by quality improvements, will be discussed in Chapter 5.

Ironically enough, the Gershuny mechanism may be even more widespread in the production of public services than in private services. This contributes to the financial problems of governments, and has led to a stagnation in the production of public services since the mid-1980s, as shown by Table 4.1. Both in private and public service production, there are pressures to counteract the mechanism by such restructuring measures as standard reduction, use of cheaper types of labour (e.g. unemployed persons on retraining programmes), new technology, better organization, better adaptation of products to needs, increased user self-service, centralization to gain scale economies, and so on. Government policies directed towards public services will be discussed below.

As regards the service purchases of households from the private sector, there is no doubt that in current prices, these purchases normally form an increasing share of total private consumption (data from several countries collected by Green 1985; Fontaine 1987; Elfring 1988; ECONAnalyse 1995). Figure 4.5 illustrates this process in France.

Figure 4.5 shows that the service share of consumption for all income classes has grown from 1979 to 1989. It also shows that rich households consume relatively more services than poor ones (Engel's law). Notice that 1979 incomes are expressed in 1989 francs, while consumption is in current francs.

However, there are exceptions: countries and periods with only weak or no increases in the share of service purchases. Gershuny's study period in the United Kingdom as well as France in the 1970s reveals such exceptions (Gadrey 1992a). Denmark and Norway seem to form exceptions over longer periods (Kristensen 1989; Plougmann 1988; Finansministeriet 1992; Skodvin 1987; Stambøl 1988; Dale 1994). The stagnation of private service consumption in Scandinavia may be explained by the high standard of public services, but also by the high levels of taxation which incite consumers to shift service production to the informal economy.

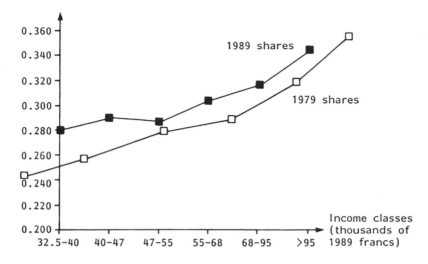

Figure 4.5. Share of household consumption used for services (except housing), France 1979 and 1989. *Source:* Reproduced and translated with permission from J. Gadrey (1992a) *L'Economie des Services*, Paris: La Découverte.

The development of the service share of household consumption in constant prices is of course less positive (especially if the irrelevant housing component is left out), due to the relative price increases of services. In most countries, the share has been more or less unchanged, though increasing shares have been observed in France in the 1980s and in Japan. (There are major problems connected with the measurement of service purchases in constant prices or volumes, as discussed in Chapter 5.)

There are, however, differences from one type of services to another, and the consumption of many services has increased rapidly, e.g. tourism, childcare, banking services, education, entertainment, telecommunications and health services. On the other hand, some of Gershuny's examples of purchases of goods substituting purchases of services because of differences in their price trends have been supported by the Danish findings of Kristensen (1989) and Finansministeriet (1992): the substitution of maids by household machines, of laundries by washing machines, of cinema and theatre visits by TV, and of machine repairs by new machines. On the other hand, Rappoport (1987) finds little difference between the price trends of such pairs in the United States. As regards the price relations between public transport and private cars + petrol, these have varied a lot from period to period. But reservations must be made against all such paired price trends which do not take changing quality differences into account.

It should be noted, too, that Engel's law must be differentiated according to type of services. The relative insensitivity of (household) services to business cycles, described in Chapter 1, indicates that in contemporary societies, some services do not have a luxury character, but fulfil fairly basic needs.

The theories of Gadrey and Silver as regards the influence of household type on the purchase of services have been confirmed by the findings of Ecalle (1987), Skodvin (1987), Stambøl (1988), Bonke (1988) and Archambault (1987): the growing number of small, childless households have above-average service purchases, while the declining number of couples with children have below-average service purchases.

ARE CONSUMERS MANIPULATED?

A different question connected with household consumption should be mentioned here, but will not be discussed in any detail: who determines the composition of consumption? The neo-classical notion of consumer sovereignty clashes with consumption theories which claim that producers manipulate consumers to buy what they produce—and not only the composition, but also the total volume of consumption. Dale (1994) maintains that consumers, at least partly, are able to understand their own needs and act accordingly, while Marshall and Wood (1995) point towards the decisive influence of the retailing chains.

GOVERNMENT POLICIES

In Western countries, governments influence household services in two ways: they produce some services themselves, and they may regulate and promote private services.

PUBLIC SERVICES

The problems connected with the volume, quality, and financing of public services in Western countries have traditionally been explored by such disciplines as political science, management research and public finance. There are, however, results of service research that are relevant to the discussion.

The problem is that after a period of rapid expansion of the public services in the 1960s and 70s, governments everywhere ran into the dilemma that people were no longer willing to pay increased taxes to pay for them ('tax revolts')—though at the same time people expressed the need for still more public services, e.g. in the field of childcare which ever more women wanted in order to be able to work in the formal economy.

Part of the explanation is of course that it is not the same groups of the population that are for and against more public services. There are other explanations, such as pressures from the vested interests of public personnel, and the lack of proper incentives to improve the production of public services. The aspect which has been pointed out by service research and which indicates that the problem will be difficult to solve, is the 'Gershuny mechanism' according to which the population has to pay ever more taxes only to get an *unchanged* amount of services.

It is only possible here to hint at various measures which may at least offer improvements, though not necessarily providing any final solution to the dilemma (Pinch 1989; Urry 1992):

1 The possibilities of increased productivity which after all exist may be used, including new technology, better organization, better adaptation of capacity to changing demand, better motivation/incentives as well as better adaptation of the services to the needs they are to fulfil (the latter is rather a question of effectiveness than of productivity, see discussion in Chapter 5). Scale economies may in some cases be obtained through concentration into bigger institutions, but this will reduce the geographical accessibility of the services. Operations may be privatized in the hope that private firms can seize opportunities of increased productivity better than public institutions.

2 The quality of the services may be reduced, thus making them cheaper. This will rarely be admitted by governments, but is often the reality behind changing such standards as the number of children per teacher, employing personnel with lower qualifications and hence lower salaries, and behind privatization.

3 In the case of conscription, governments force their subjects to do military service at extremely low wages. Various programmes in some countries in reality force unemployed persons to work, usually in public service activities, for their social benefits, which are lower than normal salaries.

4 Financing may be shifted from the taxpayers to the users, at least partly, either through payments or through unpaid user participation in production. Alternatively, voluntary work may be involved (e.g. local parents' associations, charities).

POLICIES TO PROMOTE PRIVATE SERVICES

Western governments have not until recently done much to promote private service activities. Public policies regulate private services, for instance as regards opening hours, hygiene standards, and in certain sectors requirements concerning the qualifications of the service producers. In the context of this book, the most interesting regulations concern locations allowed by physical planning. However, it is not the purpose here to discuss regulatory policies.

As long as laissez-faire philosophies of the role of governments prevailed, they clearly excluded any policy of promotion of private service activities—the development of economic activities should be left to the 'invisible hand' of market forces. In the Keynesian period after World War II, however, governments still did not try to influence the development of private service activities, but for a different reason. The prevailing idea was, as mentioned in Chapter 2, that manufacturing and agriculture formed the 'basic' activities, the motors of the economy—most clearly formulated in a regional context as the economic base model discussed in Chapters 12 and 16. If these sectors thrived, a multiplier effect would automatically lead to derived growth in the service activities, too. Only service activities with a basic character, such as tourism, were actively promoted.

In the last decade or two, these attitudes have started to change. While the general development of private service activities is still left to market forces, governments in particular have increasingly become aware of the importance of service activities, not only for the satisfaction of needs and for the well-being of people, but also for the productivity, innovation and competitiveness of all economic activities. (This is discussed in more detail in Chapters 2, 6, and 10.) Another reason is that it has become increasingly clear that the manufacturing sector in Western countries is unable to create the amount of jobs required to eliminate unemployment, and that an expansion of public services would be very difficult to finance. Hence, there is currently a broad debate in Western Europe as to whether some private household services should be supported, since they appear to be the only ones able to reduce the high unemployment among the unskilled population. Governments have observed, with envy, the much lower unemployment rates in the US, where many low-skill jobs are created in household services (see Chapter 12). But these American jobs are not well paid, and conditions of employment are not considered acceptable (see Commission of the EU 1993, the 'Delors White Paper'), so West European governments are not prepared just to abandon regulations and hope that market forces will create jobs in household services.

The problem for them is to find a solution to this dilemma, which basically is similar to the problems of public services, already discussed. A number of official reports from various countries (Greffe, Arnaud & Leprince 1990; Finansministeriet 1992; Department of the Taioseach 1993) have pointed towards ways of supporting various household services, in order to create jobs in the formal economy for unskilled persons, e.g. through subsidies or tax reductions to firms or wages. However, there are also arguments against such programmes:

1   Switching jobs from the black to the white sector is only ornamental.
2   Self-servicing has a value in reducing alienation.
3   Subsidies that favour low-productivity activities may 'crowd out' other sectors.
4   Such programmes in one way or another would take money from the poor (average taxpayers) and give it to the rich (service-buying households).

Nevertheless, some programmes have been launched, for instance in Denmark, where subsidies are given to certain service firms. And in France where subsidies are given to the service-buying households in the forms of tax deductions and, from 1995, service-buying vouchers. However, so far the effects on the total amount of unemployment appear very limited (*Le Monde* 7.12.1994).

CONCLUSION

In the 1980s there was a vivid theoretical debate on the causes and perspectives of household service developments. There now seems to be some consensus about the following notions (Illeris 1989c): the main tendency has been an externalization of service production from households to the formal economy, as a part of the increasing division of labour. The increases have to a large degree happened in the public sector, but in most countries and periods services also form an increasing share of private consumption when measured in current prices.

The basic reasons are probably (a) the development of new types of households which are not able to produce the services themselves, (b) the increased need for services which societal developments create, (c) that higher productivity and lower prices are possible in some cases, and (d) as argued in the three-sector theory, that growing affluence leads to increasing consumption of certain types of leisure, health and similar services with high income elasticities.

This conclusion, which largely corresponds to the ideas of Gadrey and Silver, does not exclude the mechanisms described by Gershuny and Skolka, however. They exist, but have in recent decades influenced only limited sectors, limited periods, or few countries, such as the Scandinavian ones. Ironically enough, they seem to have been most pronounced in the public sector (ignored by Gershuny), and to have contributed to the 'crisis of the welfare state'—in spite of clearly unfulfilled care needs. Various policies to overcome these problems have been discussed in the chapter.

The lack of time of many households probably has contributed to the externalization of some services, but at the same time limits the purchase of services which it takes time to consume (Plougmann 1994). If, in future, telecommunications radically substitute travel—for instance by promoting home work and reducing commuting—it might save time that can be used to consume services. Another barrier is the relative lack of innovations in household services (Sundbo 1994).

There has been relatively little research on household services for some years. However, private household services are now coming back into focus, mainly because of the employment problem. The question is whether this sector can employ the large number of unemployed, largely low-skilled persons in Western Europe—given that no other sector seems able to do so. Programmes to support some activities in this sector have recently been launched in several countries, but so far with limited success.

5 Productivity and Effectiveness

The concept of productivity, denoting the result of economic activity per unit of resource input, is extremely important in all economic thinking. The economic difference between ourselves and palaeolithic men may be boiled down to our infinitely higher productivity.

Not least in service research, the preceding chapters will have shown that most theory-building is based on the productivity concept. In particular, the debates of the 1980s on the development of household services, referred to in Chapter 4, revolved around the postulated low growth of productivity in service activities. Consequently, the debate led to a closer scrutiny of the concept and of the possibilities of measuring productivity in a satisfactory way. This scrutiny, taking place in the late 1980s and early 90s, resulted in severe criticism of the current measurement of productivity, especially in service activities. The arguments summarized in this chapter have been presented by, inter alia, Strassmann (1985), Gadrey (1986b, 1988a, b, 1991a, 1992a), Barcet (1987), Ruyssen (1987a), Delaunay and Gadrey (1987), de Bandt (1988, 1991b, c, 1994a, 1995), Block and Burns (1988), Illeris (1989d), Siniscalco (1989), Hansen (1990), and Stanback and Noyelle (1990).

Other ways of evaluating the outcome of service activities will also be discussed, and an attempt will be made to assess current tendencies as regards the results of service activities in relation to the use of resources.

THE CONCEPT AND MEASUREMENT OF PRODUCTIVITY

The productivity concept became widely accepted and operationalized in the largely industrial economy of the 1930s and 40s, when national accounts were set up under Keynesian inspiration (see e.g. Petit, 1985, and Madsen, 1989).

The absolute productivity values are rarely interesting. The focus is on comparisons: is the performance better or worse than last year's, than another sector's, than another country's?

In principle all resources or factors of production should enter into the denominator. In agricultural studies, area productivity is often measured, such as yield per hectare. However, in economic studies, attention is more often than not focused on labour productivity—output per number of persons or (better) the number of working hours employed—and 'productivity' will also be used in this sense in this book.

The criticism of the denominator is that while a 'person' or 'working hour' previously were entities which could reasonably well be compared between periods, sectors or countries, since labour primarily was 'manpower', this is no longer the case. As discussed in Chapter 7, in the contemporary economy the different qualifications of different groups are so decisive for economic activities that it makes little sense just to relate the results of production to the number of persons or working hours. However, little has been done to differentiate inputs in an operational way.

Even worse problems, however, are met on the numerator side. The definition above assumes that the economic activity results in a 'product' or 'output' that can be identified, measured, and meaningfully compared to the results of economic activities earlier or elsewhere. For instance, how many tons of wheat were produced, how many tons of steel? Clearly, this assumption is satisfied in the production of simple, standardized goods in agricultural and mass-producing industrial societies. But already in industrial societies with a more differentiated production, there are problems. It is still possible to identify the products, of course. But if no comparable products were made previously, it is not possible to calculate the development of productivity.

It is still worse when we come to services. Some service products appear to be reasonably well defined, e.g. the air travel of a person from London to New York, but even in such cases it may be questionable what is really produced: seat kilometres or passenger kilometres. However, the most typical service activities do not produce identifiable outputs. As discussed in Chapter 2, they are relations, the results of which are changes in the condition of a person, or of a good belonging to a person. But such relations are typically unique—there are never two identical relations—and so are the changes, which may furthermore be extremely difficult to measure in a precise way. To this, one has to add the time horizon: whereas the production of goods immediately results in a product, and there is a clear distinction between the production activity and the consumption activity, the consumption of most services cannot be distinguished from the production, and the effect of service activities (the change) is in many cases obtained only in the long run.

The purchase of advice from a management consultant may illustrate the point. This is clearly a relation, or a dialogue, where the clients must describe their ways of functioning and their problems as accurately as possible. A tangible 'product' may be a report with recommendations. But obviously this report is not interesting in itself. The essential question is whether the client follows the recommendations, and whether this, in due course, leads to the solution to the problems; in other words, whether the needs of the customer are met.

Teaching may be used as another example. The Danish law on schools states that the purpose of the teaching is to promote the many-sided development of the pupils: their wish to learn; their creativity, their ability to assess questions independently and be citizens in a democratic society. Obviously, these are effects which are difficult to measure, which can only be evaluated after many years, and which are influenced by many other factors than the schools. There is no well-defined 'product' that can be related to the number of teachers' hours and compared to the 'productivity' of teaching in other periods or countries. Standard measurements, e.g. the number of pupil-hours taught per teacher per year, have obviously extremely little to do with the effect which should be measured.

Firms which buy advertising are not interested in the number of advertisements they get for their money, but in the amount of customers and sales which are the effect of these advertisements. The effect is influenced by the information 'overkill' in contemporary societies—the production of information is enormous, only little of it has any effect.

In the late 1980s, the Danish Ministry of Finance issued a number of instructions to all government agencies, ordering them to increase their productivity by several per cent annually. They stopped, however, when the question was posed to them as to how they could meaningfully measure their own work (preparing bills, policies and budgets, writing and negotiating circulars, etc.). Clearly, the number of bills and circulars would be an extremely irrelevant expression of the result of the ministry's work, which should be an efficient use of economic resources in the society as a whole and in the public sector in particular. In this case, it is not even possible to identify the users of the services precisely. It is a case of 'pure public services', just like police and defence.

The focus on immediate products and productivity is very widespread in our societies, still thinking in terms of industrial economies with well-defined outputs. But very often, such attempts at productivity measurement remind one of the drunkard looking one dark night for his lost key under a street lamp. Asked by a policeman whether that was where he had lost his key, he answered 'No, but this is the only place where there is light enough to look for it'.

While the result of some service activities may be identified and measured in the same way as the result of the production of goods, this is impossible in the case of typical relational service activities. For half a century, statisticians who have been socialized into the economics of goods production have tried to do so, considering service products as just 'immaterial goods'. But these measurements are often painfully irrelevant. They simply do not measure what they intend to measure. Or in scientific language: they are not valid.

Thus, the concept of 'productivity' does not tell us enough about the results of the activity and the use of resources. It remains important, of course, that the service producer uses resources in an efficient way. But in the case of typical service activities, the immediate, direct results, the 'output', cannot be identified in any meaningful way, and hence no meaningful 'productivity' can be measured. Instead of that, we must focus on the long-term effects or 'outcome' of the activities, which divided by the resource input is called 'effectiveness'. Both sets of concepts may be relevant, but they answer different questions. And effectiveness can usually not be measured quantitatively, but must be evaluated in softer terms. There is now a growing interest in studying the performance of whole systems with many uses of resources, in spite of the difficulties of such studies.

As it is said popularly: 'Effectiveness answers the question of whether the right thing is done. Productivity answers the question of whether it is done in the right way'.

But there are more problems connected with the productivity concept in services. One of them is the participation of the users in typical services. This means that not only the producers and their efficient use of resources influence the activity, but also the motivation and qualifications of users. For instance, it is infinitely easier to obtain good outcomes in a school receiving children from a group of the population with commonly held norms that learning is a good thing, than in a school receiving children from a group with heterogeneous and conflicting norms.

A final problem is that the effect of services is often obtained in another economic unit or sector than the one which produces the service. Business service activities—for instance research and development activities—may possibly show modest productivity increases if measured as an isolated sector. But if the effects of their services are large productivity increases among their clients, the only meaningful procedure is to consider the system of service producers and users as a whole. At least, comparisons are only meaningful if the delimitation of the system is the same in all cases. If business services which previously were produced internally in the user firms are externalized (see discussion in Chapter 6), the user sectors may—all other things being equal—suddenly show increases in productivity, which are pure statistical illusions. Indeed, many service activities with an infrastructural character (education, health services, etc.) may be said to improve the functioning of the society as a whole, and the outcome can only be evaluated in this context.

HOW TO MEASURE PRODUCTIVITY IN SERVICES

In the measurement of productivity of service activities, there are not only the theoretical problems discussed above, but also a number of practical problems in the measurement of products or outputs and their comparability over time and space, especially on the numerator side. Of course, it is only meaningful to compare productivity if the resource inputs are used to produce identical outputs.

Within a firm or a sector, the simplest output measures are physical ones, for instance how many tons of wheat or steel are the output of a given activity, using a certain amount of resources? In office work, a few of the simplest, now often computerized, operations may be counted: how many invoices sent in a certain period? Such measures are often used internally in firms or sectors. But as products become more differentiated, even such measures pose problems. Steel, for instance, is now produced in so many varieties that meaningful comparisons can only be made for each variety separately. *The Economist* of 22 October 1994 had an interesting example of lamps. Official statistics show a slight fall since 1800 in the price of lamps, in constant prices. However, if the quality—which can be measured quite precisely in lumen-hours—is taken into consideration, the price reduction becomes 1000 times greater! Services, too, often become better over time. Just think of the speed and comfort of railway travel in continental Europe. In *The*

Economist of 28 January 1995, the reliability of productivity measures in contemporary economies is questioned, since they tend to ignore advances in quality. As regards travel, a first class railway trip on a high-speed train is clearly another 'product' from a second class trip on a slow train.

When the question is the total productivity of a firm or a sector, the problem is that they make many products. If these products are sold on a market, they may be measured in money terms, a question which will be discussed later. But public institutions which do not sell their products on a market often apply measurements in physical units. The problem is then whether 'products' can be identified which in a valid way reflect the total activity. It may be accepted that for libraries, the number of books lent forms such an indicator, even if the library performs other activities as well (giving advice, etc.). In research, it is debatable whether the number of citations in recognized international journals is a valid expression of the purpose of increased understanding and knowledge—at least the number of publications or pages is not. Most of the indicators applied to measure the effect of schools and hospitals fall far short of being meaningful or valid. When governments put pressure on public service producers to increase productivity, the results are often just reduced quality, for instance more students per teacher.

Comparisons over broad sectors, or between sectors, make it necessary to measure output in money terms (the purpose of money is of course to provide a common yardstick for the value of different commodities). However, in order to measure productivity—to relate the result of the economic activity to the resource input—one has to measure the product as 'value added', that is the price less the price of raw materials and services bought to produce the product. (When measuring the products in physical terms, one ought to have done the same thing, but that is not possible.)

Productivity measurements in money terms confront several problems. The first is that the prices of different products vary from period to period and from place to place. While in some circumstances, it may be meaningful to compare products at 'current price' or at 'exchange rates', the concept of productivity requires that the price of the product (as well as the price of raw materials and services bought) is kept constant—otherwise the comparison between two measurements would not show whether the same product was produced with more or fewer resources. There has been little discussion of geographical comparisons at constant prices, but a lot of discussion of comparisons over time, using deflators in order to obtain constant prices.

Here, the main problem is that the prices of different products develop differently over time. Hence, when one compares the productivity of large sectors or whole economies, it is necessary to use a large number of deflators, to calculate the development of each product, or at least group of products, separately, and then to add them according to their weights. Furthermore, the prices of raw materials and services bought must also be deflated separately ('double deflation'). Actually, for the calculation of national accounts the statistical offices use thousands of deflators.

However, as products get more and more differentiated—there are now not thousands, but rather millions of different material products—and 'last' for shorter and shorter periods before they are changed radically, this whole system of double deflation tends to become less and less meaningful. An example is that in the American national accounts, there were no deflators of computers before 1985 (Block & Burns 1988).

It is bad enough that many industrial products are changed frequently, so it is difficult to consider really comparable products. But as already stressed, typical services are relational, and there are never two identical relations, which tends to make comparisons of the productivity of typical services nonsensical. Undoubtedly, there is a tendency towards quality increases in many services. With increasing understanding and improving technical support, a physician, a teacher or an engineer can produce better services than before—which is never expressed in simple indicators like the number of consultations, lessons or project-hours, but which may be the most important factor behind increasing service prices.

Another problem with productivity measurements in money terms is, of course, that public non-marketed services financed via taxes do not have a price. In national accounts, their value is then put equal to the costs (primarily wages and salaries) of their production. But that means that the productivity is defined as the resources used for their production, divided by the resources used for their production! As regards comparisons over time, then, only a single deflation is applied, which means that productivity increases are defined as equal to salary increases, which anybody with the slightest knowledge of the public sector would characterize as nonsense.

However, there are also private service sectors where it is more or less impossible to identify products and prices meaningfully. In the financial sector, where money is at the same time the object and the price of the activity, no 'product' can be identified. Some calculations apply the margin between deposit interests and lending interests as an expression of the 'output', but of course this depends on many other factors than the efficient use of resources. In trade, gross profit is applied, but the same criticism is relevant here. Indeed, in times of intensified competition, retailers and wholesalers tend at the same time to reduce their gross profit and increase the efficiency in their use of resources! In business services and many other services, no standard products exist which can be compared. In these cases, deflation is based on the development of input prices (salaries), with the weaknesses mentioned in connection with public services.

The many problems connected with the measurement and deflation of products, and in particular with services, are 'solved' differently by statistical authorities in different countries. In some countries, e.g. Sweden, they have completely given up in some sectors and quite arbitrarily chosen to calculate with a 2 per cent increase in productivity per year! As a result, the frequently quoted international comparisons of productivity increases are totally ramshackle.

De Bandt (1995) mentions that official French statistics in 1993 reported a decline in GDP which led to currency speculation and to the breakdown of the European currency system. However, this reported decline—largely influenced by a decline in the production of services—was probably false. His estimate is that service production in constant prices increased, but that prices went down while salaries (used to calculate output in constant prices) at the same time increased.

One may also inverse the problem and say that a given measured development in productivity may be due to widely different factors. For instance, Gadrey, Noyelle and Stanback (1991) by detailed studies in food retailing measured parallel developments in productivity in France and the United States in 1978–86. But the backgrounds were very different. In France there was a considerable sector of old-fashioned groceries with low productivity growth plus an expanding high productivity hypermarket sector. In the United States, the former type hardly existed any longer, but a large part of the modern sector was in a process of quality increases (better information to customers, etc.) which was measured as stagnating productivity.

THE DEVELOPMENT OF PRODUCTIVITY IN SERVICES

From the above, it will be understood that I shall not attempt to present detailed quantitative data showing the development of productivity in services. They are not credible. But as already said, it *is* important how service activities develop in relation to the resources used—in particular the amount of human work. An assessment in qualitative terms might include the following considerations.

In some service activities, the use of capital goods is so important and expanding that there is no doubt that the result in relation to the work input is rapidly increasing. This is the case in transport, telecommunications and in service activities, spread over several sectors, where microelectronics play a large role. Some of the latter activities are clerical and banking, where it was feared in the late 1970s that computerization might lead to dramatically reduced employment. Such reductions did not occur in the 1980s, but there were other effects, such as the upskilling discussed in Chapter 7. However, in the 1990s, the reduction has started in banking and may again be feared in clerical work. The delay could be explained by the many organizational adaptations required to fully exploit new technology.

But the capital-intensive service activities remain exceptions. In most services, especially those consisting in relations, there are many factors which limit the possibilities of productivity growth:

1   Many service activities are so unique and different from case to case that only limited rationalization is possible. This is especially the case in the person-related services (bodycare, health, childcare, care for elderly, education). But also information services (business services) and maintenance and repair of physical objects are often individualized, see Chapter 3.

2   The need for the service producer and the service user to be together at the same time and place means that many service producers have few customers and much unused capacity in some periods, and that they may have to use time

travelling to the users (of course, in other cases the service users travel to the producers).

3 The need for proximity between service producers and users also means that many service activities have a local monopoly, or at least that they are little exposed to international competition. Hence the incentive for productivity increases is reduced. In particular, public services are often totally sheltered against competition.

4 In many cases, service markets are opaque, as discussed in Chapter 2. The customer does not know in advance what is bought. This may lead to authorization arrangements, and to high customer loyalty—all factors which reduce competition and hence the incentive to increased productivity.

5 In most service activities, it is difficult to substitute machines for men. Economies of scale remain modest.

6 The relational character of typical services means that the result depends much on the quality and motivation of the service users—factors which may vary considerably.

7 In the United States, the low wage levels for unskilled work have probably had the effect of allowing an amount of low-productivity service work with no equivalent in Western Europe. This has had the effect of reducing overall productivity growth in US service activities.

As mentioned in Chapter 4, there are also forces which pull towards more rapid productivity growth in service activities, for instance standardization and computerization. But altogether, I find it likely that productivity increases are slower in most service activities than in the production of goods.

Whether the slow increases have had the effect postulated by Baumol (1967), of reducing the total growth of productivity in economies where service activities become dominating, remains an open question. Baumol regarded the individual sectors as isolated cases. But as argued above, they are not: service activities with modest internal productivity increases may contribute to productivity increases in other sectors, and in society as a whole. There is no evidence that productivity increases should generally be declining in advanced economies.

A shift towards 'self-service', as an effect of slow productivity growth in the formal economy, as postulated by Gershuny (1978) and Skolka (1976), probably exists in some cases, see the discussion in Chapter 4. But price increases may also reflect increased quality of services, or increased demand as argued by Rappoport (1987).

CONCLUSION

Whether resources are used efficiently in economic activities or not is important. Productivity and effectiveness remain key concepts in the arguments of this book as well as elsewhere, in all economic theory. However, in the case of service activities, it is more often than not impossible to measure and compare productivities in any meaningful or valid way, for a number of theoretical and practical reasons. Given the weight of service activities in contemporary economies, the many economists, statistical authorities, governments and firms which base their analyses and policies on the decimals of productivity data are victims of illusions. At best, productivity data can be used in a very crude way— differences of several percentage points probably indicate real differences in performance.

Basically, the measurement of productivity belongs to the mass-producing industrial society with its long series of identical, well-defined products. A type of production which of course still exists, it is none the less gradually being superseded by much more differentiated economic activities largely consisting of service relations.

As a tool to assess activities, the focus should be more on effectiveness studies, bearing in mind that such evaluations are qualitative.

With these reservations, there are good reasons to believe that the increase of productivity is slower in typical service activities than in the production of goods. But services may cause productivity increases in other sectors, and there is no evidence that the growth of service activities should reduce productivity growth generally in advanced economies.

6 Development of Producer Services

Producer (or intermediate) service activities, whose products are used by firms and public institutions, form a small but rapidly growing part of service activities. They are partly performed internally in the user organizations by persons in service occupations, partly by firms whose main outputs are services and which therefore belong to the service sector. The producer service firms are predominantly private, but transport and communication are public services in many countries (though currently candidates for privatization).

Producer service firms are spread over several of the classes of official statistics. The most important subsectors are wholesaling, goods transport, cleaning, leasing —all dealing with things—agencies of temporary labour, dealing with persons, and business services (consultants, computer services, etc.) dealing with information. Business services, requiring high qualifications and showing particularly rapid employment growth, correspond to Reich's 'symbolic analysts' and have attracted by far the most service research of recent years. In addition, there are a number of subsectors serving both households and firms which have attracted more specialized sectoral research, e.g. passenger transport, hotels, finance and insurance.

Some producer service products can only be sold or delivered over short distances and are not directly traded internationally. They may be sold in other countries via branch offices or partners, as discussed in Chapter 13. Other producer services are more independent of proximity to customers. Many details in the Appendix, presenting case studies of engineering consultants, computer services, and management consultants, may illustrate the more general discussion of producer services in this chapter.

The production of most producer services is, as discussed in Chapter 5, difficult to measure meaningfully, but employment figures are presented in Table 4.1 and Figure 4.1. In Table 6.1, employment data for the narrower class of business services are shown. The table illustrates the rapid employment growth in business service activities, which in most countries have more or less trebled their share of total employment between 1960 and 1987.

Until the 1970s, producer services were largely ignored by research. Early approaches were from a physical planning point of view ('offices', e.g. Goddard 1975), from a contact and communications point of view (Törnqvist 1970), or from a demand and growth point of view (Illeris 1972). It was only in the 1980s that more researchers focused on this sector, partly motivated by its high growth rates and partly by its key role in the emerging 'post-Fordist', 'service' or 'information society', see discussion in Chapter 14. Over the last 10 years, there has been a massive wave of research on producer services.

Table 6.1. Employment in business services in five countries, 1960–1987. *Source:* J. Gadrey (1992b) Complexité et incertitude au coeur du besoin de services de conseil, pp. 157–175 in J. Gadrey et al, *Manager le conseil.* Reproduced by permission of Ediscience International, Paris.

	% of total employment	
	1960	1987
France[a]	1.9	5.5
West Germany[b]	1.4	3.6
UK	2.1	5.8
Japan	1.5	6.2
USA	2.1	7.5

[a] 1962 and 1987.
[b] 1961 and 1987.

Researchers have primarily focused on the interaction between producer service activities and manufacturing industry, asking themselves if the former just supported the latter, or if the economic dynamics were based on the interaction between them (see discussion in Chapter 2). However, it must be stressed that except for a few special cases like Germany, all input–output tables and case studies show that the producer service sector sells more to other service activities than it sells to manufacturing and other secondary sector activities. For instance Beyers and Lindahl (1994a), interviewing 180 legal, engineering and architectural, and management consulting firms in the United States, found the market composition shown in Table 6.2.

More information on the market composition of producer services is found in Chapter 8. It confirms that they normally sell considerably more to other service establishments (firms and public institutions) than they sell to goods-producing firms.

The question which will be discussed in this chapter is: why does employment (and presumably output) in producer service activities grow so rapidly?

First, it will be discussed whether the growth might be a statistical illusion, created by a tendency for firms to externalize service functions which previously were performed internally and thus registered as an activity of the user firm and

Table 6.2. Current markets of 180 business service firms, USA 1993. *Source:* Calculated from Beyers and Lindahl (1994a), Table 3.

	%
Households	3
Agriculture, etc.	4
Manufacturing	22
Construction	5
Governments	20
Other services	46
Total	100

sector (just as an externalization of service activities from households was observed, see Chapter 4). The externalization question has given rise to much research and will be discussed thoroughly. Second, other causes of growth in producer service activities will be taken up, in particular increasing demand and its background.

EXTERNALIZATION AND INTERNALIZATION OF PRODUCER SERVICES

How important are the externalization tendencies in producer service activities? Are they counterbalanced by tendencies towards internalization? What are the causes? Or to use the many other terms that are applied to the same phenomena: Make or buy? Bundling or unbundling? Hierarchy or market? Vertical integration or disintegration? Insourcing or outsourcing? Technical or social division of labour? These questions will now be discussed. But it will also be asked whether the question of externalization *or* internalization is a false one. Is it not, rather than either-or, a question of both-and? Rather than substitution, a question of complementarity?

IS THE GROWTH IN PRODUCER SERVICE ACTIVITIES A STATISTICAL ILLUSION?

The question of whether the rapid growth observed in the producer service sector in the 1980s was false, just a shift in the organization of activities that earlier had taken place inside the user organizations, can be answered by a categorical no. While firms generally tend to buy more external services, there is no doubt that at the same time, the internal service activities in the user firms grow, too, rather than decline. It is hardly possible to obtain meaningful production data on internal services, but employment data on occupations show that, for instance, in the manufacturing sector, the share of service employment in total employment is not declining.

Most data available refer to rather crude distinctions between blue- and white-collar workers, or between salary and wage earners, and tend to underestimate service occupations. Thus, official statistics said that 30 per cent of the employees of the toy factory Lego (Denmark) were salaried in 1986, which is usually taken as a characteristic of white-collar workers. But a detailed study by Nielsen and Sørensen (1987) found that 46 per cent worked in non-production departments. However, the share of salaried personnel in Swedish manufacturing grew from 24 per cent in 1964 to 31 per cent in 1987, in Denmark from 24 per cent in 1971 to 32 per cent in 1989, and according to Ecalle (1989), employment not directly involved in production increased from 32 to 40 per cent in West German manufacturing 1961–82. In some countries, the share of service workers seems to stagnate in the 1980s, but there is no decline (with the exception of the UK, see

Marshall 1989). More detailed occupational classifications of employment in the US manufacturing sector 1970–86 show that managerial, professional and technical jobs increase both as a share of total employment and in absolute numbers, while clerical, sales and lower service workers decline as a share, but still grow in absolute numbers (Kutscher 1988).

Another argument in favour of the 'statistical illusion hypothesis', brought forward by e.g. Scharpf (1985), is that declining manufacturing employment plus the growing producer service employment together tend to make up a constant share of total employment. Hence, there should be no above-average producer service growth, only a shift into external firms of some of the former manufacturing employment. However, this argument is not valid. As was mentioned above, more than half of external producer services are sold to other service activities. So the external producer service employment behind these sales cannot be added to the manufacturing employment. Thus, there *is* a net growth in the total share of service employment, and a reduction in the total share of, even enlarged, manufacturing employment.

A tendency of split-off of service activities into more or less independent subsidiaries was recognizable in Sweden in the early 1980s, but declined later (Statens Industriverk 1989). Bonamy (1988) and Perry (1990) conclude, too, that such split-offs are insignificant, but when they occur, they attract the attention of the media. De Bandt (1995) notes that for skilled service employees, the only way to obtain an increased remuneration may be to break out of their parent firm and sell their services directly on the market.

MORE GROWTH IN INTERNAL OR EXTERNAL SERVICE PRODUCTION—AND WHY?

On the question of how many and what producer services are internal, how many and what external, one theory has dominated the discussion, namely the so-called transaction cost theory (Williamson 1985). It represents a further development of the discussion following the question Coase posed in 1937: why are economic activities organized in firms? His answer was: because there are often lower costs connected with the coordination of activities and allocation of resources by management than there would be by coordination and allocation by the market. Firms will grow until the marginal costs of internal management exceed the marginal costs of external transactions—such as costs connected with the search for partners, negotiations, monitoring of contracts, the risk of opportunistic behaviour, and so on.

In Williamson's opinion, external transactions will have low costs when they are rare and do not require specific resources (qualifications or equipment which cannot be applied to other tasks), while transaction costs will be high and internal solutions preferable when the commodity in question is needed frequently and/or requires specific resources. The theory relates to the provision with inputs of both goods and services. But since the quality of most services is difficult to foresee and control, and markets are opaque, external transaction costs tend to be high.

A main weakness of this school is that it is almost purely theoretical. It is difficult to test its statements empirically, especially the costs of internal management. (One of the purposes of corporations, when they split off service departments, is exactly to force them to quantify the real costs of service production.) By focusing on the costs of external transactions, the theory has a bias in favour of internalization. Indeed, Tordoir (1993) argues that the 'transaction costs' may very well be just as high for internal procurement—especially in large, bureaucratic and complex organizations—as for external, but they are not known in the internal case. Barcet and Bonamy (1994b) stress that through the establishment of long-term networks with external service suppliers, users can reduce transaction costs—these are regarded as investments that should yield benefits in the long run. Apart from this, the choice between internal and external production is influenced by factors that can hardly be called 'costs'. Examples will be presented later.

In recent decades, flexibility has gradually become a decisive quality for firms, as 'Fordist' mass production for stable markets of mass consumption is increasingly superseded by segmented and turbulent markets. This process is discussed in more detail in Chapter 14. One way to increase flexibility is by disintegration of large, vertically integrated corporations into more independent divisions. Such divisions, as well as small enterprises, may then cooperate in networks and exchange goods and services in a flexible way. In other words, firms optimize their competitiveness by being slim and concentrating on their core skills—and then buy goods and services which require other skills.

Many scholars suggest that this process results in a tendency to net externalization of producer services, e.g. Lambooy (1989), Andersen (1991), Gadrey (1992a), Hansen (1994). It is particularly interesting that some industrial corporations in recent years have externalized most manufacturing production and concentrated on strategy and management, research, development and design, possibly logistics and distribution (Quinn, Doorley & Paquette 1990). Thus, they regard these service functions as their core activities, while the material production itself is understood as a more peripheral task. Sjøholt (1994) and Barcet and Bonamy (1994b) think that the recession of the early 1990s led to a net reinternalization, while Schamp (1995) has the opposite view.

However, empirical evidence on the development of externalization or internalization over time is scarce. Ochel and Wegner (1987) calculated the service consumption of West German manufacturing industry and found that the external part increased from 28.3 per cent in 1975 to 30.7 per cent in 1982. Gruhler (1990) calculated the degree of externalization in German manufacturing to be 35.5 per cent in 1970 and 36.0 per cent in 1980, and in the US to be 49.7 per cent in 1972 and 51.2 per cent in 1982. Using a questionnaire survey in British manufacturing, O'Farrell, Moffat and Hitchens (1993) observed a slight net tendency towards internalization of producer services, while Perry's surveys in New Zealand (1990, 1992) showed a slight net externalization, and Fournier and Axelsson (1993) found a slight increase in the share of external services in Swedish manufacturing from 47.6 to 48.8 per cent in the three-year period 1986–1989.

Beyers and Lindahl (forthcoming) found a slight tendency towards externalization in a study of American business services.

Altogether, the empirical evidence indicates no strong tendency towards either externalization or internalization of producer services. The increasing use of producer services seems to be more or less equally distributed between external and internal production, though in most cases with a slight preponderance of externalization.

For individual types of services, there may be a clear tendency. Thus, Perry as well as Gruhler notes an externalization of advertising and an internalization of computer services, the latter supported by the introduction of personal computers (see discussion in the Appendix). In Denmark, most local governments used consultants for their physical planning. But when new legislation in 1977 increased their tasks, the amount of work became sufficient to employ internal staff, and this destroyed the consultancy market, except for very specialized services. In recent years, there has been a tendency towards externalization of a large number of services from the public sector in many countries (Pinch 1989; Dale 1994; Allen & Henry 1995).

While empirical evidence on development over time is scarce, many cross-sectional surveys have been made. Table 6.3 shows the results of a study, commissioned by the Commission of the European Community (1990). Other studies are quoted in Chapter 8.

Table 6.3 shows that the degree of externalization does not systematically depend on the size or sophistication of user firms—though a tendency to greater externalization may be distinguished among medium-sized users (confirmed by Gruhler 1990). This may be explained, on the one hand, by the limited resources of small users—they cannot afford to buy external services, and it may be against their enterprise culture—and, on the other hand, by the fact that very large users can internalize even quite specialized service activities.

As regards the different types of producer services, book-keeping, management, marketing, staff management and recruitment, R&D, and storage tend to be predominantly internal activities, while advertising, banking, insurance, legal and tax-consulting services as well as transport and cleaning are bought externally (in some cases, this is mandatory due to legislation). Computing services are often co-produced. Evidence on engineering is contradictory. Generally, frequently used services tend to be produced internally, and rare ones to be bought externally.

Tordoir (1993) and Gallouj (1993) find that the internal production of business services is considerably more important than external purchase. Independent firms tend to use relatively more external services than branch firms.

TOWARDS A REVISED THEORY: MORE FACTORS ARE INFLUENTIAL

In recent years, a number of empirical studies have investigated the reasons that lead service users to choose internal provision or external purchase of producer services: Larsen (1992), Gallouj (1993), Rekkavik and Spillum (1990), Wood

Table 6.3. Externalization of business services in the European Community 1988. *Source:* Reproduced by permission from European Commission, communication III/89/2234/EN/ rev2 (1990).

Sector	Origin of the service (%)		
	Solely external	Solely internal	Combined
Engineering and related	56	14	30
Management consultancy	35	37	28
Advertising	49	24	27
Public relations	11	59	30
Computing services	22	26	55
Research & development	12	58	30
Legal services	41	21	38
Operational services	58	22	20
Country			
Germany (West)	32	47	21
France	56	30	14
Italy	47	33	18
Netherlands	39	18	43
United Kingdom	34	23	43
Size (employment)			
0–50	37	44	19
51–500	56	22	22
501–1000	38	29	33
1001–5000	39	35	26
5000+	37	33	30

(1994), Tordoir (1993), Poulfeldt (1990), Beyers and Lindahl (1994b), Strambach (1994), and Gruhler (1990). These studies have applied various interview and questionnaire methods among both service producers and users, and it is not possible to summarize the results in one table. However, together they give a picture that is radically different from the deductive one drawn up by Williamson. By far the most important reason for externalization is simply that the user firm does not possess the needed expertise. This can only indirectly be called a question of comparing costs and frequency, if one argues that the user might alternatively employ the necessary experts, but that these then would be very expensive if there were no work for them most of the time. Other important reasons for external purchases are to supplement one's own capacity in peak periods (where the same argument may be applied), to minimize perceived (fixed) costs and increase flexibility, and some totally non-economic factors: to obtain impartial assessments of problems (independent of internal 'political' groupings); to bypass the manning or wage demands of strong unions; and to get fresh inspiration/'new eyes'. Reasons for choosing internal provision have been less studied, but unwillingness to let outsiders interfere in strategic problems was mentioned several times. The specificity-factor was rarely mentioned.

On the basis of the empirical evidence, theoretical analyses have been carried out by these authors as well as by Maillat (1990), Goe (1990, 1991), Gadrey (1992c), Hansen (1990), de Bandt (1994a, 1995) and Perry (1992). Their main points of view are as follows.

Through internalization, the user firm secures better control; which in many cases is essential, given the uncertainty surrounding services which cannot be standardized in the same way as goods. Furthermore, users wish to keep services and knowledge of strategic importance confidential and regard them as core functions, e.g. R&D and design. If they use consultants, it is primarily for analysis and advice, not for implementation.

Factors pulling towards externalization, on the other hand, are those that increase flexibility. The user firm substitutes variable costs for fixed costs. In American labour market research (see Chapter 7), externalization has been stressed as one of the ways in which corporations could get more flexibility in their use of manpower (Noyelle 1990b; Christopherson 1989). However, Gadrey (1991b) stresses that not only low-skill personnel, but also experts are used in a more flexible way through externalization. The flexibility consideration applies to other kinds of costs, too. The risks of fluctuating demand are shifted to the subcontractor. Large, rigid and bureaucratic organizations are broken down.

Externalization is attractive for functions which are of peripheral significance, such as cleaning, legal problems and environmental improvements. This may be one of the reasons why, in manufacturing firms, numbers of low-skill service personnel expand less than for high-skill service personnel, as mentioned above (though peripheral services are not necessarily low skill, as illustrated by the environment example).

However, specialized services are often externalized, too. The reason is that, compared to internal production, the external specialized service producer is able to minimize costs and gain economies of scale, compared to a user who only needs the services infrequently and in between would have unused capacity. The external producer is also able to reach higher specialization and quality levels by getting experience from a variety of tasks, which is very important. It is important, too, that there are several services which many small user firms cannot possibly produce internally. For them, the choice is between buying them or not using them at all (Christensen 1994), and a lack of local external service suppliers may be a serious problem, as discussed in Chapter 10.

De Bandt (1994a) argues that the transaction cost theory is quite wrong: for business services, the opaque markets and high search costs as well as the high degree of specialization should lead to total internalization—which has not happened. As regards the provision of specialized services, the externalization is explained by the typical expert not being firm-specific and rarely used. An extreme example is the expert who knows how to stop oil well fires.

Besides, there are advantages of a non-economic kind connected with externalization. First, the use of external service providers may be a way to circumvent internal 'political' problems or to legitimate decisions already taken by management. Second, as stressed by Porter (1990), it is crucial to get external impulses and inspiration, to avoid 'inbreeding'. Innovation in business services seems primarily to be created in the interaction between users and external providers (Maillat 1990). Finally, some services are required by legislation to be bought externally, in particular auditing, or else they have a collective nature and must be shared by many users (insurance).

Altogether, there are advantages and disadvantages connected with both ex- and internalization. It may be chance whether a certain innovation was invented ex- or internally. There may be a certain room within which the users are free to act without disastrous consequences. This conclusion is strengthened by international differences, such as those shown in Table 6.3 and those referred to in Chapter 12. It is clear that different solutions are practised in different countries, according to national traditions and enterprise cultures. An extreme case is Germany with its strong tradition for firms to keep service production 'in house' (Lambooy 1989; Goe 1991). However, the former East-Central European systems seem to have had virtually no external service provision. The lack of external impulses may have been a main factor behind the disastrous lack of innovative capacity in their production systems.

SUBSTITUTION OR COMPLEMENTARITY?

The above discussion of external *or* internal provision of producer services was based on the competitive logics inherent in Williamson's theory: a given service input must either be produced internally or bought externally. Empirical support of this notion has been presented by Pousette and Lindberg (1990) who, in a survey of Swedish manufacturing firms, found a negative correlation between their use of internal and external services.

However, many authors have challenged this notion and stress the complementarity and interaction between internal and external services (e.g. O'Farrell, Moffat & Hitchens 1993; Cuadrado 1990; Gadrey 1992a; Tordoir 1993; de Bandt 1994a, 1995). The customer of a consultant, for instance, must contribute by expressing their problems, offer feedback in a reciprocal learning process, absorb the results and mediate them in their own organization. In the extreme case, the role of the consultant is a 'Socrates model': to provoke the user to solve the problem himself. Tordoir distinguishes 'sparring' services, consisting of interaction on broad management problems, and specialized, technical 'jobbing' services, defined by and absorbed by the client—in neither of these cases is there a real choice between internal and external provision. As stressed in Chapter 2, such services are typical relations with considerable co-production from the user side. If a user—e.g. a government agency—does not devote sufficient resources to these functions, the money with which they pay the consultant is wasted. (Another case is that of a government which finances consultants to serve a third party, e.g. a Third World service user. In this case, the government needs only to monitor the consultant, not to absorb the services.)

Empirical support of this notion is given by the high degree of combined production in Table 6.3, as well as by Pedersen (1986), who in a study in Esbjerg, Denmark, found that the more internal services firms produced, the more external services they bought—because they had staff who knew what could be supplied externally, could communicate with providers, and absorb the results. Tordoir (1994) reached similar results in the US: there was a high positive correlation between the use of external professional services and the range and development of internal professional functions. Beyers and Lindahl (forthcoming) found in an American study that the clients of most business service firms either did not have a department producing the same kind of services, or had one which did produce them, but was complementary to rather than a competitor of the external supplier.

Undoubtedly, there is some truth in both notions. For well-defined, standardized services without strategic importance—by Tordoir called 'selling' services—the logics of substitution dominate (and that must carry most weight in Pousette and Lindberg's material): firms and institutions either do their own cleaning, or they pay others to do it. And the choice is primarily made on the basis of costs.

On the contrary, as regards information services of strategic importance for the future competitiveness of the user firm, the logics of interaction and complementarity are much stronger. There is no either-or, but a both-and. And the criteria behind the choice of composition are not primarily input costs, but rather expected output quality. These aspects are not taken into consideration by a transaction cost analysis.

As regards the contribution of externalization to the growth of the producer service sector, the conclusion is that there are cases where a clear externalization takes place, but altogether it is not likely that a major part of the recent growth in producer service activities is caused by such a shift. Indeed, in many business services, the 'either-or' question is a false one: internal and external service production mutually reinforce each other. And in most cases, both grow simultaneously.

OTHER CAUSES OF PRODUCER SERVICE GROWTH

Let us now turn to other causes explaining the rapid growth of producer service activities. Beside externalization, four reasons have been suggested.

The first reason—not mentioned by most authors—is commonplace: that a *general growth in the economy* causes all its sectors to grow (all other things being equal). Of course, this factor does not explain the above-average growth rates of most producer service activities.

Second, if the output growth rate in the sector follows that of the total economy while productivity growth is below average, it means an above-average employment growth, merely to *compensate for lagging productivity*. As discussed in Chapter 5, it is hardly possible to measure in a meaningful way whether this happens, but there are good reasons to believe that this is the case in many subsectors.

Then there are components which represent net above-average employment growth which does not compensate for possible productivity lags. The third factor is such a component, namely *exports*. Most West European countries as well as the United States are net exporters of producer services and more or less compensate for net imports of goods in this way.

Finally, a fourth component is *relatively increasing net domestic demand* from firms and institutions. Many studies performed in recent years point out a number of factors which cause a rapid growth in the demand for producer services and in particular business services, performed internally in the user organizations or externally. To mention only some of them: Barcet, Bonamy and Mayère (1983), Lambooy and Tordoir (1986), Beniger (1986), Ruyssen (1987c), Bonamy (1988), Marshall et al (1988), Gruhler (1990), Martinelli (1991a), Coffey and Bailly (1991), OhUallacháin and Reid (1991), Gadrey (1992a, b), Tordoir (1993), Senn (1989), Beyers and Lindahl (forthcoming).

The best way to understand this increasing demand may be to consider the situation of the user organization, whether it produces goods or services. Let us try to describe the situation of a typical manufacturing firm some decades ago and now—even if such descriptions inevitably must be much too simplified—in order to show why more producer services are needed.

Previously, the production itself absorbed most of the man-hours of the typical firm. The planning and marketing of the products were relatively simple affairs, since there were few standardized products and methods of production. The inputs of raw materials, capital and labour force were standardized, too. The markets, mainly domestic, demanded well-known goods and services for mass consumption, and the distribution system was simple. Legal regulations and collective wage bargaining formed a standardized framework. Management largely consisted in combining these factors in such a way as to minimize costs and prices, and sending the corresponding orders down the hierarchy.

Today, the direct production of goods and some services has largely been taken over by machines, though other services still require many man-hours. But all the other functions of firms have become much more complex, unstable and risky. This is true of the relationships both between departments and actors within the firm, and between the firm and the surrounding world. Many types of mediation are required:

1 Markets are much more segmented and turbulent, and in many cases international. The marketing, advertising, and distribution functions have become more demanding, and it has become essential to find out what these diversified markets want, to gather and analyse relevant information, and to communicate conclusions back to management.
2 Product innovation (R&D and design) is necessary in order to meet these diversified and changing demands—adaptation of qualities to demand rather than prices being the crucial parameter of competition. Innovation of production processes and internal organization with the required flexibility

subsequently becomes an essential function, too. The inputs of producer services increase productivity, as noted in Chapter 5.

3 Financing and raw materials can be obtained in an increasing number of forms, and specialists are required to find the forms that are best adapted to the different product lines.

4 The regulatory framework becomes more complex—for instance individual contract bargaining, environmental requirements, physical planning, public subsidies—in spite of government efforts to deregulate some areas. Legal, accounting, environmental services and others expand.

5 Firms have increasingly to communicate with the outside world, not only to buy inputs, sell outputs and adapt to regulations, but also to keep themselves informed about new developments in technology, markets and other factors, and to optimize public relations generally. In a world with a deluge of information, middlemen are required to take care of these flows of communication.

6 In order to perform those operations that are not bought externally, it becomes absolutely essential to employ human resources with high, specialized and changing qualifications, including motivation and other social qualifications. Recruitment, personnel management and upskilling services become crucial.

7 Coordination of all these factors has become immensely more complex and changing, and requires the use of new information technology. Most of the personnel are preparing production, instead of producing themselves. Top management must concentrate on strategic planning, while many integrating decisions must be taken on decentralized levels, thus obliging all units to devote resources to administrative functions.

Even in agriculture, the knowledge inherited from parents is far from sufficient for today's farmer, who needs many services to keep his skills up to date.

In Figure 6.1, Tordoir (1993) has summarized the business ('professional') service functions as mediators between the firm and the complex outer world.

Another attempt to summarize the needs for producer services was made by Dicken (1992), who structured them according to their use before, during, or after the (industrial) production, see Figure 6.2.

Altogether, the growth of internal and external producer services and especially of business services is intimately linked with the emergence of a 'post-Fordist', 'service' or 'information society', which will be further discussed in Chapter 14. Generally, firms increase their competitiveness by integrating and using producer services. Noyelle (1991) claims that the extensive use of business services in the United States service sector underlies its high international competitiveness.

Some authors have attempted to find out how much the service activities contribute to the final product of the user firm, even when this is a good. Thus, Giarini (1988) as well as de Bandt (1995) write that four-fifths of the price of a good may represent services, Bannon, Brassil and Murphy (1994) note 75 per cent, Selstad (1987) 50–75 per cent, Britton (1990) quotes a figure of 75 per cent of the

SOCIAL & INSTITUTIONAL CONDITIONS   PUBLIC OPINIONS

FINANCIAL MARKETS	- finance & ins. consultancy - financial information	- legal consultancy - fiscal consultancy - (political) lobbying	- public relations - external commun.	

COMPETITORS

LABOUR-
MARKETS
	- recruitment
	- external
	  training
		- personnel management - internal
		- internal training communicat.
			- economic
			  analysis &
			  information

DEMAND
MARKET

KNOWLEDGE
&
TECH-
NOLOGY

MATERIAL
SUPPLIES

-management- & organization - corporate
development   planning

FIRM CORE

- technical
  information

- research &
  development   - engineering

- EDP support

- purchasing
- external
  logistics

- internal logistics
- operations management

- facilities management

- financial
  accountancy

- quality
  accountancy

- market
  research

- marketing &
  advertisemt

- relations
  management
- distribution

CLIENTS

- design & maintenance
  of physical infrastructure

- relations with
  the natural environment

PHYSICAL INFRASTUCTURE   NATURAL ENVIRONMENT

Figure 6.1.   Positions of specific professional functions. *Source:* Redrawn after Tordoir (1993).

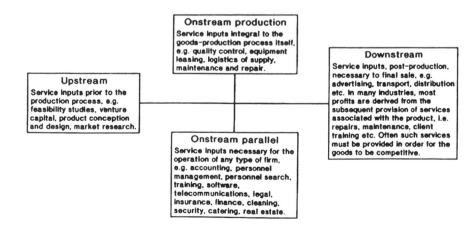

Figure 6.2.   The interconnections between services and production in the production chain. *Source:* Reprinted with permission from P. Dicken (1992), *Global Shift.* Copyright © 1992, Paul Chapman Publishing Ltd, London.

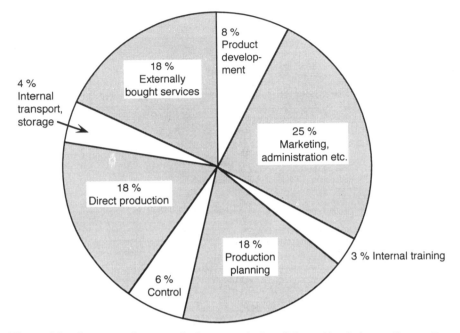

Figure 6.3. Structure of wage and salary costs in Swedish machine industry. *Source:* Data from Eliasson (1990).

value added of the goods production in the USA, and Hansen (1994) 75–85 per cent of the costs of a TV set and 85–90 per cent of the costs of a personal computer. Gruhler (1990) has calculated that in German manufacturing industry, service activities constituted 63 per cent of all activities in 1982, but 68 per cent in 1987— while at the same time, external service purchases increased from 11.6 per cent of the gross production value in 1975 to 14.0 per cent in 1987. Figure 6.3 offers a more detailed picture of the structure of wage and salary costs in Swedish machine industries with over 200 employees in 1986. Service activities here account for 82 per cent of these costs. (Other costs also include some services, e.g. distribution.)

The increasing demand for producer services and their high share of the total input in production constitute evidence of their great importance in the total economy. It might also be attempted more directly to assess the impact of producer services on the performance of their clients. This has not been done in many cases, in spite of the importance of the question. One recent study by O'Farrell and Moffat (1995), however, shows that client satisfaction generally is high, and that most recommendations of the consultants are implemented fully or with minor modifications. This finding may partly be due to the fact that the client often is a co-producer, or that the client is responsible for the hiring of and the brief given to the service firm. As the authors observe, it remains to be studied in more depth what the effect of the services is on the performance of the user.

To sum up, it may be said that the growing complexity of societies and firms, the increasing division of labour, and the growing uncertainty in contemporary economies require firms to use more services in order to increase their control over their environments. No economic activity can exist today without substantial use of services. Evidence quoted in Chapter 8 shows that more sophisticated firms use more services than less advanced firms.

Governments have not interfered much with these processes, but largely left them to market forces, apart from supplying 'soft infrastructure' (education, research, etc.). Policies have, however, been applied in the field of technological innovation and transfer, which seems to interest politicians and media more than organizational skills for instance. Thus many governments have created public or semi-public technological service agencies to improve the dissemination process, assuming, often implicitly, that the market does not result in an efficient transfer of technological knowledge.

CONCLUSION

The recent employment growth in producer services is due to several factors:

1 net externalization from user organizations;
2 growth in the total economies;
3 compensation for lagging productivity;
4 exports;
5 increasing domestic demand.

It is not easy to find out in what proportion these factors contribute. A few authors have set up quantitative models, but they tend not to include all the factors, and use data of questionable validity. Thus, Elfring (1988) has calculated the factors behind total service employment growth, based on seven countries during 1973–84. The model did not work in West Germany. In the other countries 40–60 per cent of employment growth was due to productivity lags, 20–30 per cent to growth in final demand, and 10–40 per cent to growth in intermediate demand. Kutscher (1988) found that 43 per cent of GDP growth in US producer services 1972–86 was explained by general GDP growth, and 55 per cent by changing 'technical coefficients' in the input–output tables (covering both externalization and real growth in demand). Stabler and Howe (1992) note that according to Canadian input–output tables, no externalization happened between 1974 and 1984, the growth in service production being real.

Other attempts to determine the components are based on the amount of activity externalized from user firms to producer services. Thus, in Sweden, jobs externalized from manufacturing were estimated to represent 50 per cent of the growth in producer service jobs in 1977–82—but the proportion is said to have declined later (Statens Industriverk 1986). In a study by Perry (1990), business service firms in Auckland said that only to a modest degree did they get their business from externalization (except from the public sector). The author calculates that the employment growth in the business service sector during 1976–86 is three times bigger than the total number of internal service jobs in manufacturing, so most of the growth must be due to increased demand. A study of new business service firms in the UK by Keeble, Bryson and Wood (1992) showed that for 91 per cent of the firms, less than 10 per cent of their work had been externalized from client firms.

Though the evidence is weak and heterogeneous, the general impression is that net increasing demand is considerably more important than externalization as a source of increased activity in the producer service sector. Sayer and Walker (1992) call this aspect of the increasing division of labour 'indirect labour', but they forget that most of it is used by other service activities, not by the manufacturing sector.

As regards the question of externalization or internalization, the theory most often applied is Williamson's 'transaction cost' theory, which focuses on cost differences, whereby especially frequent and highly specific services should preferably be produced internally. However, recent empirical studies and theoretical work show that this, narrowly economic, theory has not focused on the most important factors. What pulls toward externalization is primarily the need for high-quality, specialized services, the need for flexibility (e.g. substituting fixed costs by variable costs, and buying extra capacity in peak periods), the need for new inspiration, and the need to have problems assessed by outsiders. On the other hand, the need for control and confidentiality about strategic decisions pulls toward internalization.

Furthermore, the substitution logics of the transaction cost theory are not always valid. They may be so in the case of simple services of peripheral importance, for example cleaning: it is either done by the user firm or bought from outside. But high-quality business services are rather created through an interaction process between service producers and users, and follow a both-and logic: the more and better services users produce internally, the more they buy externally.

At any rate, producer services now form an extremely important component in advanced economies, accounting for 75 per cent or more of the input costs of many manufactured goods.

Of course, there is no guarantee that the growth in the producer service sector will continue, though the structural changes behind it seem to form a major long-term trend. Some producer service subsectors suffered rather heavily from the recession of the early 1990s. And Sjøholt (1994) notes that at least as regards banking employment in Scandinavia, this is not only a business cycle fluctuation. Barcet and Bonamy (1994b) think that increasingly qualified service users are losing confidence in the skills of some external service producers—e.g. in management consulting—a point also made by Sjøholt. However, as mentioned in Chapter 1, service output declined less than manufacturing output in this recession. And at least in North America, business services have not stopped increasing their share of total employment, both during and after the recession (Sofianou 1994).

7 Qualifications and Conditions of Work

Employment is of course an extremely important aspect of service activities: in developed countries, most persons work in service sectors and/or service occupations. And for most service activities, the personnel form both the largest cost item and the most important resource. While the quantitative trends in employment are discussed in Chapters 1, 4, and 6, the purpose of the present chapter is to discuss two qualitative aspects: the qualifications of the service personnel and the conditions under which they work—two questions which are usually treated together in the literature. However, they have not been studied much in the service activities, though the books edited by Noyelle (1990a) and Gadrey and Gadrey (1991) must be mentioned. In this chapter, I shall first discuss methodological problems and empirical findings. Then the theoretical issues will be treated.

METHODOLOGICAL AND EMPIRICAL ASPECTS

HOW DO WE MEASURE SKILLS?

It is not easy to determine what skills or qualifications are required for a given job. A detailed study of what the worker actually does is needed, and then an assessment of what skills are required to do it, and a classification of the skills. While some studies of this detailed type do exist, many scholars have relied on proxy variables.

Occupational data form one possibility: the number of persons employed in different types of jobs, such as managers, secretaries, teachers, nurses, waiters and cleaners for example. These data do, in a crude way, tell something about the skill requirements. But they suffer from two drawbacks: first, in official statistics, they are much scarcer than sectoral employment data, and much less standardized internationally (though a UN classification does exist, as mentioned in Chapter 3). And second, they are not very well defined. The specific work performed by an occupational group may differ as between countries and firms, and certainly changes over time: a nurse (now male or female) does much more skilled work today than a century or just a generation ago—and the latter work is now often done by other occupational groups.

Another possibility is the formal education or training which workers have. It is then assumed that the work they do corresponds to their education (which of course is not always the case). Data on educational achievements are fairly well defined, but again the detailed 'contents' change over time and vary from country to country (though the EU attempts to harmonize exams and diplomas required for certain jobs). Another drawback is that it says nothing about skills acquired outside the formal education and training system. Data on formal education also ignore the 'social' or 'general' qualifications of motivation, precision, ability to cooperate, innovativeness, independence and so on, which in an increasing number of jobs are recognized as being crucial. A number of studies on creators of new producer service firms indicate the importance of skills not shown by official diplomas. The entrepreneurs usually have experience from employment in other firms in the same sector, or in customer firms, coupled with the social qualification of a strong motivation to be independent. Furthermore, they tend to be older than manufacturing entrepreneurs (Keeble, Bryson & Wood 1992; Cappellin 1989; Beyers & Lindahl forthcoming; Birley & Westhead 1994).

A third proxy variable which is sometimes used—though it says even less about skills—is the earnings: it is assumed that the higher a person's wage or salary is, the more skilled is his or her work. There are problems about these data, too, not to mention their reliability. First, it is difficult to compare them from country to country and over time, because of differences in price levels, tax levels and structures, social security systems and other factors. Second, wages and salaries depend not only on skills, but also on the value of the work for the firm, the responsibility and prestige connected with it, the labour market balance between supply and demand and so on. Third, while wages and salaries in some countries are determined by market forces, they are in other countries highly regulated by legislation, or collective bargaining between employers and unions, and the regulations vary from place to place and over time.

SKILLS IN SERVICE ACTIVITIES

There is no doubt that compared to manufacturing industries, the tertiary sector has a higher share of low-skill jobs and of high-skill jobs, but a smaller share of medium-skilled jobs (though they are numerous in banking for instance). The skilled manual workers, important in the secondary sector, have only few counterparts in services, while it is easy to distinguish a large number of unskilled personnel, such as cleaners, sales workers, truck drivers, nursery assistants. On the other hand, there are highly skilled doctors, computer specialists, musicians, accountants, aeroplane pilots (if we discount the service occupations of manufacturing activities, the latter will be left with extremely few highly educated persons). This may be illustrated by Table 7.1.

In this situation, averages are not very meaningful. It may be noted, however, that though average earnings in services in the US are lower than in manufacturing, the level of formal education is higher (the latter is also true for France, according to Gadrey 1992a).

There are undoubtedly differences in this pattern from country to country. As will be discussed in Chapter 12, many West European countries have 'lacked' some

Table 7.1. Labour force composition (excl. independents) in the USA 1987. *Source:* Calculated from Applebaum and Albin (1990) Tables 3.8, 3.9 and 3.10.

Sector	% in occupations			% with college degree	Median earnings US$ 1986/hr
	Executive, professional, supervisor	Mechanic, craft, operator	Sales, clerical, service operator		
Extractive, manufacturing, construction	31	53	16	15	7.96
Services	43	12	45	27	6.91
Total	39	25	36	23	7.24

of the low-skill, low-wage jobs which have been found in the American service sector, and 'compensated' by higher unemployment rates. The traditional American low-skill service jobs are not only badly paid, but the work is 'Taylorist', dominated by repetitive operations. The jobs offer fewer career opportunities than other jobs, and show higher unemployment risks. These 'bad jobs' are largely held by women, blacks and Hispanics (Browne 1986; Sheets, Nord & Phelps 1987).

Part-time jobs, usually performed by women, are connected by most authors with 'bad jobs'. This is a questionable connection, however. It is true that in Anglo-Saxon countries most regulations ensuring workers' rights do not apply to part-time jobs, but in continental EU countries they do. And even if top managers rarely work part-time, a considerable number of persons with university degrees and similar skills do so. At any rate, though labour unions who feel that they represent those who '*have* to work for their living' do not like to admit it, there is no doubt that most people working part-time do so by their own choice and preference (Christopherson 1989; Christopherson & Noyelle 1992).

A special type of low-skill enterprise has emerged in recent decades and attracted considerable attention, namely the so-called 'back offices'. These are establishments in which repetitive routine tasks are performed which have no face-to-face contacts with customers. Typically, they perform computerized operations (data entry, data processing) on data forwarded by telecommunications, e.g. concerning wages, accounts, invoices, subscriptions, and bookings. Results are also returned via telecommunications. They will be discussed in more detail in the Appendix. Suffice it here to say that the total number of jobs in back offices is relatively limited, and that a certain level of qualifications is required: typically high school education plus such social qualifications as carefulness and stability.

CHANGES IN SKILLS

The best representation of changes in skills is undoubtedly offered by the interview studies carried out in various sectors by Bertrand and Noyelle (1989) for the

Table 7.2. Traditional and new skills in banks. *Source:* O. Bertrand and T. Noyelle (1988), Employment and Skills in Financial Services: A Comparison of Banks and Insurance Companies in Five OECD Countries, *The Services Industries Journal*, **8**, No. 1. Reproduced by permission of Frank Cass & Co. Ltd.

OLD COMPETENCES	NEW COMPETENCES
COMMON EMERGING COMPETENCES	
1. Ability to operate in well-defined and stable environment	Ability to operate in ill-defined and ever-changing environment
2. Capacity to deal with repetitive, straightforward and concrete work process	Capacity to deal with non-routine and abstract work process
3. Ability to operate in a supervised work environment	Ability to handle decisions and responsibilities
4. Isolated work	Group work; interactive work
5. Ability to operate within narrow geographical and time horizons	System-wide understanding; ability to operate within expanding geographical and time horizons
SPECIFIC EMERGING COMPETENCES	
Among Upper-tier Workers	
1. *Generalist competences.* Broadly, largely unspecialized knowledge; focus on operating managerial skills	*The new expertise.* Growing need for high-level specialized knowledge in well-defined areas needed to develop and distribute complex products
2. *Administrative competences.* Old leadership skills; routine administration top down, carrot-and-stick personnel management approach; ability to carry out orders from senior management	*The new entrepreneurship.* Capacity not only to manage but also to set strategic goals; to share information with subordinates and to listen to them; to motivate individuals to go after new business opportunities
Among Middle-tier Workers	
1. *Procedural competences.* Specialized skills focused on applying established clerical procedural techniques assuming a capacity to receive and execute orders	*Customer assistance and sales competence.* Broader and less specialized skills focused on assisting customers and selling capacity to define and solve problems
Among Lower-tier Workers	
1. Specialized skills focused on data entry and data-processing	Disappearance of low-skill jobs

OECD, and similar studies. Some examples may illustrate the changes occurring currently.

The widespread introduction of network-connected personal computers in the 1980s meant that persons on low hierarchical levels got access to much information. They became able to combine this into individual solutions to the problems they were dealing with. At the same time, purely routine operations became fully automated, such as the withdrawal of money from bank accounts. Thus computerization resulted, unexpectedly, in increasingly skilled and diversified work, for instance in banks (Borum 1987; Bertrand & Noyelle 1988; Littek, Heisig & Gondek 1991). Bertrand and Noyelle summarize their findings in Table 7.2.

When all staff members of an organization get personal computers, the tasks of secretaries change from being predominantly typing into more diversified and responsible administrative work, such as taking care of filing systems (Bertrand 1988).

Increasing demand from customers for qualified and individual service also pulls towards increased skill requirements and improved conditions of work for 'front workers'—the persons at the bottom of the hierarchy who meet the customers face to face and serve them. This has long been recognized by the 'service management' school (Normann 1984). Examples are found in banks, in American up-market retailing, and so on (Gadrey 1994a).

Noyelle (1990c) has studied selected business services (accounting, management consulting, computer software) in the US. In these—already highly skill-demanding—sectors, he found increasing requirements of qualifications and specialization, leading to a breakdown of the earlier internal labour markets in the firms. He notes the importance for professionals of their personal networks. Other examples of upskilling are found in Hirschhorn (1988) and Hutton and Ley (1987).

As regards the back offices, employment in developed countries is reduced partly by removal to the Third World, partly by automation (data are increasingly transmitted directly from the operations that create them). Whatever employment remains tends to be relatively skilled (Wilson 1994).

The validity of statistical evidence must be considered much inferior to primary data, as already noted. However, it is worthwhile showing the changes in service occupations, see Table 7.3. Thus, according to Kutscher, employment growth rates in the US are clearly higher in high-skill than in low-skill service jobs, while in absolute numbers, growth has been highest in low-skill jobs. This is the interpretation which has dominated the debate (e.g. Ecalle 1989). However, as shown in Chapter 12, it now seems that high-skill jobs account for most of the growth in US service employment. This interpretation is supported by the fact that the hourly wage rate in the service sector has increased from 0.91 per cent of the all industry average in 1960 to 0.99 per cent in 1993 (Kelly 1995). However, the development of wages and salaries varies from country to country and from period to period. French wage data from 1975–80 show a relative improvement of earnings in low service categories (Gadrey 1987). But in the 1980s, deregulation measures and deteriorating working conditions in the public sector have in some countries had the opposite effect (Elfring & Kloosterman 1990). Externalization from the public sector to private enterprises (for instance of cleaning work) is another measure which has led to deteriorating conditions of work (Pinch 1989; Allen & Henry 1995).

Reich (1991) classifies jobs into three broad groups (plus a residual group), as mentioned in Chapter 3. 'Routine production workers' including back offices are

Table 7.3. Per cent change in service occupations, USA 1972–1986. *Source:* Kutscher (1988). Reprinted with permission from *Technology in Services: Policies for Growth, Trade and Employment.* Copyright © 1988 by the National Academy of Sciences. Courtesy of the National Academic Press, Washington, DC.

Executive, administrative, managerial	73.7
Professional	57.5
Technicians etc.	74.5
Sales workers	54.6
Clerical & admin. support	35.2
Private household workers	−31.9
Other service workers	45.9

declining in share of total employment in the US because of competition from low-wage countries and because of automation. 'In-person service workers' include most of what have here been called low-skill jobs in services. Their number is increasing because of growing demand, and they are not exposed to international competition and can rarely be automated. Finally, the number of 'symbolic analysts' increases, too, due to added demand and the impossibility of automation. In many cases, there is international competition, but OECD countries are generally competitive.

In Britain, a distinct research tradition has focused on the characteristics of the highly skilled service personnel, calling it the 'service class' (Savage, Dickens & Fielding 1988).

To conclude: the growth in service employment takes place both in highly skilled and in low-skill jobs. The most valid information indicates a broad increase in skill requirements, corresponding to the generally increasing educational level of the population. But the trend differs from country to country and from period to period, deskilling may occur in isolated cases, and low-skill jobs are relatively more important in the US than in most of Western Europe. However, the growth in low-skill service jobs indicates that the solution of high structural unemployment in Western Europe may partly be found in this sector, as discussed in Chapter 4.

TOWARDS NEW THEORIES OF SKILLS AND WORKING CONDITIONS IN SERVICES

In the present chapter, I have chosen to present the empirical evidence before entering a theoretical discussion, because the dominating body of theory, deriving from 'industrial sociology', is highly questionable. It has largely focused on manufacturing industries (in particular the car industry) in America, and tended to generalize from this area to other sectors and countries. The point of departure for many authors has been Braverman (1974) who painted a picture of a dual labour market. On the one hand, an internal labour market within large corporations, with secure and well-paid work and good promotion opportunities. On the other hand, a marginal labour market among small firms, characterized by low skills, low wages, and insecurity. Generally, technological development led to deskilling, or at least an increasing bipolarization between the few with high skills and the many with low skills. In the deindustrialization debate of the 1980s, the 'good' jobs were even seen as identical with manufacturing jobs and the 'bad' jobs as identical with service jobs (e.g. by Cohen & Zysman 1987).

Authors who have made detailed skill studies in services criticize this theory. Here, there is no room for the peaceful cooperation between schools which I mentioned in the preface. 'The representation of a bipolarization of qualifications might well be for the Keynesian–Marxist theory of the 1980s, what the thesis of pauperization of the proletariat was for the Marxism of the 1950s: a good intention, but an error' says Gadrey (1987). 'A re-conceptualization of the labour market, as it has been transformed in the United States over the past two decades or so, demands a sharp break from earlier models and theories' (Christopherson & Noyelle 1992). Littek et al (1991) put it this way in connection with the theories of 'critical' German industrial sociology on salaried workers: 'It proved to be downright impossible to interpret the experience and understandings of the respondents according to our hypotheses ... the premises ... have turned out to be false.' Even authors with a Marxist basis today reject the deskilling theory (Sayer & Walker 1992).

Attempts to modify the theories have primarily focused on the concept of dualism. Noyelle (1990b) suggests replacing it with a division into three segments: (a) the core of management and skilled internal workers; (b) skilled contingent workers: specialized workers, more orientated towards their profession than towards the firm; and (c) unskilled contingent and marginalized workers. Thus the size of the firm is not seen as the most important criterion, but rather the skills of the workers and their specificity.

Gadrey (1991b, 1992a) has further developed these ideas into the 'model of flexible segmentation' shown in Figure 7.1. The top segment is the core of management, specialists and full-time, permanently employed staff. The bottom right-hand segment consists of workers on flexible employment terms (part-time, time-limited contracts), many of them front workers. The tendency here is towards upskilling and improved employment conditions. The—increasing—bottom left-hand segment consists of external and hence flexible workers, partly temporaries, partly subcontractors (here we touch upon the externalization question discussed in Chapter 6), and partly freelance specialists.

Gadrey observes that this model is based on the assumptions that (a) the supply of labour exceeds the demand, which is not always the case, especially among specialists; (b) the institutional framework allows a high degree of flexibility, which is much less the case in (continental) Western Europe than in the US (and the UK); and (c) wages are very low for the bottom right-hand segment—again an assumption which is more realistic in the US than in Western Europe. Because of these weaknesses, Gadrey suggests that the model of flexible segmentation may be supplemented by one of 'bureaucratic employment systems' with predominantly permanent employment, applied partly in 'Fordist' private firms, partly in professional public and private organizations.

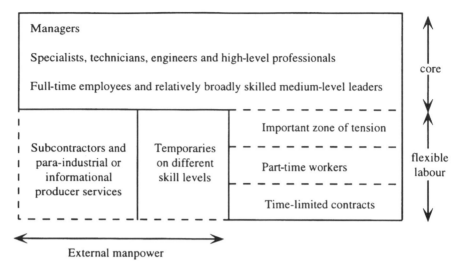

Figure 7.1. Gadrey's model of flexible segmentation. *Source:* Reproduced and translated with permission from J. Gadrey (1992a) *L'Economie des Services*, Paris: La Découverte.

These models certainly correspond much better to the observed realities in contemporary service activities than Braverman's does. Still, it may be suggested that they are based too much on criteria of only secondary relevance, such as the internal/external distinction and the permanent/flexible employment distinction. They still have a hint of considering personnel as costs. Possibly more fruitful theories might be based on the notion, so dominant in contemporary management literature, that personnel is primarily to be considered the most important resource of the firm, and that the conditions of employment tend to reflect this (Beaverstock 1990 for instance stresses attractions and rewards). But of course, there are variations between different types of work and different institutional arrangements. And though there is no deskilled majority, there is a low-skill minority with severe employment problems.

Theorizing along these lines would also bring skills more into focus. The knowledge gained by empirical studies ought to be fully valorized. And in all thinking about an emerging service, information or knowledge society (see Chapter 14), the importance of human resources is absolutely fundamental. Is it possible to devise a theory of employment that reflects this?

CONCLUSION

The service sector employs relatively more high-skill and low-skill, but fewer medium-skilled, persons than the goods-producing sectors. However, there are substantial differences from subsector to subsector and from country to country, in particular the US has a relatively large number of low-skill, low-wage service jobs.

The general tendency is towards upskilling, not least in the US. At the same time, such general qualifications as flexibility, creativity, independence and responsibility become increasingly important. These trends mean that the dominant theory, Braverman's dual labour market theory postulating widespread deskilling, is contradicted by empirical evidence. It seems that even critics of this theory depend too much on its concepts, and that future theoretical work might look towards contemporary management literature in which personnel is considered a resource rather than a cost.

Part III

LOCATION OF SERVICES AND REGIONAL DEVELOPMENT

8 Inter-urban Distribution of Service Activities

In this part of the book, the focus will be on geographical aspects. Where are service activities located, and why? How do they interact locally with other economic factors? What is their role in regional economic development?

Most of the discussion will focus on inter-urban questions: in what cities, rural districts and regions are service activities located, and why? In Chapter 11, the focus shifts to the intra-urban level: in what parts of the cities are service activities located, and why? The factors that are important on the inter-urban level are somewhat different from the intra-urban level, so it is important to distinguish between the levels.

By way of introduction, this chapter will present data on the geography of service activities. There are two radically different sets of questions and data-sources. First, the distribution of service activities between regions and between levels of the urban hierarchy is highlighted by official statistics. Second, trade and interaction between service producers and service users in different areas are illustrated, largely by data from survey studies in different countries.

STATISTICAL DATA ON THE LOCATION OF SERVICE ACTIVITIES

In this section, data on the geography of the total service sector will first be presented, then household and producer services will be distinguished. Of course this is a very crude way of describing the service sector. Household services are both local (e.g. food shops) and high-level (e.g. specialized hospitals). Producer services cover many types, too, from those providing small and medium enterprises with unsophisticated services, to highly specialized expert consultancy, to 'back offices' offering routinized operations. A group of internalized service functions, namely corporate headquarters, will briefly be discussed, too. Furthermore, a first analysis of the changing geographical distribution of service activities will be presented, focusing on the changes which are caused by the different structure of the service sector in different areas.

A general problem is that geographical statistical data on service activities are scarce, compared to data available on the goods-producing sectors. In particular, regional data on service production are very scarce and, as discussed in Chapter 2, of questionable validity. The geographical distribution of service activities must

Table 8.1. Geographical employment in services, Denmark 1984–1991. *Source:* Labour force statistics.

Place of work Region	Empl. 1984 (× 1000)	Empl. 1991 (× 1000)	Growth 1984–1991 (%)
Copenhagen reg.	725	736	1.5
Rest of islands	295	314	6.4
East Jutland	290	318	9.7
S, W & N Jutland	408	440	7.8
Urban class[a]			
Over 1 million	725	736	1.5
20 000–300 000	561	610	8.7
5000–20 000	244	256	4.9
Rural	191	205	7.3
Total[b]	1730	1817	5.0

[a] Whole communes, plus peri-urban communes.
[b] Including approx. 10 000 with no fixed place of work.

usually be illustrated by employment data, from countries where such data have been available.

TOTAL DISTRIBUTION OF SERVICE ACTIVITIES

The geographical distribution of total service employment in Denmark is shown in Table 8.1. Relative to the distribution of population, services are over-represented in the Copenhagen region. In the 1980s, however, a clear shift to other regions and smaller towns took place.

Table 8.2 shows the distribution of total service employment in the United

Table 8.2. Employees in services in British regions 1981–1993. *Source:* Regional trends, 1994.

Region	1981 (× 1000)	1991 (× 1000)	Growth 1981–1993 (%)
North	631	740	17
Yorks & Humber	1025	1259	23
East Midlands	747	956	28
East Anglia	408	557	37
South East	5037	5508	9
South West	988	1262	28
West Midlands	1059	1290	22
North West	1451	1648	14
Wales	563	671	19
Scotland	1231	1431	16
Northern Ireland	326	398	22
Total	13 472	15 718	17

Table 8.3. Employees in services, Belgian provinces 1983–1990. *Source:* Annuaire de statistiques régionales.

Region	1983 (× 1000)	1990 (× 1000)	Growth 1983–1990 (%)
Antwerp	288	350	22
Brabant	632	736	16
Hainaut	185	212	15
Liège	172	194	13
Limburg	91	126	38
Luxemburg	34	42	23
Namur	66	78	19
East Flanders	175	222	27
West Flanders	159	207	30
Total	1802	2167	20

Kingdom. Service employment is relatively concentrated in the South East (the London region). In the 1980s, a clear shift from the South East to other southern regions occurred. The total growth rate in the South of England has been slightly below the national average.

Table 8.3 shows the distribution of total numbers of employees in service activities in Belgium. Here, services are over-represented in Brabant (with Brussels). In the 1980s, however, growth rates were higher in peripheral provinces than in the Brussels area and the old industrial regions. Generally, service growth rates have been higher in Flanders than Wallonia, reflecting the trend in population and other economic activities.

Table 8.4 shows the distribution of the total number of Dutch service sector employees, and Table 8.5 the distribution of French service sector employees. In

Table 8.4. Employees in services, Dutch provinces 1984–1991. *Source:* Regionaal statistisch zakboek.

Region	1984 (× 1000)	1991 (× 1000)	Growth (%)
Groningen	106	136	28
Friesland	92	124	35
Drenthe	66	89	35
Overijssel	175	222	27
Gelderland+Flevoland	329	466	41
Utrecht	235	338	44
North Holland	582	756	30
South Holland	745	929	25
Zeeland	60	78	31
North Brabant	360	505	40
Limburg	182	238	30
Total	2952	3880	32

Table 8.5. Employees in services, French regions 1982–1992. *Source:* INSEE: Statistiques et indicateurs des régions françaises, 1995.

Region	1982 (× 1000)	1992 (× 1000)	Growth (%)
Alsace	311	370	19
Aquitaine	507	621	22
Auvergne	224	260	16
Bourgogne	288	335	16
Bretagne	498	577	16
Centre	421	503	19
Champagne-Ardennes	241	277	15
Corse	44	56	26
Franche-Comté	175	209	19
Ile-de-France	3000	3518	17
Languedoc-Roussillon	339	454	34
Limousin	130	153	17
Lorraine	406	467	15
Midi-Pyrenées	425	541	27
Nord-Pas-de-Calais	636	776	22
Basse-Normandie	236	295	25
Haute-Normandie	316	371	17
Pays-de-la-Loire	513	626	22
Picardie	284	340	20
Poitou-Charentes	272	316	16
Provence-Alpes-Côte d'Azur	833	1001	20
Rhône-Alpes	978	1214	24
Total	11 077	13 280	20

the Netherlands, there is a clear concentration in the Randstad Holland (provinces of North and South Holland and Utrecht). In the 1980s, however, a decentralization took place, especially to the 'intermediate' zone.

In France, there is a clear concentration of service employment in the Paris region (Ile-de-France). Between 1982 and 1992, however, growth rates were below average in this region, as well as in most of central France, while they were above average in most southern and western regions.

In all five countries under consideration, services are over-represented, relative to population, in the largest urban areas. In all five countries, the tendency in the 1980s was towards regional decentralization, but in some provincial regions, growth rates have been considerably higher than in others.

HOUSEHOLD SERVICES

Regional data on employment in service activities aimed at households are not easy to get, since no ISIC classes (see definition in Chapter 3) correspond well to this sector.

The general impression is that household services are distributed much like the population, and that the change pattern largely corresponds to the changes in population. However, there is no doubt that in most Western countries, the smallest villages have lost a good deal of service activities over the last decade.

PRODUCER SERVICES

Due to the recent research focus on producer services, and in particular on the more narrow class of business services, more data are available on these activities. Table 8.6 shows the distribution of producer services in Denmark. Employment in producer services is strongly concentrated in the Copenhagen region, while there is little in rural areas. However, growth in the 1980s was slightly more rapid in the rest of Denmark (especially in the medium-sized towns) than in the Copenhagen region.

The regional distribution of business services in the Nordic countries in 1991 is shown in Figure 8.1, using location quotients (compared to the distribution of total employment). The figure shows a clear concentration of business service in the national capitals, which have about half of total national employment. Only a few other counties with major cities have location quotients above 1, while the smallest and least densely populated counties have location quotients of only about 0.5.

The recent growth in business service employment in the Nordic countries is illustrated by Figure 8.2. This shows a complicated growth pattern. In Finland and Norway, one can speak of a clear decentralization tendency, where the capitals have below average growth rates. But only in Norway do the peripheral counties have systematically above-average growth. In Denmark and Sweden, on the other hand, the capitals have growth rates close to the national averages. In the province,

Table 8.6. Geographical employment in producer services in Denmark 1982–1991. *Source:* Labour force statistics.

Place of work Region	Empl. 1982 (× 1000)	Employment 1991 (× 1000) (% of resid. pop.)		Growth 1982–1991 (%)
Copenhagen reg.	175.6	199.7	11.6	ı 14
Rest of islands	49.0	57.3	5.5	+17
East Jutland	56.2	70.3	7.5	+25
S, W and N Jutland	71.4	85.3	6.0	+19
Urban class[a]				
Over 1 million	175.6	199.7	11.6	+14
20 000–300 000	103.0	127.2	7.4	+23
5000–20 000	42.1	48.3	5.8	+15
Rural	31.6	37.3	4.2	+18
Total	362.4	420.6	8.1	+16

[a] Whole communes, plus peri-urban communes.

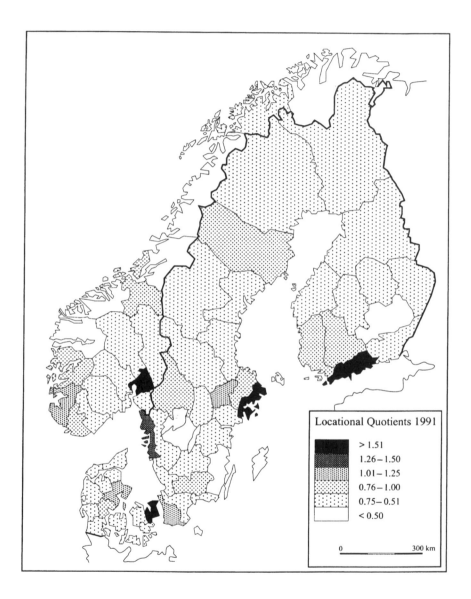

Figure 8.1.   Location quotients for business services in the counties of the Nordic countries 1991 (country averages 1.00). *Source:* Illeris and Sjøholt (1995).

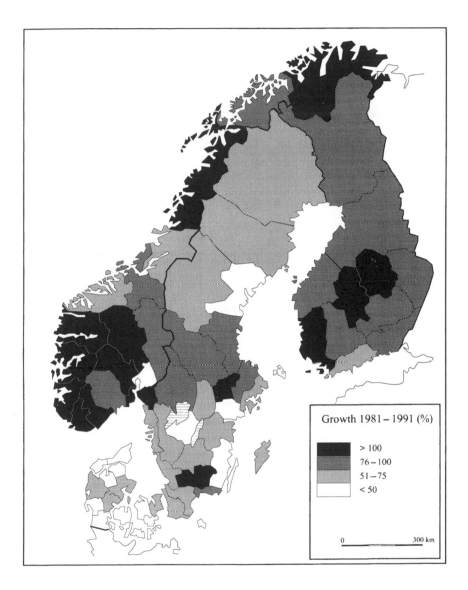

Figure 8.2. Growth percentages in business services in the counties of the Nordic countries, 1981–1991. *Source:* Illeris & Sjøholt (1995).

Table 8.7.   Employment in business services, British regions 1981–1991. *Source:* based on Wood (1993b).

Region	1981 (× 1000)	1991 (× 1000)	Growth (%)
North	32	52	64
Yorks & Humber	54	97	79
East Midlands	42	76	81
East Anglia	23	47	104
South East	494	805	63
South West	57	108	89
West Midlands	72	124	72
North West	87	147	69
Wales	25	42	68
Scotland	65	118	82
Northern Ireland	14	21[a]	52[a]
Total	965	1635	69[a]

[a] For Northern Ireland 1991, 1989 data are used.

some counties are considerably more dynamic than others, forming a mosaic with no clear pattern.

In the United Kingdom, the regional distribution of employment in business services 1981–91 is shown in Table 8.7. The South East (with London) has about half of British business service employment. In the 1980s, growth was below average in the South East, but above average in the other South English regions. Taken as a whole, the North and South of Britain both have growth rates close to the national average.

In West Germany, Figure 8.3 shows the share of business services in total employment, by Regierungsbezirke. It shows that the highest shares are found in the largest city areas: Hamburg, Frankfurt, Munich and Nuremberg, while the lowest shares are found in the relatively rural areas along the East German and Czech borders.

Figure 8.4 shows the 1980–91 development in business service employment. It shows that the highest growth rates were found in the South of Germany (and in West Berlin), which corresponds to the general southward shift of the West German economy. There is no correlation between city size and the growth rate of business service employment.

In France, Figure 8.5 shows location quotients of salaried employment in business services, by regions. This shows a strong concentration of business service employment in Ile-de-France (with Paris), which had 39 per cent of total French employment. On the other hand, more rural regions—especially in the eastern Paris basin and the Massif Central—had relatively little business service employment.

Table 8.8 shows the 1981–91 development of salaried business service employment, in absolute numbers and per cent of the total number of employees. It shows that the share of the Paris region declined, and the same occurred in the second and third largest concentrations, the Lyons region (Rhône-Alpes) and the Provence-Alpes-Côte d'Azur. However, the other regions have developed in very

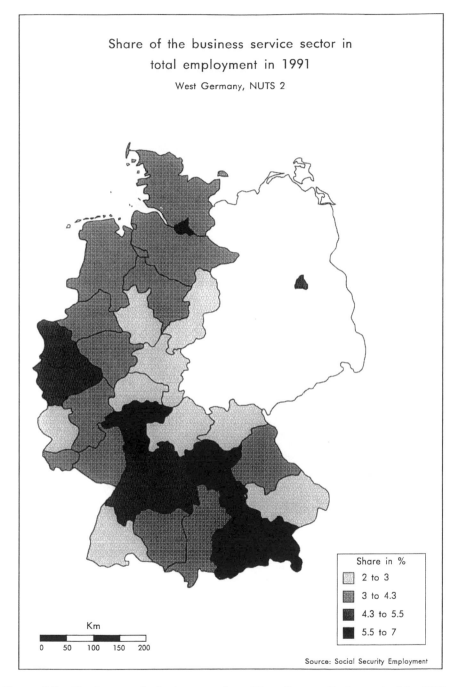

Figure 8.3. Employment in business services, West German Regierungsbezirke 1991.
Source: Gäbe & Strambach (coord.) (1993).

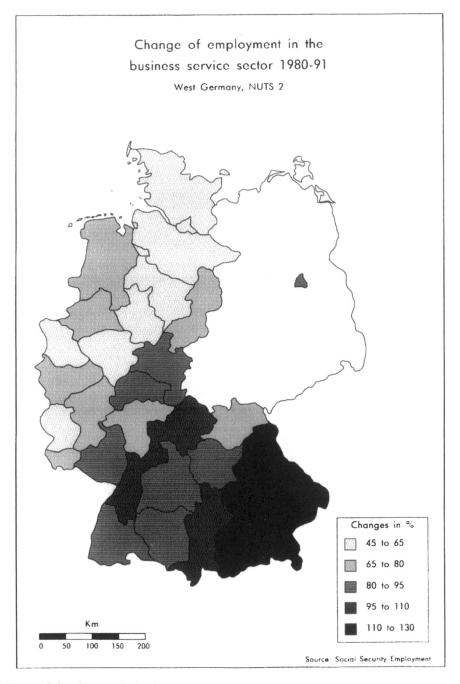

Figure 8.4. Changes in business service employment, West German Regierungsbezirke 1980–1991. *Source:* Gäbe & Strambach (coord.) (1993).

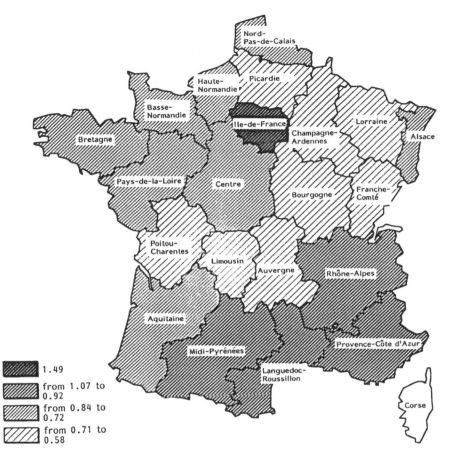

Figure 8.5. Business services, regional location quotients, France 1991. *Source:* Reprinted from *Progress in Planning*, **43**, F. Moulaert and C. Gallouj, Advanced Producer Services in the French Space Economy, pp. 2–3, Figure 2, copyright © 1995, with kind permission from Elsevier Science Ltd, The Boulevard, Langford Lane, Kidlington, OX5 1GB, UK.

different ways, forming a complex pattern. Most western regions have increased their shares, while most eastern and central regions have changed relatively little.

In the United States, the distribution of employment in business and professional services 1976 to 1986 are shown in Table 8.9. This shows that business service employment, which is largely concentrated in metropolitan areas with over 1 million inhabitants, decentralized in the 1976–86 period. The share of the largest metropolitan areas declined—according to the authors, mainly in the four largest ones—while the share of non-metropolitan counties (including towns of up to 50 000 inhabitants) increased.

In Belgium, Moyart (1995) has analysed the change in the number of producer service employees in 1982–92, by urban classes. In Brussels, the number grew by

Table 8.8. Employees in business services, French regions 1981–1991. *Source:* Reprinted from *Progress in Planning*, **43**, F. Moulaert and C. Gallouj, Advanced Producer Services in the French Space Economy, pp. 2–3, Table 3, copyright © 1995, with kind permission from Elsevier Science Ltd, The Boulevard, Langford Lane, Kidlington, OX5 1GB, UK.

Regions	1981	%	1991	%
Nord-Pas-de-C.	45 670	4.95	75 527	5.20
Picardie	15 576	1.69	27 905	1.92
Ile-de-France	374 124	40.55	567 447	39.09
Centre	26 670	2.89	43 127	2.97
Hte-Normandie	27 055	2.93	38 447	2.65
Basse-Normandie	12 544	1.36	22 393	1.54
Bretagne	25 233	2.73	43 348	2.99
Pays de Loire	33 328	3.61	54 501	3.75
Poitou Charentes	12 368	1.34	21 090	1.45
Limousin	6 151	0.67	9 375	0.65
Aquitaine	30 968	3.36	48 996	3.37
Midi-Pyrénées	25 410	2.75	47 878	3.30
Champ.-Ardennes	13 113	1.42	20 752	1.43
Lorraine	24 082	2.61	37 129	2.56
Alsace	22 172	2.40	37 659	2.59
Franche-Comté	9 634	1.04	15 996	1.10
Bourgogne	16 033	1.74	24 692	1.70
Auvergne	9 876	1.07	15 247	1.05
Rhône-Alpes	104 695	11.35	159 987	11.02
Languedoc-Rous.	20 105	2.18	34 364	2.37
P.A.C.A.	66 344	7.19	103 519	7.13
Corse	1 579	0.17	2 375	0.16
Total	922 730	100.00	1 451 754	100.00

Table 8.9. Employment in business and professional services, USA 1976–1986. *Source:* B. OhUallacháin and N. Reid (1991), The Location and Growth of Business and Professional Services in American Metropolitan Areas, 1976–1986, *Annals of the Association of American Geographers*, **81**, 2, Table 1. Reprinted by permission of Blackwell Publishers.

Metropolitan category	Employment (thousands)		Percent share	
	1976	1986	1976	1986
Total metropolitan	2665.9	5641.9	96.4	93.7
Large metropolitan[a]	1916.4	3947.1	69.3	65.5
Intermediate metropolitan[b]	734.7	1661.0	26.6	27.6
Small metropolitan[c]	14.8	33.8	0.5	0.6
Nonmetropolitan	100.6	380.8	3.6	6.3
U.S. Total	2766.5	6022.7	100.0	100.0

Sources: U.S. Department of Commerce (1976, 1986a).
[a] Population of Metropolitan Area equal to or greater than 1.0 million in 1980, n = 39.
[b] Population of Metropolitan Area less than 1.0 million and greater than 100 000 in 1980, n = 241.
[c] Population of Metropolitan Area equal to or less than 100 000 in 1980, n = 25.

55 per cent, in other arrondissements with cities over 50 000 inhabitants by 102 per cent, and in the remaining arrondissements by 127 per cent.

To summarize: it is very clear that producer service activities are strongly concentrated in the largest city areas, while rural and peripheral areas have relatively little activity in this sector.

The trends in the 1980s are less clear. Shifts out of the largest city areas have been observed in Finland, Norway, the United Kingdom, France, and the United States, but not very clearly in Denmark, Sweden or West Germany. The regions that have gained most can in some countries be identified as the generally most dynamic ones, e.g. southern England except London, and southern Germany. The peripheral regions have only systematically improved their situation in Norway, while in Sweden, the United Kingdom and France, their growth rates have been close to the national averages.

As regards the urban hierarchy, information from Denmark, West Germany, and France does not indicate any systematic upward or downward shift tendency, while a clear decentralization has taken place in the United States and Belgium.

CORPORATE HEADQUARTERS

A group of internalized service functions, the corporate headquarters, have attracted special attention. In the United States, Holloway and Wheeler (1991) have

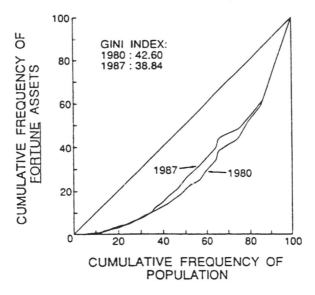

Figure 8.6. Lorenz curves of American corporate headquarters 1980 and 1987. *Source:* S.R. Holloway and J.O. Wheeler (1991), Corporate Headquarters Relocation and Changes in Metropolitan Corporate Dominance, 1980–1987, *Economic Geography*, **67**, 1, Figure 4. Reprinted by permission of Economic Geography, Clark University.

shown that corporate headquarters are much more concentrated in large cities than the population. The changes in the 1980–87 period are illustrated by Figure 8.6. The figure shows a decreasing degree of geographical concentration in American corporate headquarters. In particular, New York and other large North-Eastern cities are hit, while the winners are large second-rank cities (Drennan 1989; Holloway & Wheeler 1991; Noyelle 1994; Lyons 1994).

In Britain, a slight shift from the peripheral regions to the South East occurred between 1971 and 1987, as measured by the number of headquarters of the 500 largest corporations (Marshall 1994); in other words, a slight geographical concentration tendency.

CHANGES IN DISTRIBUTION DUE TO THE COMPOSITION OF SERVICE ACTIVITIES

On the basis of the statistical description of service activities in Chapter 4 (Table 4.1 and Figure 4.1) and this chapter, a preliminary analysis of the causes of the changing geographical distribution of service employment can be conducted. Data in both chapters show (a) that producer services have higher growth rates than household services (especially in recent years when the growth of public services has slowed down). Data in this chapter show (b) that producer service activities are more concentrated in large urban areas than household services.

If all other things were equal, the result of (a) and (b) would have been that total service employment increased by higher rates in large urban areas than elsewhere. The data show, however, that this is not the case. All other things were not equal. Inside each subsector, there were different growth rates in different geographical areas, which shifted employment between them. Or in shift-share terminology: the structural (or share) component was not decisive for the total geographical development in service employment.

As regards corporate headquarters, the losses of New York cannot be ascribed to the composition of activities, either.

PROVISION OF SERVICES

Important questions concerning the geographical role of service activities in our economies are: Where are services sold and bought? How much trade or interaction is there between service producers and service users in different areas? Input–output data tell us a little about these questions. More knowledge has been created through cumbersome surveys made by a number of researchers. Unfortunately, such studies only cover producer services.

The purpose of this section is to present the findings of such surveys and input–output data and, as far as possible, to extract general conclusions from them. It should be noted that the surveys not only include geographical information, but also information on the use of services, the internal or external provision, as well as information on the sectors to which services are sold (questions also discussed in Chapter 6).

Undoubtedly, more survey studies exist than those referred to here. Often their findings have been published in reports with a limited circulation. I have chosen to limit the presentation to studies carried out after 1984 and covering at least two subsectors. Some earlier studies have been summarized in Illeris (1990), and another compilation has been carried out by Gallouj (1995).

Generally, the results of the various studies cannot be compared directly or in a quantitative way. The time and methods of data collection, the definition of services and regions, as well as the selection of user sectors and services vary too much for that. For instance, the results depend on how fine-grained the classification of services is: the more fine-grained, the fewer will use all services. Valid conclusions from these heterogeneous studies can only be drawn about general tendencies of the type 'bigger user firms distinguish themselves from smaller user firms by ...'.

In the surveys, purchases and sales have been referred to very different geographical units. In the following tables, they have been summarized under the headings 'local' (the locality itself and its immediate surroundings up to a distance of 20–30 km), 'regional' (up to a distance of 50–100 km, in one case 150 km), 'capital' (if not situated in the local or regional zone), 'rest of country', and 'abroad'.

The question of service use and provision has been approached from both sides. First, studies investigating service users will be presented. Next, studies conducted from the service producer side. A special section will be devoted to evidence on the development of service provision over time.

STUDIES OF THE USERS OF PRODUCER SERVICES

Thirteen surveys of user firms (one of which studied two areas independently) will be reported here. They have typically used postal, telephone or interview questionnaires, asking 'Do you use service X?' and 'From whom and where do you get service X?'. They specify between 8 and 47 services, mainly advanced information services, whereas they have not focused much on less sophisticated services such as cleaning. The studies are:

- Schamp (1987) received 278 answers to a postal questionnaire, sent to manufacturing firms (independent firms and corporate headquarters with over 20 employees) in four parts of Lower Saxony.

- Delgado (1991) interviewed 54 small and medium manufacturing establishments in an industrial estate in Porto.

- Gallouj (1993) received about 500 answers to a postal questionnaire, sent in 1987–88 to firms in the region Nord-Pas-de-Calais. Some of the questions made a comparison with a similar survey in 1978 possible. This will be reported later.

- Lensink (1989) conducted 282 telephone interviews with wholesalers and business service firms in four rural Dutch areas in 1986, asking them about their service inputs (and, as will be presented later, their service outputs).

- Lamonde and Martineau (1992) carried out 34 interviews with firms in four different parts of the province of Quebec in 1991.

- Townsend and MacDonald (1994) conducted 39 interviews with business service firms with more than five employees in Edinburgh in 1993, asking them about their service inputs (as well as their service sales, to be reported later).

- Tordoir (1994) received 148 answers to a postal questionnaire sent to very large firms in a number of cities in the North Eastern United States in 1991.

- Tordoir (1991) received about 600 answers to a postal questionnaire, sent to offices with over 100 employees in the Randstad Holland.

- O'Farrell, Moffat and Hitchens (1993) conducted a postal survey among manufacturing firms in Scotland and South East England. The presentation of the 233 Scottish answers and the 210 South East answers will be made separately.

- Pedersen (1986) received 229 answers to a postal questionnaire sent to firms in the Esbjerg area in 1985.

- Daniels (1987) conducted a telephone and postal survey among firms in Merseyside in 1985–86, receiving 278 answers.

- Jönsson (1986) made 3060 telephone interviews among Swedish manufacturing establishments with over 10 employees in 1986.

- Illeris (1991e) received 181 answers to a postal questionnaire sent to small–medium, exporting manufacturing establishments (6–1000 employees) in peripheral Jutland in 1990.

Only the Esbjerg study discusses the distinction between service products and the firms that provided them. In this case, the geographical distribution of external purchases is based on a question of what firms were the suppliers. The distribution between internal and external provision refers to service products, as it necessarily must.

The total use and provision of services in these surveys are shown in Table 8.10. It should be noticed that most authors have not calculated averages over all types of services. In my opinion, such a calculation is possible, the provisos necessary are not stronger than the provisos already made concerning the whole exercise.

The data on the share of respondents that use the various services—resulting in percentages between 40 and 72—do not tell much. It depends on which services they have been asked about.

The studies which highlight the internal and external provision of services show them to be roughly of the same order of magnitude, while the provision from parent companies forms a smaller part of the total service provision. But again, the results depend on the questions, which usually have been selected to focus on services which it is possible to externalize.

The majority of external services are bought locally, except in the Dutch and Quebec cases where the areas under study were deliberately limited to rural areas and small towns. In the other studies, the shares bought locally vary from 47 to

Table 8.10. Use and provision of producer services

	Use (% of respondents)	Provision (from % of users)			Provision (from % of externally bought services)				
		int.	parent firm	ext.	local	regional	capital	rest of country	abroad
Lower Saxony	72[a]	58[a]	—	42[a]	45[b]	24[b]	9[d]	31[b]	13[d]
Porto	68[c]	68[c]	—	32[c]	78[d]	—	9	—	11
Nord-P-d-C	71[e]				54[f]	25[f]			
Rural Netherl.					39[g]			61[g]	
Quebec	69	7		93	45	—	31[h]	21	3
Edinburgh					52	16	27		5
North-East US					25[i]	41[i]	—	33[i]	6[i]
Randstad Holl.					47[j]	39[j]		18[j]	
Scotland	52	44[k]	10[k]	46[k]	70[l]		12[l]	16[l]	3[l]
South East UK	52	50[m]	7[m]	43[m]	83[n]			16[n]	0[n]
Esbjerg	40	45	9	46	58	32	9		2
Merseyside	58[o]				57[p]	16[p]	14[p]	12[p]	0[p]
Sweden					64	—	13	23	—
Periph. Jutland	95	49[q]	4[q]	47[q]	63	—	8	24	5

[a] Unweighted average of 6 size classes, Figure 16.4 (Schamp 1987).
[b] Weighted average of the data in Table 16.5 (Schamp 1987). For peri-urban Hannover, Hannover is counted as intra-regional.
[c] Unweighted average of 37 types of service, Table 5 (Delgado 1991).
[d] Percentage 'dominant location' of 29 types of service, Table 10 (Delgado 1991).
[e] Unweighted average of 28 types of service, p. 78 (Gallouj 1993).
[f] Unweighted average of 32 types of service, table in Gadrey and Gallouj (1988)
[g] Unweighted average of 8 types of service. Table 6.9 (Lensik 1989).
[h] Montreal.
[i] Unweighted average of 11 types of service, weighted by number of answers in each area, Table 4 (Tordoir 1994).
[j] Reduced to give a sum of 100%.
[k] Unweighted average of 12 types of service, excl. firms supplied from several sources, Table 2 (O'Farrell et al 1993).
[l] Excl. firms supplied from several regions. Capital = South East. Table 4 (O'Farrell et al 1993).
[m] Unweighted average of 12 types of service, excl. firms supplied from several sources, Table 2 (O'Farrell et al 1993).
[n] Excl. firms supplied from several areas, Table 5 (O'Farrell et al 1993).
[o] Expressing that the service is necessary.
[p] Unweighted average of 12 types of service, reduced to give a sum of 100%.
[q] Reduced to give a sum of 100%.

85 per cent, while the shares bought outside the region (i.e. more than 50–100 km away) vary between 11 and 37 per cent. It is noteworthy that where we have information about it, the national capitals only supply 8–14 per cent of external services (again except in the Quebec case, where Montreal plays a bigger role). Imports from abroad form 0–13 per cent of externally bought services.

As already stressed, the use and provision of producer services depend on the user firms. Some of the older studies, summarized in Illeris (1990), contain data on the service use of different types of user firms, while this is rarely the case in the above-mentioned surveys. From Illeris (1990), the following conclusions, which are supported by the few new data, may be quoted:

1   Independent firms and branch establishments seem to use services to roughly equal degrees.
2   Branch establishments get more services from their parent company and buy fewer services externally than independent firms.
3   Independent firms buy more services locally than branch establishments do, and less from other regions.
4   Big establishments use more kinds of services than small establishments.
5   The shares of internal and external service provision do not vary systematically by user size.
6   The shares of local and distant provision of external services do not vary systematically by user size.
7   More sophisticated user firms use more services than less sophisticated ones.
8   More sophisticated user firms use both more internal and more external services than less sophisticated users.
9   The degree of sophistication has no clear influence on the shares of local and distant provision of external services.

As already mentioned, some of the studies referred to in Table 8.10 are more explicit as regards the use and provision of different types of service. Among the types mapped in at least seven studies, accounting, advertising and legal services form one group of services which are used by most respondents. These are usually bought externally, and usually from local or regional suppliers. On the other hand, engineering consultancy, management consultancy and market research are used by less than half of the respondents and are not so often bought from external suppliers, but if so then quite often from distant suppliers (except engineering).

STUDIES INVESTIGATING SERVICE PRODUCERS

Twelve studies have asked producer service firms questions like 'How big are your sales of service X, to whom, and where?'. Obviously, these studies are only concerned with externally supplied services. The studies are:

• Porterfield and Pulver (1991) received 712 answers to a postal questionnaire sent in 1986 to producer service firms in the Upper Midwest (Wisconsin and surrounding states).

- Mayère and Vinot (1991) received 2841 answers to a questionnaire sent to business service firms in the four largest cities of the region Rhône-Alpes in 1989, in cooperation with the statistical authorities.

- Wood, Bryson and Keeble (1993) interviewed 120 small (less than 12 professionals employed), independent management consulting and market research firms in three areas of England in 1991.

- Hessels (1992) received 737 answers to a postal questionnaire sent to business service firms with more than four employees in the four large city areas of Randstad Holland in 1989–90.

- Gallouj (1993) received 582 answers to a postal questionnaire sent to business service firms in the region of Nord-Pas-de-Calais in 1987–88.

- Lensink (1989) conducted telephone interviews with 118 business service firms with more than five employees in four Dutch rural areas in 1986.

- Coffey and McRae (1990) carried out 168 interviews with and received 330 answers to a postal questionnaire sent to producer service firms in Vancouver in 1986.

- Townsend and MacDonald (1994) interviewed 39 business service firms with more than five employees in Edinburgh in 1993.

- Michalak and Fairbairn (1988) received 173 answers to a postal questionnaire sent to business service firms in Edmonton in 1987.

- Daniels (1995) conducted a survey of 1303 business service firms in the United Kingdom in 1991.

- Beyers and Lindahl (forthcoming) carried out 444 telephone interviews with producer service firms in the US North West and in Chicago in 1993.

- Daniels (1987) conducted a telephone survey of 151 and a postal survey of 28 producer service firms in Merseyside in 1985–86.

The distribution of service sales between economic sectors and between geographical zones is shown in Table 8.11. The table shows that in most cases, producer service firms sell considerably more to other service firms and public service institutions than they sell to manufacturing and other goods-producing firms. But there are exceptions, and of course the result depends on the selection of investigated firms. In some cases, the studies show considerable sales to households, due to the inclusion of some 'mixed' sectors in the survey.

Concerning the geographical distribution of producer service sales, the different studies yield surprisingly similar results. Most of the services are sold locally and regionally, less in distant regions. However, considering the fact that only three of the studies include the capitals of the countries in question (the England, Randstad, and UK studies) it is an unexpected finding that the distant sales are quite important: typically, only 40 per cent of the services are sold in the city itself and its immediate vicinity (up to 20–30 km). Within a distance of 50–100 km, this share only increases to typically 65 per cent. On the other hand, about 35 per cent are normally sold in remote regions, including often more than 5 per cent exports. This finding has great importance for the theoretical discussion on the need for

Table 8.11. Service sales, by sector and by location of customers

% of all sales	Households	Goods produc. sector	Private serv.	Public sector	Local	Regional	Capital	Rest of country	Abroad
Upp. Midwest					68		—	31	1
Rhône-Alpes	2	56	22	20	33	24	15	21	7
England	—	40	49	9	28	28	—	36	9
Randstad Holl.	8	72		20	40	20	—	23	17
Nord-P-d-C					39	26	14	15	7
Rural Netherl.	6	50	33	11	61		37		2
Vancouver	24[a]	15[a]	44[a]	17[a]	66		19		15
Edinburgh	24	15	52	9	52	29	12		7
Edmonton	12	17	41	27	64		33		3
UK	6	76		18		87			13
US					65[b]	11[b]	19[b]		5[b]
Merseyside[c]	—	31	45[d]	26	20	27	6	31	15

[a] Calculated from Table 4.4 (Coffey & McRae 1990).
[b] Weighted by number of interviews in each area, Table 12 (Beyers & Lindahl forthcoming).
[c] Sectoral distribution according to postal survey, geographical distribution according to telephone survey.
[d] Incl. other establishments within same organization.

proximity to customers, see Chapter 9. It corresponds to the results of earlier studies, reported in Illeris (1990), as well as to the results of Gallouj (1995).

Some of the survey reports publish results for individual sectors. They show that in most sectors, sales to service firms are considerably more important than sales to manufacturing firms. Engineering consultants constitute an exception, with manufacturing, construction and the public sector as the main markets.

The different producer service sectors have different geographical markets. Accountancy and legal services are primarily sold on local and regional markets. Computer services and management consultancy, on the contrary, are to a high degree sold on distant markets. Again, these results corroborate those of earlier studies (Illeris 1990) and those of Gallouj (1995). The latter author adds R&D services and engineering consultants to the category which sells much in other regions. He also notes that less specialized service producers and branch offices primarily sell to local customers, while the market orientation does not depend on the size of the service firms.

THE DEVELOPMENT OF SERVICE PROVISION OVER TIME

Information on changes in service provision over time is scarce. Still, a few sources exist. The Nord-Pas-de-Calais study on service users in 1987–88 is to some degree comparable to a study carried out in 1978 (Gallouj 1993). The average of 71 per cent of respondents which used the services in 1987–88 corresponds to an average of 54 per cent ten years earlier. The use of producer services had increased. While 79 per cent of the externally purchased services were supplied from the region itself in 1987–88, this was only the case with 49 per cent of the services ten years earlier. Thus, the regional supply of services had increased its ability to cover the regional demand—a 'catching up' had occurred, which corresponds to the relatively high growth rate in this region shown in Tables 8.5 and 8.8.

In the major survey of producer services carried out by Beyers et al (1985) in the Puget Sound area (with Seattle), the firms were asked about the location of their customers over the last five years. The result was that sales outside the local area had increased from 46 to 55 per cent of total sales.

In some cases, inter-regional input–output studies have been repeated with unchanged methods. Stabler and Howe (1988, 1992) have analysed data on trade between the Canadian provinces in 1974, 1979, and 1984. They found that sales out of provinces had increased from 17 per cent of all service sales in 1974 to 22 per cent in 1984. On the top of this, there is a considerable increase in inter-provincial trade in services embodied in goods. It is noteworthy that service sales out of Saskatchewan—which has no city with over 200 000 inhabitants—formed just as high a share and increased just as fast as the sales from provinces with large cities, such as Alberta and British Columbia (1979 results).

The survey by Gallouj (1995) confirms that the share of extra-regional service sales increases over time.

CONCLUSIONS

Household services are, on the whole, distributed between regions, as well as between cities and rural areas, according to their population. Producer services and corporate headquarters are strongly concentrated in the largest city areas. As a result, services as a whole are geographically more concentrated than the total population and economic activity.

The geographical changes of the 1980s display tendencies of decentralization in some countries—total employment in producer services has had higher growth rates outside the largest urban areas. But the decentralization has been selective, not general in all peripheries or low order centres. Increased concentration has not been observed in any of the countries investigated. Household services tend to follow shifts in the distribution of population, though the most dispersed services tend to concentrate in the second lowest level.

If the structure of the service sector (the composition in terms of household and producer services) had alone been responsible for the geographical development of the sector, it would have grown more in large city areas than elsewhere, since the rapidly growing producer services are over-represented there. However, this has not happened, which shows that other locational factors have been at work. In Chapter 9, such factors will be discussed.

The main findings from the data on the use and provision of producer services and the inter-regional trade in services are the following:

1 As regards the use of services, big establishments use more kinds of producer services than small ones, and more advanced establishments more services than less sophisticated users. Independent firms and branch establishments seem to use roughly the same amount of services.
2 As regards internal and external provision, branch establishments buy fewer services externally and (of course) more services from parent companies than independent firms. There is no evidence of differences between big and small or between more and less sophisticated users.
3 The majority of external services are purchased/sold locally or regionally, within distances of 50–100 km. However, service trade between regions is considerable—if measured as a share of total sales typically about 35 per cent— and not only sales from national capitals to other regions, but also upwards and across in the urban hierarchies.
4 Independent user firms get more of their services locally than branch establishments. Some kinds of producer services are almost exclusively sold on local and regional markets, such as accountancy and legal services. Other kinds, e.g. management consultancy and market research, are to a high degree traded between regions.
5 Over time, inter-regional trade in services is increasing, as a share of total sales. This fact does not exclude an increasing local provision of certain types of producer services.

9 Factors of Inter-urban Location

The purpose of this chapter is to discuss the factors influencing the inter-urban location of service establishments. In other words, to answer the question *why* service activities are located and change their locations in the way described in Chapter 8. There is no simple answer to this question, and a number of factors are discussed. First, studies into the service firms' own assessment of the factors of location are presented. Second, traditional theories of service location are dealt with, focusing on minimization of distance to customers and to sources of information inputs, respectively. Third, the changing influence of transport and telecommunications is discussed in more detail, the importance of accessibility as well as improved transport and communication technologies. Fourth, other factors are discussed, in particular the possibilities of recruiting skilled personnel. Finally the conclusions are drawn.

SURVEYS OF LOCATION FACTORS

The simplest way to investigate why service producers are located where they are, is to ask them. This method, however, has a number of pitfalls.

First, it has to be made clear exactly what is meant by 'where'. It is important to distinguish between the precise location (where in the urban area?), and the location in a broader context (in which urban area?). But not all authors make this distinction.

Second, it is also important to distinguish between the reason why the service firm was located there originally, and why this location now improves or hampers its competitive situation, compared to other locations. Often, the former question is uninteresting, especially if it is the firm's first location—the usual answer is then that the founder lived there.

Third, answers have to be interpreted critically. Many respondents have only vague and unclear ideas about the advantages and disadvantages of their locations. The most interesting investigations have studied firms which have moved recently.

Fourth, the questions and circumstances vary so much from study to study that they are difficult to compare.

Fifth, factors may not be mentioned if the respondents take them as a matter of course. This may be the case with transport and telecommunications in countries where the infrastructure is good everywhere. It must also be kept in mind that it is 'free' for the respondents to want better infrastructure as long as they do not themselves have to contribute to finance it.

Unfortunately, not many studies of the locational factors of service firms have been carried out. In particular, surveys of household services do not seem to exist. Presumably, proximity to customers is so evident a factor that it has not stirred the curiosity of researchers. As regards producer services, however, there are a few useful surveys. But it should be emphasized that the evidence is weak.

Beyers (1989) in a study in Washington state found that proximity to customers was mentioned as by far the most important factor of location. A much smaller number of respondents mentioned the quality of telecommunication systems, direct access to major highways, quality and reliability of electricity service (a factor which undoubtedly is taken for granted elsewhere), cost of office space and property, need to be close to other business, and quality of life in community (which must be interpreted both as the owner's residential preference and as being a factor behind the availability of skilled labour).

Kristiansen (1992) in a Norwegian study found that proximity to customers was the most important factor, followed by a large local market, availability of qualified labour, and the entrepreneur's own residential preferences. He put questions about the factors which were important for the decision of where to live and found that the following were important: (a) closeness to friends and family (which must be interpreted as a conservative factor, a wish to stay where one is or to return to where one has been); (b) climate—in particular summer climate; (c) availability of water sports; (d) availability of open air attractions, in particular mountains; (e) educational facilities for children; (f) labour market for spouses; (g) availability of one-family houses; (h) professional milieu; (i) attractive urban environment; and (j) sport and cultural activities for children. Other factors scored low, including some indicators of business milieu and of accessibility.

RESER (1995) found, in a study of six West European cities, that proximity to the market was important for many service producers (but unimportant for others). The possibility of recruiting qualified staff members was important for up-market firms (though less of a bottleneck during recession). Other factors were mentioned less often, such as access to information and impulses, easy access to an international airport, low costs, and image and prestige.

In a study of business services in the United States, Beyers (1994) asked about competitive edge factors. He found that among the 13 factors specified, some were geographical, namely 'proximity to clients' (no. 7) and 'proximity to suppliers' (no. 11). No transport or communication factor is mentioned, though many services are said to be delivered via telecommunications.

Illeris and Jakobsen (1991) interviewed computer service firms in Denmark. Recruitment of qualified staff was mentioned most often, especially by up-market firms. The possibilities were optimal in university cities, but large labour markets and amenities could also attract qualified people. The stability of staff-members was important, too, and in this respect provincial places had an advantage over Copenhagen. Second, proximity to customers was mentioned. And third, good accessibility for business travels, especially for up-market firms. But the latter was said not to be a problem anywhere, and the construction of a bridge over the Great

Belt would not change anybody's competitive situation much. Of secondary importance were the local professional milieux as well as salary levels, and costs of premises were totally without significance.

To summarize: Proximity to customers is considered important by producer service firms, as well as recruitment of qualified personnel (the latter especially by up-market firms). As factors of secondary importance, proximity to information/ business milieux as well as accessibility factors were mentioned, and in some studies cost factors.

PROXIMITY TO SERVICE USERS: THE ECONOMIC BASE MODEL AND THE CENTRAL PLACE THEORY

When research on the location of service activities began, the first theories focused on the need for service producers to locate close to the service users. These theories were developed in a deductive way in the 1930s—theories which in the 1960s became widely known and accepted. The two elements of these theories were conceived independently of one another, but are logically consistent and supplement each other.

The common basis for these theories is the notion that service users buy services as near as possible, in order to minimize transport costs. (As mentioned in Chapter 2, it is a fundamental characteristic of most service activities—as opposed to manufacturing—that producers and users have to meet face to face, and the transport of persons is expensive, especially if it has to be frequent.) Hence, and in contrast to manufacturing, service producers get a competitive advantage if they locate as close to their customers as possible, and the geographical distribution of service activities becomes largely determined by the distribution of customers. Service firms cannot sell on remote markets, because customers there will buy from local suppliers. In other words, the development of service activities in a given area is limited by the purchasing power of customers in that area.

The first element in this body of theory, known as the economic base model, deals with the relations between economic sectors. According to this model, which is illustrated by Figure 9.1, the economic base of a given area—for instance a city—is formed by the sectors which are able to sell their products outside the area. These activities are primarily the goods-producing sectors, agriculture and manufacturing industry, though tourist activities and shipping may be included, too. The money which the basic activities bring into the area is partly redistributed inside it as the wages and salaries which they pay to their personnel, i.e. local households. The latter demand services, and the service producers have, as mentioned, to locate close to them. In a second round, these service producers employ people who again demand other services. Thus, basic activities have a multiplier effect, while the total volume of service activities in an area is determined by the purchasing power which the basic activities bring into it. The service activities are 'non-basic' and play a passive role in the economic

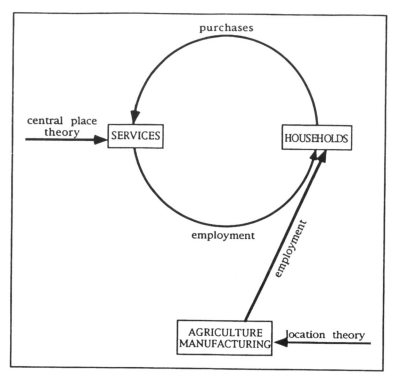

Figure 9.1. The economic base model

development of the area—a question which will be further discussed in Chapter 10, where modifications of the model will be suggested, too.

The economic base model was invented between the world wars by various authors independently of each other. The Dutch version (as used for example by van Dinteren 1989) has the advantage that it explicitly focuses on the critical parameter of the model, namely the size of the 'area' inside/outside which non-basic/basic activities can sell their products. The Dutch version acknowledges a hierarchy of activities: some may be locally non-basic, others regionally non-basic but locally basic, others again nationally non-basic but regionally basic, and so on. This hierarchy is identical with the lower and higher order service hierarchy of central place theory, presented below.

The second element in this body of theory, called central place theory, may be seen as a further elaboration of the need for proximity between service producers and customers, focusing on different types of service producers. It was conceived by Christaller (1933). What distinguishes the different types of service producers from one another is their different need for turnover in order to operate profitably, and behind the turnover, the different needs for minimum customer and purchasing power bases, their 'thresholds'. Services with low thresholds are able to operate profitably in small towns or villages (low-order central places) they serve small areas within short ranges. On the other hand, service activities with high thresholds require large customer bases, they locate only in big towns (high-order central places) and have long, but still limited, ranges.

On each level in this hierarchy, the service activities agglomerate into central places—for instance, the chemist, the bookstore and the clothes shop locate close to one another. This is explained by the competitive advantage they gain when the customers from the hinterland can economize on transport costs by combining visits to several service suppliers in one trip.

In this way, a hierarchy is created. At the bottom, there is a large number of low-order central places with service activities that need only a modest customer base from a small area. At the top, there is a small number of high-order central places which not only contain the low-order service activities, but also high-order service activities that require large customer bases and serve large areas (including many low-order central places). Figure 9.2 illustrates the hierarchy and the service flows in it. Later, recent modifications of this model will be discussed.

If governments attempt to offer public services in such a way that they are as accessible for all as near as possible, in other words that the travelling costs of citizens are minimized, while the services are produced within given cost constraints and hence at a given scale, the central place theory may apply to the location of non-marketed services, too.

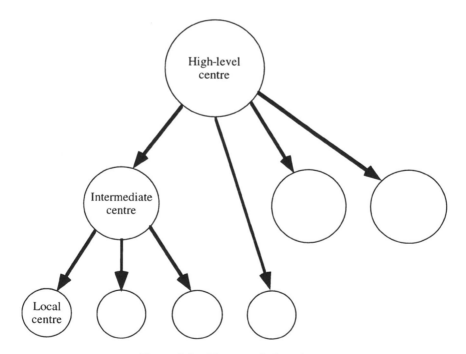

Figure 9.2. The central place theory

Christaller developed the theory under extremely simplifying assumptions, e.g. of evenly spread customers, which led to the result that central places should form a pattern of regular hexagons, and that there should be clear steps between the levels of the hierarchy. Empirical testing in the 1960s focused on such characteristics and found it difficult to confirm this version of the theory. This fact as well as other problems with the economic base model and the central place theory led to severe criticism in the 1970s. The worst problem probably is that they are developed within a neo-classical framework and form static equilibrium models which ignore the processes of change.

However, today the above-mentioned unrealistic assumptions tend to be relaxed, and scholars focus on the more general (and commonplace) statements. Most service activities (especially household services) do locate in such a way as to minimize distances to their customers, as confirmed by the evidence in Chapter 8 and in the above-mentioned surveys. Service activities locate in central places of higher and lower orders, and higher order central places also contain all services of lower order. But a number of problems with the theories exist, in particular when the theories are applied to producer services which nobody thought about in the 1930s or 1960s. These problems will be discussed for the two theories as a whole.

THE NEED FOR PROXIMITY BETWEEN SERVICE PRODUCERS AND USERS

As already mentioned, Christaller reasoned on the basis of a crude minimization of distance, implicitly assuming that customers' costs would be more or less proportional to distance. He paid little attention to the fact that the required frequency of transport is also an important factor: the more frequent, the higher the total costs and the distance sensitivity. Improved methods of storage (deep freezers, etc.) have in some cases reduced the need for frequent shopping trips and hence distance sensitivity (Illeris, Kongstad & Larsen 1966).

More important, improved means of transport, in particular increased private car ownership, have reduced transport costs, especially time costs. Again, the distance sensitivity has been reduced—if one cannot walk to a shop, it makes little difference whether one drives 3 or 6 km (Dale 1994). Thus, while people still buy services near to their homes, they are increasingly willing to go a little farther in order to obtain higher qualities and/or lower prices.

As regards producer services, in some cases the distance between producers and users is unimportant, either because the services can be transmitted via telecommunications, or because the travelling costs are insignificant in relation to the price of the services. These cases will be discussed later.

But in other cases, where face-to-face contact remains necessary, and distance minimization is important, the central place theory is to some degree applicable (Ellger 1995). Contrary to widespread notions, this is more often the case with commonplace and cheap producer services, especially if they are used frequently, than with sophisticated and expensive services (Illeris 1994a; Tordoir 1994).

In order to understand the need for face-to-face meetings between service producers and users, recent research has focused on the nature of their interaction, especially in the case of producer services. In some cases, for instance in management consultancy, the user participates actively in the creation of the service (Gadrey 1994c). Face-to-face contact is required. If persons or things are the objects of the services, they also have to be performed where these objects are. However, in other cases, such as that of engineering consultancy, proximity is not necessary while the core service is produced, but in other stages: proximity facilitates the search for customers, the contract negotiations, and later the supervision of the execution (RESER 1995). Thus, it is not only transport costs in a narrow sense that are reduced through proximity, but the total costs of having transactions with external partners (Daniels 1993b).

There may be other barriers to interaction than distance barriers. This will be discussed in more detail in connection with international trade in services (Chapter 13). But even inside countries, cultural barriers may play a role, as between French- and English-speaking Canada (Coffey & Polèse 1990).

GEOGRAPHICAL CONSEQUENCES: CONCENTRATION OR DECENTRALIZATION

Curiously enough, in the literature there are many contradictory statements like 'The consequence of the need for proximity to service users is geographical concentration of service producers' and 'The consequence of the need for proximity to service users is geographical decentralization of service producers'. (Both 'concentration' and 'decentralization' are here used to describe a state—more or less concentrated than economic activities in general—not a change over time).

Such statements show that the authors generalize from one part of the picture. The simple fact is that some service activities, especially business services, serve customers which are most easily reached from large cities, and hence concentrate there. Other service activities serve customers that are located in a dispersed way, and for them, the need for proximity pulls towards decentralization.

The former case, concentration in a few large cities, is characteristic of high-order service activities which minimize total transport costs by locating at the top of the central place hierarchy. Often, their customers are themselves concentrated in large cities and form large local markets there. Service producers not only minimize transport costs by concentrating, they also reduce business uncertainty and risks—May (1994b) talks of 'the insuring metropolis'. An example of a concentrated market is the corporate headquarters which are important customers of many sophisticated business services. Another example is that of newly developed business services which still only have few customers (an early life-cycle stage) and most easily serve them out of a large city.

The opposite case, decentralized location in order to minimize distances to dispersed customers, means that the service activity is of a relatively low order. There is a considerable group of producer services which can find sufficient business within a small area, namely the not very specialized service producers which serve the almost ubiquitous retailers, artisans, small manufacturers, and farmers. According to the evidence in Chapter 8, lawyers and accountants who sell their services within a distance of 50–100 km belong to this category. (Of course there are also specialized firms in these sectors.)

Studies of the technical and computer sectors, described in more detail in the Appendix, have shown them to include subsectors which provide unsophisticated clients with commonplace services adapted to their individual needs (Illeris 1994a). They form a kind of all-round 'house consultant'. They need to be close to their clients, not only because the travelling costs of these services are high relative to the price, but also because they must be able to arrive at short notice—a couple of hours—in case of emergencies, and because of the low cultural barriers: their intimate knowledge of the clients, and their ability to 'speak the same language' are among their most important qualifications. They fulfil a very important function in the total economy.

Special characteristics of local demand may attract or repel special types of service producers. Retirement regions need above-average health services (Glasmeier & Borchard 1989). Specialized industrial districts, such as the 'Third Italy', attract producer services providing for their special needs (Jaeger & Dürrenberger 1991). The aircraft and space industry in Toulouse has attracted a large number of R&D organizations and computer services (Gilly 1990). On the other hand, if less sophisticated users dominate, as in old industrial regions and underdeveloped peripheries, there is only a poor market for advanced services. This is the case in Nord-Pas-de-Calais (Gallouj 1993), Scotland (O'Farrell et al 1993) and the Italian Mezzogiorno (Cavola & Martinelli 1995).

CHANGING PARAMETERS

As already stated, central place theory has a static character: given a certain distribution of customers and purchasing power, and given minimum turnovers or thresholds for profitability, it determines the location of service activities. If these parameters change, the locational pattern must also change.

The geographical distribution of customers often changes. Chapter 8 showed examples of household services adapting to changes in the distribution of population, though with a time lag. Earlier attempts to model the changing location of service activities also show that they have followed changes in the distribution of population (Illeris 1989e).

The distribution of producer services has been influenced by a growth in the number of relatively dispersed independent small and medium enterprises over the last decades (Philippe & Monnoyer 1989; Moulaert, Tödtling & Schamp 1995). Even if these firms use rather few services, as shown in Chapter 8, their growth has contributed to an increasing local demand. On the other hand, there is a large and sophisticated demand from advanced enterprises and corporate headquarters in large cities. However, Marshall has pointed out that a decentralization of functions and decision-making in large corporations will tend to disperse the demand for producer services (Marshall & Jaeger 1990; Marshall 1994). Of course, a devolution of powers from national to regional and local governments—which has happened in most Western countries over recent decades—influences the public sector demand for producer services in the same direction.

Changes in the total purchasing power and in the composition of demand also influence the demand for household and producer services. In Norway's rural areas, agricultural subsidies increased purchasing power in the 1970s and kept the demand for household services high (Dale 1994). On the other hand, declining agriculture in the US weakened rural services in the 1980s (Glasmeier & Howland 1994). In recent decades, the rapidly increasing demand for public services (childcare, secondary and higher education) has meant that these could be supplied in lower order central places than earlier. The same is true of a number of leisure and bodycare services. On the other hand, in countries where the consumption of cinema services has decreased, cinemas have had to concentrate geographically.

Producer services which develop from early to mature life-cycle stages experience an expanding market, where local areas offer sufficient business—in other words, thresholds are reduced. This process has played an important role in recent decades (Monnoyer 1993). Computer services may serve as an example, see the Appendix. Such sectors change from being high-order to low-order services. Entrepreneurs create new firms to serve growing local markets, and old large-city firms form networks with local firms or set up decentralized branch offices, which have the extra advantage of being able to offer sophisticated services by calling in headquarter specialists.

Internal developments within service activities—increasing or decreasing economies of scale—may also change the thresholds. It is not always possible to measure these factors in quantitative terms. In mental hospitals, the professionals now try to break up the large institutions of former times, because of the qualitative advantages of therapy in smaller institutions. This tendency combines with a preoccupation with better contact between the institution and the surrounding society (in central place terms: shorter ranges). This constitutes a decentralizing factor.

However, in most cases economies of scale seem to increase, or the need for specialization grows and pushes up threshold values: hospitals with the most specialized equipment and staff that can only be used by a small part of the patients require a large population basis. Increasing economies of scale, and hence geographical concentration, currently take place in retailing. In banking, household services are split between routine operations carried out by decentralized cash-dispensing machines and more specialized services offered in increasingly concentrated establishments.

CONCLUSION ON PROXIMITY TO SERVICE USERS

Proximity to customers, in order that transport costs between service producers and users as well as other transaction costs can be minimized, remains a decisive factor of location for household services and many producer services. For them, traditional central place theory remains valid, though it must be modified in details —customers use nearby service providers, but not necessarily the nearest ones.

Central place theory is static. However, the many locational changes observed in service activities which depend on proximity to customers may be interpreted as changing parameters pulling towards new equilibria: changes in the geographical distribution of customers, in their purchasing power and in the composition of demand as well as internal changes in the service activities leading to in- or decreasing economies of scale. Some of these changes pull towards increasing concentration in higher order central places with larger markets, others towards decentralization into lower order central places based on smaller markets.

PROXIMITY TO SOURCES OF INFORMATION

The statistical evidence in Chapter 8 clearly showed that producer service activities are highly concentrated in large city areas. There are several factors behind this concentration, but according to most of the literature, the main explanation is the need for proximity to sources of input. For wholesaling, this may mean proximity to their suppliers of goods, but this question has not been studied much. In most cases, it is a question of proximity to sources of information, which is the factor to be discussed in this section.

WHY DOES PROXIMITY TO INFORMATION SOURCES LEAD TO GEOGRAPHICAL CONCENTRATION?

The main argument is that service activities that treat information—business services, a few household services such as cultural activities and mass media, and similar activities performed internally in other firms—need a lot of information inputs, especially if they are to be innovative. In particular they need sophisticated information, non-standardized and complicated information with a strategic value. As the importance of innovation, market knowledge and understanding of the surrounding world increases, access to sources of information becomes more and more crucial. This is obtained through 'orientation contacts' (Thorngren 1970) which often have the form of face-to-face meetings.

The search for these inputs is costly, uncertainty is high (Cappellin 1988; Daniels 1991b). The costs are minimized through location in large cities where there is a concentration of sources such as other firms, organizations, mass media and research institutes. To quote an anecdote from the computer service field: you get more new ideas from spending a night in a Silicon Valley bar than from reading and telephoning a whole year.

The notion is widespread that proximity to sources of information plays a decisive role as a factor which pulls information services towards concentration in information-dense environments, in particular large cities. It is found in well-known books dealing with general economic and societal development, such as Porter's (1990) and Reich's (1991). (The latter, however, modifies his ideas about the concentration of 'symbolic analysts' and writes that they 'can work almost anywhere there exist a telephone, fax, modem, and airport'.) Andersson (1985) describes the outbursts of creativity which took place in cities, due to synergies based on frequent face-to-face interaction, for instance in Athens in the fifth century BC, in Florence in the Renaissance period, or in Vienna around the turn of the last century. (The irony is that this highly original book, claiming that creativity is the future of the large city, was written while the author worked in the small and remote Swedish town of Umeå.) In the locational literature, the classical work arguing this point of view is Gottmann's (1961).

The fundamental societal trend behind the need for information inputs is the increasing division of labour between economic units—including recent tendencies of externalization and vertical disintegration. This clearly makes it more important to reduce the costs of external transactions and interactions and enhances the importance of proximity to sources of information as a factor of location (Hansen 1990; Daniels 1991a).

ADVANTAGES OF AGGLOMERATION AND NETWORK-BUILDING

As argued above, the easy and cheap access to sources of information is a main reason why information services agglomerate in large cities. Other agglomeration advantages are infrastructure and the labour and office markets, to be discussed later. Some authors also include in the concept of agglomeration advantages proximity to customers, discussed above.

However, interaction between information service producers is rarely a one-way flow, but rather a reciprocal process. It has a dialogical character (Planque 1984) in which information in- and outputs cannot be clearly distinguished, and where synergies are created. Thus many authors stress that economic actors build networks in order to supplement one another, and that network partners primarily are found in the same urban area (RESER 1995; de Jong, Machielse & de Ruijter 1992; Mayère & Vinot 1993).

Since large cities not only offer advantages of local interaction, but also are the places with the highest interregional and international accessibility, they attract information services which need both close international connections and local contacts (Sjøholt 1992b). 'World cities' are those which have the densest international contacts (Daniels 1993b).

Areas with high densities of information exchanges may develop into 'innovative milieux' (Maillat 1990) or just professional milieux. As mentioned above, business services concentrate in large cities in order to serve corporate headquarters, but headquarters also locate there in order to be close to business services. Together, these functions constitute complexes which are the motors of most metropolitan areas (Noyelle & Stanback 1984) and the meeting places of the power- and knowledge-élites (Ellger 1988).

SMALLER CENTRES OF INFORMATION EXCHANGE

The largest geographical concentrations of information sources are the big metropolitan areas. But more modest concentrations exist elsewhere and offer good locations for some information service activities.

Generally, as one descends the urban hierarchy, the concentration of information sources gets poorer. Small towns offer so little that information services have to pay the costs of obtaining their inputs from the outside, usually from big cities. Selstad and Lie (1987) show that this is what happens in Norwegian provinces, and O'Farrell et al (1993) stress the handicap that this constitutes for Scottish business service firms.

However, not all information service activities interact to the same extent. Studies in metropolitan areas have shown that the interaction pattern is split into clusters of interrelated activities, typically a financial and trading cluster, a publishing and advertising cluster, and an engineering and construction cluster (Goddard & Morris 1976). If a small centre is specialized in such a way that it contains a sector or cluster of activities which need particularly intensive mutual interaction, it may, within this special field, offer sources of information that equal those of much bigger cities.

One type of specialization is found in 'industrial districts'. As an example, the Herning-Ikast textile district in West Jutland contains such information services as education, R&D, designers and trade organizations (plus other services such as exhibition and transport facilities and wholesalers), all specializing in the needs of textile and garment producers, and all having close mutual cooperation (Hjalager 1986).

Another type of specialization consists of administrative capitals and related service activities (mass media, trade organizations, etc.), in countries where these functions have been placed outside the largest cities, such as the United States.

A third type is found in university towns—again in countries where these are placed outside the large cities. Here, R&D units may profit from synergies with university departments (Malecki 1987; Thwaites & Alderman 1990). The many science parks or 'technopoles' that have been created in recent years are attempts to reap such synergies. However, the same effect may also be obtained on much more modest levels, for instance where general practitioners cooperate in a medical centre in order to support one another professionally (Dale 1994).

EMPIRICAL EVIDENCE

Though some of the statements concerning proximity to information inputs are empirically based, many of them have been developed primarily by theoretical reasoning. The empirical evidence of the above-mentioned surveys indicates, however, that producer service firms only consider proximity to sources of information a factor of location of secondary importance.

CONCLUSION ON PROXIMITY TO INFORMATION SOURCES

In much of the literature, it is argued that for business services and other information services, proximity to sources of information is a decisive factor of location, due to the necessity of face-to-face interaction. It is argued that this is the main explanation of the observed concentration of business services in large cities.

There is no doubt that proximity to sources of information *is* a factor of location for this sector. Survey evidence shows, however, that the firms only rate it a factor of secondary importance. Other factors must contribute to the explanation of the observed geographical concentration of these activities.

CHANGES IN TRANSPORT AND COMMUNICATIONS

Let us now focus on the changing influence of transport and telecommunications on the location of services. As already mentioned, the importance of this factor is due to the very nature of services. In most cases, the service producer and user have to meet, which means that at least one of them must be transported. And transport of persons is—especially if it is frequent—costly, and can be less automated than the transport of goods. On the other hand, some services can be transmitted cheaply via telecommunications.

Improvements in transport and telecommunication technologies have been spectacular in recent decades. They catch the eye of the media and politicians and give rise to prophecies of revolutionary changes in our lives. On the basis of the knowledge existing in the mid-1990s, an attempt will be made here to give a sober assessment of the influence of these technological changes on the geographical distribution of service activities.

More precisely, two questions are discussed in this section. First, the influence of the accessibility of a place on the location of service activities—accessibility meaning how easy it is to get to and from the place, from and to other places (which may be measured in a variety of ways). And second, how have the changes in transport and communication technologies influenced the location of service activities—have they pulled towards a geographical concentration or decentralization? But before discussing these questions, the changes in transport and telecommunications will be summarized.

WHAT REALLY ARE THE CHANGES?

To characterize the changes, one has to measure the costs of overcoming distances. Direct expenditure on investments in infrastructure and means of transport plus the operating costs are only part of the costs. Often time costs (lost working hours of service producers or customers) may be higher than the direct expenditure. The general tendency in both transport and telecommunications is that—due to technical progress, increased productivity, and in some periods cheaper energy—

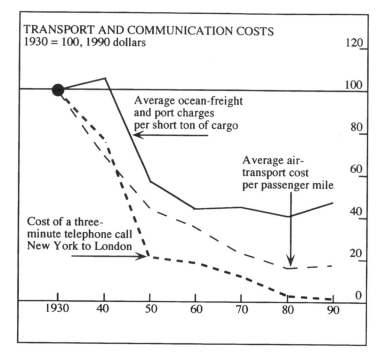

TRANSPORT AND COMMUNICATION COSTS
1930 = 100, 1990 dollars

Figure 9.3. Transport and communication costs. *Source:* based on *The Economist* 20.7.1991.

the direct costs have decreased, relative to other prices, as illustrated by Figure 9.3. Wherever travel has become more rapid, time costs have decreased, too.

It is useful to distinguish between *ubiquitous* modes of transport (by road) and telecommunications, which in the Western world reach almost every house, and, on the other hand, railways, air and waterborne transport which can only be accessed at stations, airports and ports.

As regards *transport*, the enormous increase in car ownership has meant a strong tendency towards ubiquitously higher accessibility, much more equally spread than when railways dominated the transport system. Remote places are simply less isolated than they were earlier. The construction of motorways has reduced the costs of inter-urban road transport. However, in the densely populated central Western Europe, the motorway system is now close to saturation. And within cities, traffic congestion has meant that improvements in accessibility have been limited—in inner cities it has even deteriorated, in spite of metros and motorways.

Air transport has also increased tremendously since World War II and improved inter-urban accessibility. In the 1950s, large cities—in Europe almost only capitals—were connected by regular flights. Later they were combined with shorter domestic flights, together forming a 'hub-and-spoke' system. The last decade has, however, been characterized by new lines between second- and third-level European cities, so the monopoly on high air accessibility which the capitals had earlier has been reduced (Illeris 1994b). But the system of air control, not connected electronically from one European country to another, has such a low capacity that it is saturated in central Western Europe in the summer months.

There are some question marks about the future of these two successful means of transport. They are both heavily polluting, and in central Western Europe, the infrastructure is close to saturation.

The relative importance of railways, sea and river/canal transport has decreased—in the United States to the point where passenger transport has almost disappeared. In Europe, high-speed trains have entailed an environment-friendly revival since the 1980s. They concentrate accessibility on a few large cities (but not, according to current investments and plans, only in the core of Europe).

As regards *telecommunications*, the old postal system and the newer telephone system are both ubiquitous. The postal system has since World War II only improved its performance in inter-continental connections, but it should not be forgotten that the possibility of sending information via disks is an important improvement. The cable, radio and satellite signals systems (telecommunications in a more narrow sense) have experienced a tremendous growth, due to their falling real prices and their ever-increasing capacity to carry new types of services. New technical solutions—in recent years optical fibres—have initially been adopted in densely populated areas where demand is high. But they have usually been extended to sparsely populated peripheries fairly quickly (Daniels 1993a mentions a recent British example). In Western Europe, one can hardly say that many areas lack communications infrastructure. The geographical tariff structures also influence accessibility. They vary from the postal principle of distance-independent tariffs to the cost-based principle of telephone companies, but prices of long-distance calls are falling, relative to those of short-distance calls. Altogether, the growth of telecommunications has undoubtedly favoured a geographical equalization of 'total accessibility'.

In the future too, accessibility will be important. But the current euphoria about infrastructure investments may in some instances be ill-founded. Infrastructure is expensive, and the anticipated benefits should be related to the costs (including environmental costs). In areas where the infrastructure is already good, some of the projects now planned will only marginally improve accessibility.

In some situations, transport and telecommunications are competitors: 'Can I discuss this problem with X over the telephone, or do I have to meet him/her face to face?'. The future answers to this question may be influenced by environmental restrictions or taxes on car and air transport. But seen in a wider context, it is not only a question of substitution, but also of mutual reinforcement. The wide choice of modes of transport and communications is simply both cause and effect of the ever-increasing division of labour in our societies, which is accompanied by increasing exchanges of goods, services and people.

SURVEY EVIDENCE OF THE IMPORTANCE OF ACCESSIBILITY

As mentioned above, the few results available from surveys do not indicate that transport and communication accessibility are of decisive importance for the location of service activities. But this may partly be because at least telecommunication facilities are good throughout the survey areas.

DO IMPROVED TRANSPORT AND TELECOMMUNICATIONS FAVOUR CONCENTRATION OR DECENTRALIZATION OF SERVICE ACTIVITIES?

We now turn to the second question of this section, which has been central to much research and debate in recent years.

In the 1960s and 1970s, most answers were based on the simple fact that by making it cheaper and easier to overcome distance, improved transport and telecommunications made it possible to sell an increasing amount of services over longer distances—as witnessed by the surveys referred to in Chapter 8. Technological development diminished the need for service activities to locate close to their customers and/or their sources of information. Agglomeration advantages were reduced, distances were 'shrinking'. 'There is everywhere' as Pascal (1987) said.

Visions of a future society without friction of distance were portrayed, societies in which service activities, homes and other functions could be just anywhere, because it was possible to get in contact with everybody else more or less instantly, face to face or via telecommunications.

This vision was presented in the 1960s by physical planners from California (where Los Angeles was growing as a car-based urban area with almost no agglomerated centre; e.g. Webber 1964). In 1980, stressing the telecommunication links, Toffler described how the geographical structure of society could be characterized by dispersed 'electronic cottages'.

In the 1970s, research started to explore exactly how telecommunications could substitute for face-to-face meetings. For instance, Pye (1979) both analysed actual meetings and used laboratory experiments. The results of these studies showed that many meetings could be substituted either by telephone conferences or by much more expensive video-conferences. But in reality, the numbers of face-to-face meetings continued to grow. The studies had focused too much on the easily measured, well-defined 'programmed contacts', and neglected the more complicated, unstructured and spontaneous 'orientation contacts'. And by focusing on substitution, the studies had ignored the mutual reinforcement processes, how meetings and tele-contacts supplement each other and together form an improved interaction system.

The 1980s were characterized by a realization that new technologies would not lead to a society without the friction of distance (e.g. Moss 1987; Daniels 1988; Ellger 1988; Hepworth 1989; and Selstad 1989). Some standardized services could be transmitted at low cost via telecommunications. Producers of such services, typically back offices, could indeed locate far from their customers. But in most cases, service producers and users would still have to meet, proximity would remain necessary, and advantages of agglomeration important. This would especially be the case with specialized and sophisticated information services, such as the interaction between business services and corporate headquarters. The advantages of agglomeration would be reinforced by the high standard of infrastructure of large cities and their high accessibility.

The 1990s seem to modify these answers. While maintaining that distance frictions do not vanish, it is now realized that it takes time before the opportunities offered by new technologies are taken up, and that communication technologies still improve rapidly. Services which a decade ago were too complicated or too expensive to exchange via telecommunications, are now transmitted electronically. It is also realized that by focusing so narrowly on telecommunications, researchers had forgotten the improvements and (time) cost reductions that took place in transport. These factors pull towards a reduction of distance barriers and agglomeration advantages.

Furthermore, it is now realized that the costs of travel must be seen in relation to the value of the services. To take an extreme example: if an oil well is on fire, an extinction expert is immediately flown in from wherever he can be found—nobody considers the transport costs, however high they are. High-level architects and financiers locate in Hawaii, even if they often have to visit customers all over the United States (*The Economist* 3.4.1993). Symbolic analysts can, according to Reich (1991), work almost anywhere, as long as there is infrastructure for connecting with the rest of the world.

Thus, it is not the really sophisticated service activities that depend most on proximity, even if they require face-to-face meetings. It is rather individualized low and medium quality services, custom-made to each client and often used frequently, simply because their travelling costs are higher relative to the price of the services. These are the types of service activities that still minimize transport costs by locating roughly according to central place theory (Illeris 1994a).

The traditional central place model for the location and delivery of services, as illustrated by Figure 9.2, may now be modified as shown in Figure 9.4. While the service flows of the traditional hierarchical model still exist, they have been supplemented by a number of untraditional flows, from low-order to high-order places, and horizontally and diagonally across the hierarchy. Many services are no longer bought at the nearest place.

Finally, it is increasingly understood that the question 'do the improved transport and communication technologies lead to geographical concentration or decentralization?' is basically a false question. Even if the consequence of these improvements is a relative reduction in the costs of overcoming distances, this does not in itself lead to a geographical decentralization (or concentration). They constitute a necessary, but not a sufficient condition for decentralization. Their effect is to relax constraints of proximity to customers (and sources of information). But that does not mean that all locations become equally good. It means that *other* factors of location then become relatively more important. Some of these factors—

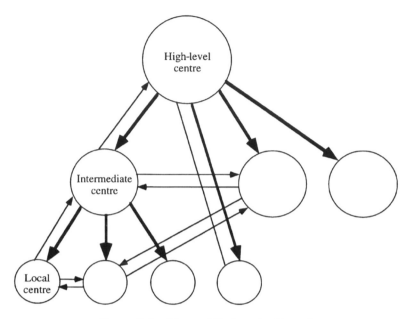

Figure 9.4. The modified service hierarchy

which are discussed later—pull towards concentration, others towards decentralization.

In other words, improved transport and telecommunication technologies are *enabling* forces. They enable, for instance, service activities in large cities to serve wider hinterlands than before. But they also enable service activities located in small, remote towns to serve customers in big cities. They increase competition— just like other forces that break down barriers, such as liberalization of international trade. Who gains, and who loses? That depends on a number of factors which influence competitive capabilities, and some of these factors are tied to the location of the competitors. Thus *other factors of location than proximity become more influential* (Illeris 1989e; Philippe & Monnyer 1989; Coffey 1990; Marshall 1990; Kellerman 1993; Richardson 1994).

This ambiguity is not a new phenomenon. The locational effects of the telephone were ambiguous. It allowed the headquarters of corporations to be geographically separated from the plants and to concentrate in large cities (Coffey & Bailly 1990) if this was optimal for some reason. But it also allowed service activities to locate far from large cities, if *that* was optimal (Abler 1977).

CONCLUSIONS ON CHANGES IN TRANSPORT AND TELECOMMUNICATIONS

Transport and telecommunications have become immensely better and cheaper in the decades since World War II. Accessibility has increased everywhere. While airlines and high-speed trains contribute to the accessibility of large cities only, cars and telecommunications are ubiquitous and pull towards an equalization of accessibilities.

However, though accessibility is important, it does not seem to be a decisive factor of location, according to survey evidence. Improved transport and telecommunications have meant that while service activities earlier were located in such a way as to minimize distances to customers (and, for information services, distances to sources of information), for some of them this constraint has now been relaxed.

Most household services and unsophisticated and cheap producer services still have to locate in the proximity of their markets, especially if the services are custom-made and if frequent face-to-face meetings are required. Distance is still a barrier. But some information services can now be transmitted cheaply via telecommunications, and firms producing them are able to locate independently of the users. This is especially the case of highly standardized services. However, improving technology all the time increases the array of services that can be delivered in this way. If transport is restricted or taxed heavily for environmental reasons, more service activities will be pushed into this category.

Other services are so sophisticated or complicated that face-to-face meetings will remain necessary. However, improving transport technologies (cars, planes, high-speed trains) have also reduced the (time) costs of travel to meetings. And travelling costs may be insignificant relative to the price of these services. Here, too, the necessity of proximity and the advantages of agglomeration are reduced.

In cases where distance barriers are reduced, it is not possible to conclude whether the effect will be a geographical concentration or decentralization of the service activities. Improved transport and communications enable the activities to locate independently of their customers. Then other factors, to be discussed later, will have decisive influence on the pattern of location.

RECRUITMENT OF PERSONNEL AND OTHER FACTORS OF LOCATION

Having found that for some producer service activities, the traditional factors of proximity to customers or to sources of information are no longer decisive, we shall now discuss the factors of location which then become influential. According to the above-mentioned surveys, the possibility of recruiting qualified personnel is the most prominent one.

RECRUITMENT OF QUALIFIED PERSONNEL

Not only the above-mentioned, but also several other studies confirm the finding that for producer service firms which are not tied to proximity to their customers, the possibility of recruiting qualified staff (meaning not only university-educated) is the most important factor of location (e.g. Keeble, Bryson & Wood 1991; Gallouj 1993; Gadrey 1994c; Thwaites & Alderman 1990).

This finding turns the traditional theory of regional development upside down. It has always been assumed that labour had to migrate to the places where the firms (for other reasons) located: 'The man must come to the job'. What we find here is that the job must come to the man. Or at least, that firms located where this type of labour prefers to be have a competitive advantage. Of course, the reason is that this segment of the labour market is a sellers' market (though less so in periods of recession). If skilled persons create their own firms, these may be located where the entrepreneurs prefer to live.

A special aspect is that qualified people shall not only be recruited, but also retained—it is expensive to search for and train new staff-members. Personnel stability is typically higher in small, provincial labour markets.

The importance of skilled personnel for the location of service activities is natural, given the fact that personnel constitute both the main cost and the main resource. Furthermore, this labour force is not very geographically mobile, and recruitment possibilities vary considerably from place to place. The skills which the service producers need may be of many kinds and be found on many levels. But they are rarely identical with those important in manufacturing. Unemployment in old industrial areas is not easily solved by growing service employment (Urry 1992).

The next question is where qualified people prefer to live. There is only limited research on this, and there has been little connection between research on service location and research on migration and residential preferences. Still, some answers seem to emerge.

First, there is a general conservative factor. People wish to stay where they and their children have their family and friends and a known environment, where they often have invested in a house for example—though the geographical mobility of professionals may be higher in the US than in Europe (Malecki & Bradbury 1990). Wood (1993a) and Marshall and Raybould (1993) report how skilled personnel use their power to resist locational change—a phenomenon well known from attempts to relocate government offices. This 'conservatism' may be a factor that favours the return to (smaller) towns of adolescence after education (in big cities), but in other cases is a factor that keeps a traditional (big city) location of service activities.

Second, places with institutions of higher education tend to offer a large supply of qualified labour. Students may get into contact with employers even before graduating—this seems to be important in science parks. Or they may start building families and be subject to the conservative factors already mentioned. Thus, firms might find it easier to recruit staff in such places. On the other hand, if local demand does not match supply, an educational institution may operate as a pump that sends the local youth away in search of the jobs for which they have been educated (Selstad & Lie 1987).

Third, the large labour market of a big city is an important way of reducing uncertainty and risks for people with specialized qualifications and a limited number of potential employers (just as it is for employers looking for persons with special skills). The importance of a large labour market has even increased, as married women have entered the arena. The spouses of specialists are often specialists, too, and such couples have little chance of finding two specialized jobs in a small town.

Fourth, the professional milieu in a place may play a role for qualified people, just as proximity to sources of information may for firms. For instance, this may be important in advertising (May 1994a). However, usually it is the internal milieu offered by the firm that seems to be the important factor—prestigious firms are always able to recruit—wherever the firm is located. However, in cases where people combine two jobs, for instance as part-time university teachers, the milieu of the agglomeration is a factor in its own right (Rasmussen 1992).

Fifth, qualified people seem increasingly to follow preferences determined by what they consider important in their leisure time. The preferences and attractions are varied: some prefer the large supply of cultural and leisure services and the 'urbanity' of large cities. Others prefer the less polluted environment, as well as the safer and closer social environment of small towns. Pleasant climates and landscapes, availability of water and winter sports, and attractive urban environments increasingly dominate the migration pattern, while it is difficult to persuade people to go to less interesting rural regions (Glasmeier & Borchard 1989, Sjøholt 1990) and forbidding, polluted old industrial areas (Gallouj 1993). Quality of life factors and amenities are thus indirectly, through their attraction to key personnel, important factors of location (Bonamy & Mayère 1987; Gillespie & Green 1987; Wood, Bryson & Keeble 1993; Malecki 1987; Haug 1991).

To summarize: many factors influence the preferences of qualified people, and thus recruitment possibilities in various places. The large labour market is a strong force pulling high-level service activities towards concentration in large cities (Selstad & Hagen 1991; May 1994b; Daniels 1993b; Coffey & Bailly 1992). However, quality of life factors may pull towards other areas, and Sjøholt (1992a) and Lundmark (1994) observe that qualification levels in certain subsectors are equally high on different levels of the urban hierarchy. But only some small towns and rural areas are able to attract qualified people.

LOW WAGES AND CHEAP PREMISES

In some surveys, costs are mentioned as a factor of location for producer service firms, though only of secondary importance. The advantages of large cities drive up the price of totally immobile factors of production—offices—as well as relatively immobile factors—the labour force. For firms which compete in high-quality markets, this seems to be unimportant. But cost-sensitive producer service activities that are not tied to proximity to customers are repelled by large cities and tend to locate in low-cost areas. This is primarily the case with back offices which use less qualified labour (Aydalot & Camagni 1986; Philippe & Monnoyer 1989; Coffey & Polese 1987; Wood 1989).

Of course, there are many degrees of cost-sensitivity and degrees of dependence on proximity to front offices, as well as degrees of labour skills. Many back offices are located in medium costly suburban settings, in order to recruit women with a good school education and such social qualifications as stability and carefulness (Nelson 1986). Other back offices are located in rural areas or national peripheries; in recent years the tendency has been towards location in low-wage countries (Wilson 1994; May 1994a). In any event, back office employment is threatened by automation, and by the increasing ability of users to reinternalize the operations.

PRESTIGE

Prestige or image is mentioned as an inter-urban factor of location in one of the above-mentioned surveys and by a few authors (Begg & Cameron 1988; Castells 1989), but seems to be more important in an intra-urban context, see Chapter 11.

CHANGES IN INTERNAL ORGANIZATION

Corporate reorganization may lead to changes in the location of internal service activities. Massey (1979) has emphasized restructuring by way of geographical separation between headquarters located in national core cities and, on the other hand, production units located in peripheries with cheap labour.

However, this school of 'corporate geography' got strangely out of contact with contemporary literature on management tendencies and on the emerging post-Fordist or service society, referred to in Chapter 14. This literature stressed decentralization of decisions and vertical disintegration of corporations. It is Marshall's achievement to have brought the theory of corporate geography out of the Fordist age (Aksoy & Marshall 1992; Marshall & Raybould 1993; Marshall 1994).

The empirical part of Marshall and his collaborators' work is a study of 20 British corporations in various manufacturing and service sectors. They showed a variety of tendencies, but the majority had slimmed their headquarters radically over the 1980s, linked to a decentralization of internal service activities (except the most strategic ones) to the divisional offices, located in many regions.

A parallel process is the devolution of government which has taken place in most West European countries (except the UK) in recent decades. Service activities have been shifted from national capitals to regional and local administrative centres.

CONCLUSION ON OTHER FACTORS OF LOCATION

Some types of producer services no longer locate as near as possible to customers or sources of information, as other factors of location become decisive. For qualified service activities, the possibility of recruiting skilled personnel constitutes the most important factor of location, which means that the residential preferences of such people become crucial. Large labour markets play an important role for them and pull towards large cities. But quality of life factors are important, too, and according to taste may pull towards attractive cities or small town and rural environments—while other rural areas and old industrial regions are unattractive.

Less qualified producer service activities that are not tied to proximity to customers—typically back offices—locate outside big cities in order to minimize wage and office costs: in suburbs, peripheral regions, and increasingly in low-wage countries.

Decentralization of power to lower levels of corporate and government hierarchies has been accompanied by geographical decentralization of internal service activities from big to smaller cities. Other factors of location, such as prestige, may play a role, but do not seem to be decisive in an inter-urban context.

OVERALL CONCLUSION ON INTER-URBAN LOCATION

The explanations behind the distribution of service activities that was described in Chapter 8 may be summarized as follows.

Household services and some producer services largely locate in the proximity of their customers. The growing demand for producer services has led to a geographical decentralization, since local markets increasingly offer sufficient turnover.

Sophisticated producer services are to a high degree concentrated in large cities. While, originally, this concentration minimized transport costs to customers and to sources of information, these costs are now insignificant relative to the price of high-quality services. Furthermore, accessibility—which is a *sine qua non*—tends to become geographically more equal. The decisive factor of location is now the possibility of recruiting qualified staff. And because of the large labour market, cultural and other factors, this is easiest in large cities. However, other locations, which are rendered attractive by quality of life factors, are possible.

For less sophisticated producer service activities, which are able to transmit their services via telecommunications, low wage and office costs have become the decisive factors of location, driving them from large cities to suburban and peripheral locations, and increasingly to low-wage countries.

An attempt has been made by Coffey and Polèse (1987) to tie the various factors together in a quantitative model of office location, based on the minimization of three groups of costs: (a) costs of information inputs, including communication costs; (b) salary costs, including costs of recruiting qualified personnel; and (c) costs of selling services, including communication costs. These costs more or less reflect the 'factors of location' which have been found to be decisive in the above summary.

10 The Role of Services in Regional Development

There are two questions to be addressed in this chapter. What is the role of service activities in the economic development of regions? How can service activities contribute to regional development policies?

RECENT MODIFICATIONS OF THE ECONOMIC BASE MODEL

As mentioned in Chapter 9, the traditional notion is that because of the need to minimize transport costs between service producers and users, service activities can only sell their services within limited distances. Thus, they cannot bring money into an area by 'exporting' to other areas ('exporting' in this connection means selling to other areas as well as to other countries). Their growth is limited by local purchasing power which depends on the amount of sales which other, 'basic' activities make outside the area. The role of service activities is 'non-basic' or passive, and there would be no sense in promoting service activities in a regional development policy.

CREATION OF EMPLOYMENT AND INCOME, SATISFACTION OF NEEDS

In recent years, the traditional economic base model has come under attack. Since service activities in each local area—as well as in society as a whole, see Chapter 1—have grown rapidly, it must be recognized that new employment, new economic development and new incomes are primarily created in service activities. The growth of non-basic activities in a local area is still limited, but the multiplier increases. Private and public service activities contribute to the increasing division of labour, to the externalization of activities from households and user firms, and thus to specialization and increased productivity.

These processes take place everywhere, but the processes are more advanced in some areas than in others. Regional service research has not discussed them much, but see Gallouj (1993) and Martinelli (1991b). Regional development policies can aim at accelerating these processes.

It must also be recognized that household services directly fulfil the ultimate purpose of the economy: to satisfy human needs. The more and better household services that are produced in an area, the higher the satisfaction of needs.

There has been more research focus on changes in the relationships between the sectors of the economic base model. They will now be discussed.

MOST SERVICE ACTIVITIES REMAIN NON-BASIC

As discussed in Chapter 9, most private and public household services and many producer services can still only sell their services within limited distances. The parameters may change, the geographical ranges get longer, but they remain limited. The economic base model—as well as central place theory—remains valid for most service activities.

Some authors argue that the modifications of the economic base model are marginal, and that attention should remain focused on the production of goods as the important economic base (Patton & Markusen 1991; Esparza 1992; Perry 1991). Coffey and McRae (1990) have drawn attention to the fact that there are institutional barriers to service trade, not only between countries, but also between regions, since local governments in reality prefer local procurement.

SOME SERVICE ACTIVITIES BECOME BASIC

However, the empirical evidence presented in Chapter 8 shows that producer services today sell many services quite far away—typically 35 per cent of the turnover is to customers more than 50–100 km away—and that this share is increasing. This cannot be ignored, and most authors agree that a number of service activities must be included in the basic sector: see for instance Kirn (1987), Hansen (1990), Harrington, Macpherson and Lombard (1991), as well as Marshall (1994) who stresses that this development has been ignored by the 'corporate complex' literature. These service activities play an active role in the economic development of the area—if they grow, the whole local economy grows.

What are basic service activities? In Chapter 9, it was argued that the distance barrier is broken primarily for two types of services: those that can transmit their services via telecommunications (e.g. back offices), and those that are so valuable that travelling costs become insignificant. The empirical documentation in Chapter 8 showed that business services such as management consultancy and market research are such branches. But of course, there are also other producer services, such as wholesaling and transport. Among household service activities, those which serve tourists are undoubtedly basic, and the same may be said of those which serve retired people who bring in their pensions from other regions (Gillis 1987). Finally, it should not be forgotten that national government and international organization activities often have a basic character for the place where they are located, e.g. in the cases of administration, military establishments, universities and so on (Townsend 1991).

The composition of non-basic service activities is more or less the same all over a country, depending only on the hierarchical level, since the demand from households and firms for unsophisticated services does not vary much. On the other hand, basic services, as well as other basic activities, are radically different from area to area (Léo & Philippe 1991; Groshen 1987; Bonnet 1991). One area may specialize in tourism, another in military establishments, a third in back offices, a fourth in engineering consultancy—and some areas do not export services, but only goods. In this way, the location of basic services contributes to uneven regional development (Marshall & Wood 1995). If the basic agricultural or manufacturing activities of an area decline—which often happens—it is crucial for the local economy that other basic activities substitute for them, and in many cases service activities constitute the only option (Edvardsson, Fureh & Karlsson 1987).

Generally, large cities sell a larger share of their service production outside the city and its immediate hinterland than small towns do; according to Daniels (1991a) often about half, but we have few data to illustrate this. But then, in the case of large cities it is difficult to distinguish between, on the one hand, services that are non-basic and minimize distances to customers (for services with high thresholds, a metropolis is the highest order central place) and, on the other hand, basic services which locate there for other reasons. At any rate, large cities do not monopolize basic service activities. As argued by Boulianne (1991) and shown by the examples in Chapter 8, many service activities can perfectly well operate in small towns, and may be located there for some of the reasons discussed in Chapter 9.

From the point of view of the local economy, it may be more valuable to have services than manufacturing as the basic activity, since service activities usually have higher local multiplier effects (Beyers, Alvine & Johnsen 1985; Porterfield & Pulver 1991; Keeble et al 1991). The reason is that service firms spend a higher share of their total expenditure on (local) wages and salaries, while agriculture and manufacturing firms use more of their expenditure to buy goods inputs elsewhere.

Service firms often choose to penetrate new geographical markets by setting up branch offices, rather than selling directly from headquarters, in order to retain the advantages of proximity (this is discussed in more detail in connection with international trade, see Chapter 12). For the market area in question, it may be a problem to house branch offices rather than independent firms, not so much because of exploitation—profits being ploughed back—but because branch offices are less likely than independent firms to develop into basic activities. On the other hand, branch offices may bring investments and skills into the area which it would not have had otherwise. And some multi-site corporations are quite ready to let branch offices specialize and 'export' services within their fields of expertise (Gallouj 1993; Illeris 1994a).

SOME NON-BASIC SERVICES BECOME INDIRECTLY BASIC

Some of the service activities that sell only to local customers and thus, by definition, are non-basic can nevertheless be said indirectly to play a basic role in the local economy and its development. There are three types of indirectly basic service activities.

First, there are producer service activities which provide strategic services to basic activities (whether these are agricultural, manufacturing, or other services). The customers would be less competitive if they did not have access to these service inputs in their proximity. These producer services are important in mediating innovations to their customers and in increasing their productivity. If the customers sell goods elsewhere, these may be said to contain 'embodied' services.

Undoubtedly, local indirectly basic producer services, for instance technological, marketing and management advice, are particularly important for relatively unsophisticated manufacturing firms. If such service activities are lacking in an area, the small manufacturing firms—which cannot produce these services internally—simply do not use them, and their competitive capacity suffers. This has for instance been observed in the Italian Mezzogiorno (Martinelli 1991c). More sophisticated and/or larger firms are better able to produce such services internally, or buy them from distant suppliers. However, relatively unsophisticated firms are numerous and play an important role in the total economy. Hence the local supply of producer services is important, too (Maskell 1987; Gallouj 1993; Illeris 1994a).

It is difficult to assess and understand the importance of these strategic, indirectly basic producer services in any precise way. Many authors have argued that in some cases they are so important that it turns the economic base model upside down. It should no longer be the location of service producers that was tied to proximity to the service users, but service users that were tied to proximity to service producers (as was discussed for service firms as service users in Chapter 9, under the heading *Sources of Information*). In a classic contribution, Blumenfeld (1955) argued that this was the *raison d'être* of large metropolises, and this has often been repeated in the literature on services (Illeris 1989e; Bailly 1994). On the other hand, Martinelli (1989a) found evidence in the 'Third Italy' that few firms considered local service supply important for their competitiveness.

Gallouj (1995) distinguishes between producer services which facilitate the functioning of customer firms, and services which are able to attract customer firms.

Philippe and Léo (1993) have a different approach to the role of non-basic producer service activities; they emphasize that growth in basic activities is amplified if their demand for inputs from producer services can be satisfied by local service producers.

A second category of indirectly basic producer services does not influence the performance of the service users, but simply constitutes a necessary condition for them, much like physical infrastructure. This is for instance the case with telecommunications (Daniels 1989) and, as has been experienced in East-Central Europe, of banks.

A third category of service activities may be considered even more indirectly basic: services which are crucial for the local supply of qualified personnel, which according to Chapter 9 again may be decisive for the location of basic service activities (as well as for other basic activities). This category comprises educational establishments—given that many young people are easier to recruit where they have been educated. It also comprises the many types of household services that contribute to the attractiveness of localities and influence the residential preferences of qualified people: cultural, leisure and other 'quality of life' services (Kirn 1987). Many of the services in this category are public, at least in Western Europe (Sjøholt 1993) and may be influenced by local development policies.

A MODIFIED ECONOMIC BASE MODEL

Altogether, the economic base model, as shown in Figure 9.1, must be modified to show a more complicated fabric of money flows and reciprocal locational influences, as suggested in Figure 10.1.

The traditional notions remain, namely that basic activities offer employment and pay wages to household members, that households generate a demand for consumer services, and that the latter activities offer employment and pay wages to household members.

The first modification is that some service activities are included in the basic sector.

The second modification is the introduction of a sector of indirectly basic services. Some basic activities depend on the local availability of these indirectly basic services and constitute a market for them. (Of course consumer service activities also constitute a market for these services, but that is less important.) Some households depend on the local availability of other indirectly basic services and constitute a market for them, and some basic activities again depend on the local availability of the (qualified) members of these households.

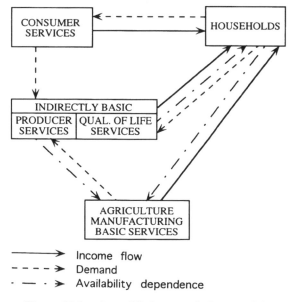

Figure 10.1. A modified economic base model

REGIONAL SERVICE POLICIES

From Chapter 8 it is clear that service activities are geographically more concentrated than economic activities as a whole. Neither the present situation, nor a possibly even denser future concentration is acceptable to West European national governments or the EU, and of course even less for regional and local governments in areas with few service activities.

Nevertheless, until recently service activities were not considered as objects of regional development policies. This was a logical consequence of the economic base model; service activities were supposed to play a passive role in (regional) economic development, not to be able to expand beyond the purchasing power of the local market, and automatically to follow the development of basic activities.

As argued above, this model must now be modified. It must be recognized that some service activities have a directly or indirectly basic character and are relevant objects of regional development policies. But of course, there are still service activities which do not contribute to regional economic development. Understandably, local politicians are also interested in policies which aim at diverting retail trade from neighbouring towns. But this will remain a zero-sum game, the total regional volume of retail trade can hardly be increased if incomes are not increased in other ways. Still, from a welfare point of view there is a case for keeping a minimum level of services in sparsely populated local areas. For instance, village shops have been the object of a conservation policy in some countries.

Thus, there is a case for a service component in regional development policies, with the aims to promote employment and incomes, to promote processes that contribute to the performance, innovation and competitiveness of the local economy, and of course also to improve living conditions and to satisfy the needs of the local population.

A number of authors have in recent years argued in favour of a service component in regional development policies: Ruyssen (1987b), Marshall and Bachtler (1987), Aasbrenn (1987), Illeris (1989b, 1994b), Martinelli (1989b), Coffey and Polèse (1989), OECD (1989), Coffey and McRae (1990), Gallouj (1993). Consequently, both the EU and national governments have, to varying degrees, included service activities as objects of their regional policies, and regional and local governments have increasingly targeted service activities in their economic development efforts. The following discussion of policy instruments is based both on suggestions and on experience with measures that have already been introduced.

I shall not discuss here the question of who should carry out a regional service policy (see Illeris 1994b). As in regional policies in general, I think there is an argument for leaving much to regional and local governments who know the local problems and opportunities best. But national and EU authorities must set the rules of the game, designate regions where the policy measures are to be applied, and redistribute financial resources to them.

Three types of instruments may be considered: (a) measures to influence the supply of services; (b) measures to influence the demand for services; and (c) measures to improve the interaction between service production and service use.

HOW TO INCREASE THE LOCAL SUPPLY OF SERVICES

The remedy closest at hand to influence the supply of service activities would be to subsidize investment, as has been done in regional policies directed towards manufacturing. In the case of manufacturing, the argument against subsidies for running costs is to avoid supporting enterprises which in the long run are economically unsound. (This consideration may be an argument against all kinds of subsidies, since cost reductions tend to lure firms into a strategy of price competition which has little future in Western countries at all, see Illeris 1994b.) In this respect, 'basic' services like tourism and expert services are in the same situation as manufacturing firms. The problem is that for most service activities, capital costs are only a small part of total costs, so investment subsidies alone may have little impact. Subsidies for running costs might be considered, at least in the early years of new activities, and possibly reserved for strategic costs such as the salaries of qualified staff.

As regards other services, with only local markets, it is questionable whether the argument against subsidies for running costs (or subsidies at all) is valid. The importance of these services does not depend on their efficiency, but on their effects. As regards business services, to contribute to the performance of their clients, and household services, to contribute to the satisfaction of the needs of the customers and make the area attractive—and for both, to offer employment. They are in any event sheltered against strong competition by distance, and will rarely show high productivities. It may be argued that in the light of the objectives of the policy, subsidies for running costs would not do much harm.

In the particular kind of negotiation-persuasion-cum-subsidies regional policy which is run by the Swedish government, about 4000 business service jobs were relocated out of Stockholm from 1987 to 1991, most of them to the northern development regions, see Figure 10.2 (Lundmark 1994). In a country with a total of 4 million jobs, this is no modest result.

Other policy instruments fall within the area of improving conditions for service suppliers. Transport and telecommunications infrastructure will be discussed later, in connection with interaction instruments. Office building is another type of infrastructure, which governments for instance have supported in France (La Défense in Paris). 'Soft' infrastructures, e.g. good local education and research institutions, are important for service producers, and both hard and soft infrastructure (cultural amenities for instance) contribute to attract qualified staff. They will be discussed in depth later. But there is also a question of 'social' qualifications, such as entrepreneurship and innovativeness, which show large regional differences, but which are difficult to influence in the short run. It is suggested that governments support service entrepreneurs with advice, courses and

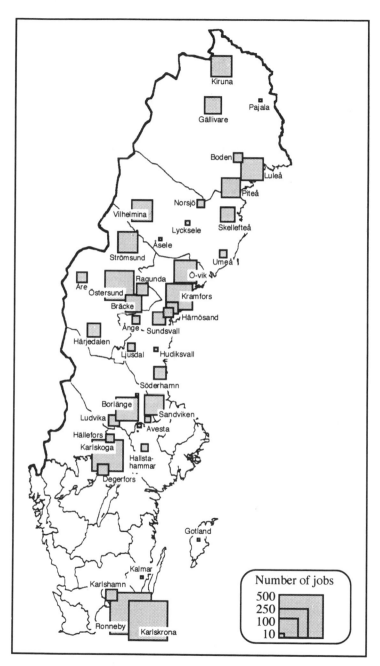

Figure 10.2. Relocation of service jobs from Stockholm, Sweden 1987–1991. *Source:* Redrawn from M. Lundmark (1994), *Databranschen i Sverige*, Stockholm, ERU, by permission of ERU.

suitable premises, whereas financial subsidies must be limited in order not to skew local competition.

The above-mentioned measures should aim at the creation or expansion of local service suppliers, as well as attracting firms from outside. From the point of view of contributing to the quality of client firms' performance, it may be advantageous to attract branch offices of major business service firms, which can draw upon the specialized expertise of headquarters, if and when required. It may even be argued that the subsidies should be offered to internal service producers within user firms.

A very important set of tools is found in the public services, which constitute conditions ('soft infrastructure') for private service suppliers. However, regional development policies may clash with government policies which pursue other objectives, and sectoral authorities, in education for instance, are not always easy to coordinate with development authorities. From a development point of view it is important that research is not too purely theoretical, which may conflict with research traditions in many countries. Training and education also should not be purely theoretical or involve learning too many facts by heart, neither should they be geared too narrowly towards today's practical skills which may be useless tomorrow.

A special policy instrument is the relocation of national government offices in provincial regions. This has been carried out in several West European countries, in particular for employment reasons. In some countries, e.g. the UK, mainly routine operations (back offices) have been relocated, while Sweden for instance has emphasized that decision-making units and research institutions with many high-skill and high-salary employees should be included in the policy. However, such operations are difficult. A devolution of powers to regional and local levels is probably much more valuable, also from a service point of view.

As regards technological services, West European governments have in many cases thought that in certain regions, private firms and organizations do not offer a sufficient supply. It has been shown that such technological agencies could meet a latent need in small and medium enterprises which have either not been aware of existing services or not been able to pay them. In several cases, the market within realistic distances has simply been too small for private service producers to operate profitably (Illeris & Rasmussen 1992). Hence, governments have established public or parastatal technological service agencies, which may be interpreted as repairing market imperfections, rather than as an attempt to compete with private service firms.

HOW TO INCREASE THE LOCAL DEMAND FOR SERVICES

Most authors agree that a regional service policy should support not only the supply of services, but also the demand, at least from firms. The reason is that regional development progresses through the interaction between business service producers and service-using firms. Since barriers may be found on both sides, it is necessary to overcome them on both sides, too. In other words, if only the supply of services is supported, such services may not find users.

The demand for services in a region may be encouraged by subsidies for the purchase of services, especially to small and medium firms. This has been done in France for some years, with considerable success. Of course, some of the purchases are made outside the region, thus losing some of the regional development purpose—and a good deal of the intensive interaction aimed at. However, provincial service users buy only a minor part of their services in Paris (Gallouj 1993). But this policy discriminates against the use of internal services. Another counter-argument is that subsidized demand incites suppliers to raise their prices, and thus to reduce or neutralize the intended effect.

In fact, barriers against the use of more services are not just cost-barriers, but often mental barriers. In small firms, the owner or manager often does not know that he can improve his enterprise through services. As mentioned in Chapter 6, the bigger the internal service production (which means qualified staff in the firm), the more likely the purchase of external services. Hence, training and information to user firm staff are important tools, as well as support to firms to hire qualified staff-members for limited periods.

The service purchases of local governments can make it possible for local service firms to increase their skills and experience. Indeed, it seems that provincial service activities perform best in countries with a considerable devolution of government. Undoubtedly, there are synergies inherent in their interaction with local service suppliers. On the other hand, these synergies may be reduced if local governments give local suppliers a real procurement monopoly—a state of affairs that the Single European Market rules will help to break up.

HOW TO IMPROVE THE SERVICE SUPPLIER–USER INTERACTION

Some of the barriers against increased use of business services are to be found in the linkage between supply and demand: constraints of insufficient transport and telecommunications infrastructure, and barriers of a social, institutional or informational kind.

Transport and telecommunication systems are necessary for the interaction between economic agents on which all division of labour depends. In particular, fast and cheap infrastructure for personal travel (airlines, high-speed trains, motorways, etc.) as well as high-capacity telecommunication systems are required for the exchange of services, as discussed in Chapter 9.

While the most developed regions are normally well equipped with physical infrastructure, this is not always the case in less developed regions, where the density of interaction and hence the microeconomic profitability of infrastructure investments is lower. This is a serious problem in Eastern Europe, but even in Western Europe and North America, there are regions with a poor infrastructure. In such cases, both service producers and service users will have an interest in improved infrastructure, and in tariff systems that do not discriminate against peripheral regions. As previously public or concessionary transport and telecommunication systems are privatized or deregulated, there is a danger that only microeconomic profitability criteria, ignoring social costs, will prevail. In such cases, subsidies earmarked for transport in less developed regions may be a part of regional policies, as is practised by Swedish railways.

However, improved transport and telecommunication systems only relax a former constraint of proximity between service providers and service users. Other factors then decide which locations are the most favourable ones. Regional policies should therefore never use the establishment or improvement of transport and telecommunication systems as an isolated policy instrument, but always supplement them with other actions that improve the performance conditions in less developed regions—such as those already suggested in this chapter.

The lack of physical infrastructure, however, is not the only barrier between service providers and service users in less developed regions. Here, due to the low density of economic agents, service markets are often particularly opaque. A regional service policy should therefore include initiatives to improve the functioning of the market. Governments could provide information, create data banks about service supply, take initiatives to combine the demand from several firms for specialized services, create local places of exchange of the knowledge and experience which exist in local firms—or encourage others to do so. Probably the most efficient instrument is to create local mediators, 'development officers' or service brokers, as are now found in many countries. Their job, in areas where they know the small and medium-sized enterprises and their problems well, is to advise on the solution of problems, in particular to create contacts between the local firms and service suppliers. Technological service agencies may have the same function, when they meet problems on which they themselves are not able to advise.

It is of vital importance that such mediators operate in an unbureaucratic way and obtain the confidence of small and medium-sized firms. This means that they, physically and mentally, must be very close to the firms they are to serve, and speak the same language. They should have business or technical training and practical experience.

Science parks or technopoles may also be seen as instruments to obtain increased synergies through improved interaction between service producers and service users at high levels of specialization. The idea is to copy the processes which have been observed in the 'Silicon Valley' around Stanford University in the San Francisco area: a close interaction between university research and high-tech firms, in an attractive area, including a spin-off of research results into commercial application.

The results from the many science parks that have been established in recent decades are mixed, however (Massey, Quintas & Wield 1992). High-tech spearheads have caught the attention of the media and the politicians to a degree which is out of proportion to their importance in the total economy. In most cases, the more humble mediators mentioned above would give better value for money. Furthermore, as discussed in Chapter 9, highly specialized and valuable knowledge services are not heavily dependent on proximity. Both producers and users of such services will typically have international contacts and networks with other high-level specialists. It is rather for less specialized small firms that local mediation is important. This does not exclude the possibility that science parks may be important locations for high-tech firms for other reasons, such as prestige and recruitment of young university graduates.

As regards the service component of regional policies, it is of course not realistic to aim at anything like a totally even geographical distribution of service activities per 1000 inhabitants. The present pattern of location will show a good deal of inertia, and not all future factors of location can be influenced by regional policies. A hierarchy of service centres, in which the supply of services will be much better, quantitatively and qualitatively, in metropolitan areas than in small towns, will continue to exist.

CONCLUSION

The traditional notion was that service activities played a totally passive role in regional economic development. Due to their inability to sell over longer distances, their growth in a given area depended on the amount of such basic activities as agriculture and manufacturing. However, it is increasingly emphasized that as service activities grow, they contribute to the development of their area by providing employment, incomes, and satisfaction of human needs.

It is also recognized that while the economic base model largely remains valid for most household services and many producer services, it needs important modifications. Some producer services have become basic; they sell important parts of their services outside their own region. This is primarily the case of back office services, transmitted via telecommunications, and sophisticated service activities for which travelling costs are insignificant relative to the price. Furthermore, a part of those activities which serve only local customers are indirectly basic services. Their customers are basic activities which depend on local service supply for their competitiveness, innovation, and productivity. To this category also belong service activities which sell education and quality of life services and thereby supply or attract the qualified labour on which the basic activities of the area depend.

Service activities are becoming a target of regional development policies, due to the recognition that many of them, especially producer services, today have a directly or indirectly basic character. A number of measures may increase the regional supply of services, but it is equally important to support the demand for producer services, as well as the functioning of the often rather opaque regional service markets.

11   Services Within Cities

This chapter is concerned with the geographical distribution of service activities within urban areas. Where are various kinds of service activities located? How does their distribution change over time? And what are the reasons for the changing location patterns?

By an 'urban area', we mean the total built-up area and the surrounding commuting zone, not only the administrative central city or municipality. One may distinguish between a core or Central Business District (CBD), an older 'inner city', and outer suburbs or periphery. But the geographical bases of data from different urban areas vary, according to the administrative arrangements.

The discussions here focus primarily on the distribution of producer services. First, the main trends of theoretical thought are outlined. Second, statistical data on the intra-urban location of service activities are presented, as well as survey evidence on factors of location. Third, an attempt is made to reach conclusions consistent with empirical evidence.

THEORIES ABOUT THE INTRA-URBAN DISTRIBUTION OF SERVICE ACTIVITIES

Many authors have theoretically discussed the intra-urban location of service activities.

Private household services are generally said to depend on proximity to their customers, even if there may be modifications in the details—customers may be attracted to other service suppliers than the nearest ones, if they are in some respect better or more easily accessible. Public services, too, are generally located in the local areas they exist to serve. On the whole, household services are distributed in the same way as the population.

Producer services—which form a large part of the office activities—were historically located in the city cores for two reasons. First, in the days when public transport had a quasi-monopoly of intra-urban transport, the central business district had the highest accessibility, firms located there could best make use of the large labour market and other externalities of big cities. Second, by locating there, firms could minimize the transaction costs of the many face-to-face meetings required to obtain information, to sell and deliver producer services, and other contacts (Goddard & Morris 1976).

From the 1960s, two theoretical directions may be distinguished. Most authors have stressed the ever-increasing importance of specialized information exchange between corporate headquarters, financial activities and business services, on which control and decisions were based, and which required face-to-face meetings (see discussion in Chapter 9). Hence, a reinforcement of the core location of producer service activities would take place (Gottmann 1961; Coffey & Bailly 1992). The emergence of a CBD in the formerly almost totally suburban Los Angeles is seen as a confirmation of this theory (Moss 1987). A recent version excepts 'back offices' with routinized functions and no need for face-to-face contacts, which are forced to locate elsewhere by the high rents of the CBD (Castells 1989; Warf 1991; Daniels 1993a).

Another school has stressed the possibilities which the car and the new telecommunications have opened for producer services to locate anywhere and still be in close contact with business connections and clients, even to meet them face to face, while at the same time reducing the commuting distances of their largely suburban personnel. Hence, the CBD would be weakened, at least relatively, but because of its low accessibility for cars often even in absolute terms. This theory was, characteristically enough, first launched in California (Webber 1964) and later argued by Kutay (1986) and Marshall and Jaeger (1990) for example. May (1994a) suggests a multipolar structure of urban areas, with a limited number of office concentrations and science parks, rather than a general dispersal.

THE DISTRIBUTION OF SERVICE EMPLOYMENT

How are service activities, as measured by employment, distributed within urban areas? And what are the current locational trends?

Private and public household services may be illustrated by Table 11.1, showing the Nordic capitals. This shows that there is more household employment in the central cities than in the suburbs, relative to the population living in the area. This is due to the fact that some centrally located service activities (e.g. entertainment) serve the whole urban area. In the Nordic capitals, household services have shifted radically towards the suburbs, following the distribution of population with some time-lag.

Producer services may be illustrated by the cases of the Scandinavian capital regions (larger than the regions of Table 11.1), see Table 11.2.

Ellger (1988) presents the data shown in Table 11.3 on the employment in information services in the Kreis of Stuttgart and the four neighbouring Kreise.

Both in the Scandinavian capital regions and in the Stuttgart region, business service employment is over-represented in the core, but a decentralization tendency has prevailed in the period.

Schamp (1995), comparing location quotients for business services during 1980 and 1991 in West Germany, notes that shifts from large cities to their fringes have been the general case.

OhUallacháin and Reid (1991) calculated location quotients for business and professional services in large American urban areas (SMSAs) in 1976 and 1986. In

Table 11.1. Employment in household services, Nordic capitals 1980–1992. Source: Labour force statistics.

		Place of work					
		Central city		Suburbs		Total	
		(× 1000)	(per 1000 inh.)	(× 1000)	(per 1000 inh.)	(× 1000)	(per 1000 inh.)
Copenhagen	1982	143.0	247	140.3	159	283.3	204
	1992	129.3	234	142.2	177	271.5	200
	growth %	−9.6		1.4		−4.2	
Helsinki	1980	95.7	198	34.9	95	130.6	154
	1991	105.8	212	59.7	131	165.5	174
	growth %	10.6		71.0		26.7	
Oslo	1980	80.9	179	25.4	114	106.3	158
	1992	99.6	210	39.6	153	139.2	190
	growth %	23.1		56.1		31.0	
Stockholm	1980	178.4	276	100.7	153	279.1	214
	1991	165.3	243	129.0	171	294.3	205
	growth %	−7.3		28.1		5.4	

Table 11.2. Employment in business services, Scandinavian capital regions 1980–1990. *Source:* Illeris and Sjøholt (1995).

		Central municip. (× 1000)	Place of work Suburban ring (× 1000)	Fringe (× 1000)	Total (× 1000)
Copenhagen	1982	29.7	16.8	8.8	54.3
	1990	34.3	25.9	14.4	74.5
	growth %	20	54	63	37
Oslo	1980	22.5	3.2	1.2	26.9
	1990	27.6	7.5	4.1	39.2
	growth %	23	136	224	46
Stockholm	1980	37.8	8.5	2.8	49.1
	1990	53.5	16.8	7.1	77.4
	growth %	42	98	154	58

almost all cases, central counties had higher location quotients in 1986 than suburban counties. And in almost all cases, growth quotients were largest in suburban counties, indicating an intra-urban decentralization.

Van Dinteren and Meuwissen (1994) have studied the distribution of business services in the core area of the European Union, see Figures 11.1 and 11.2. Figure 11.1 shows that the share of business services in total employment is highest in London, Paris, Frankfurt, Brussels, and the Randstad Holland (plus Luxembourg).

Figure 11.2 reveals that growth rates have been highest in the administrative units surrounding the above-mentioned large cities. Paris and Frankfurt which are themselves part of very large administrative units constitute exceptions, but in these cases the authors quote evidence of an outward shift, too.

A more detailed study of producer services in the four big Belgian cities of Antwerp, Liège, Ghent, and Charleroi was carried out by Moyart (1995). On average, in 1982 84 per cent of the producer service employment of the arrondissements in question was in the central municipality. But in 1992, this share had declined to 76 per cent. In other words, growth rates had been higher in the periphery.

Table 11.3. Employment in information occupations, Stuttgart 1979–1986. *Source:* based on Ellger (1988).

		Social security insured persons		
Kreis	1979 (× 1000)	1986 (× 1000)	1986 % of total employm.	1979–86 Growth %
Stuttgart	161.0	168.4	46.9	5
Böblingen	33.7	41.5	29.5	23
Esslingen	46.7	52.9	30.9	13
Ludwigsburg	40.8	46.5	32.9	14
Rems-Murr	30.7	36.2	30.1	18

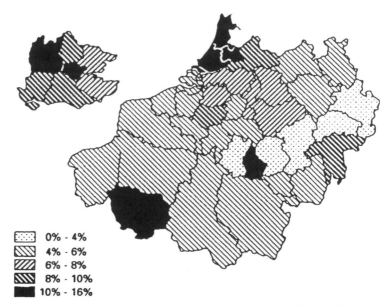

Figure 11.1. Share of business services in total employment, Central Western Europe 1990. *Source:* Reproduced with permission from J.H.J. Van Dinteren and J.A.M. Meuwissen (1994), Business Services in the Core Area of the European Union. *Tijdschrift voor Economische en Sociale Geografie*, **85**, 4, 366–370.

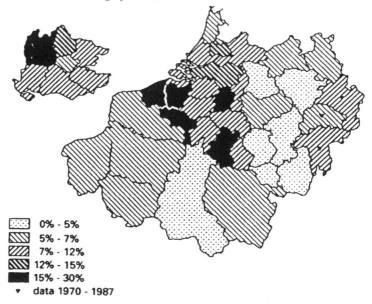

Figure 11.2. Growth of business services, Central Western Europe 1980–1990. Average annual employment growth in %. *Source:* Reproduced with permission from J.H.J. Van Dinteren and J.A.M. Meuwissen (1994), Business Services in the Core Area of the European Union. *Tijdschrift voor Economische en Sociale Geografie*, **85**, 4, 366–370.

As regards the internal service activities in corporate headquarters, suburbanization trends are observed both in the UK (Marshall 1994) and the US (Noyelle 1994).

The conclusions from the statistical evidence are quite clear; service activities, in particular producer services, are over-represented in the cores of urban areas. Currently, however, a decentralization or suburbanization tendency is taking place in the case of both household services and producer services. But the evidence is too fragmentary to say whether this is the case everywhere.

At any rate, the statistical evidence is crude and does not show that producer services outside the core are often more or less concentrated in a number of, often planned, office complexes. These may be quite close to the core, as is La Défense in Paris or Canary Wharf in London, and may be included in the central city data. Or they may be located in the periphery, as Høje Tåstrup in the Copenhagen area or the American 'edge cities'. However, not all offices are located in such concentrations. In 13 medium-sized Dutch towns, Van Dinteren (1989) found that 37 per cent of office employment was in the cores, 28 per cent in other pre-war areas, 31 per cent in post-war residential areas, and 5 per cent in areas zoned for economic activities.

It should also be mentioned that the types of producer services may differ between urban cores and peripheries. Thus in all the four large urban areas of the Randstad Holland, Hessels (1992) found that suburban business services had relatively more regional and national markets, central city business services relatively more local markets. In Edmonton, Michalak and Fairbairn (1988) found a similar pattern. In the Scandinavian capitals, technical services tend to be more suburbanized than other producer services (Illeris & Sjøholt 1995). Hessels also observes that multisite service firms tend to have suburban headquarters. Tordoir (1991) found that in the Randstad Holland, intra-urban face-to-face contacts do not decline with distance (in contrast to Goddard and Morris 1976). It may safely be concluded that back offices are not the only suburban producer service activities, and that in many cases they form only a small part of them.

INVESTIGATIONS INTO THE FACTORS OF LOCATION

For most private and public *household services*, it is obvious that proximity to the users is the most important factor of location, though they only follow the redistribution of population after a certain time-lag. Studies exist only for individual sectors, such as retailing.

The factors underlying the intra-urban location of *large public institutions* (hospitals, universities, barracks, government administration, etc.) have barely been studied. They often cause problems in physical planning, requiring both large areas and high accessibility. Once established, they are hard to shift, as witnessed by the central, historical location of government buildings, old universities and similar foundations.

As regards the question why *producer services* are located where they are, several older investigations (focusing on 'offices') as well as more recent studies exist. They are based on questionnaire or interview surveys, and as discussed in Chapter 10, this method has several weaknesses, for instance some studies have not distinguished between inter- and intra-urban locational factors.

Fich (1990) has conducted a number of interview studies in Copenhagen and Danish provincial towns. In the Copenhagen area, only a few services, some legal and financial services, really depended on core locations, because of frequent contacts with business connections. Others were centrally located because of prestige and the attraction of the urban environment in general. In provincial towns, the most important factor was (car) accessibility, which is better in suburban than in core locations.

RESER (1995) has interviewed business service firms in the largest and second largest urban areas of Denmark, France, and Italy. Easy accessibility (including parking facilities), especially for the staff, was the factor mentioned most frequently. Other factors were attractiveness and prestige (pulling in different directions, towards historical cores in some cities, and towards high-amenity suburbs in others), sufficient space, (time) distance to international airports, and rent levels. Some respondents (in Paris) mentioned proximity to clients, while others explicitly stated that all metropolitan clients could be served equally well from all locations in the urban area.

Van Dinteren (1989) conducted a postal enquiry among office firms in 13 medium-sized Dutch urban areas in which 459 firms answered an open question about factors of location. The most frequent answer was accessibility, followed by parking facilities and prestige. A special study of firms which had moved between 1974 and 1984 (mainly from inner cities to suburban areas) showed that the most important reason for leaving the old premises was insufficient room for expansion, followed by the low quality of the buildings and the low prestige. New premises were chosen on the basis of prestige, quality of buildings, car accessibility, and possibilities for expansion.

Dowall (1987) focuses on back offices which have few personal contacts with clients. His investigation in San Francisco showed a substantial suburbanization tendency, driven by a search for low rents and for labour which was cheap relative to its skills. A study by Nelson (1986) in the same urban area showed that back offices preferred female staff with some education and high stability. Such women were found in suburbs and often wanted part-time work close to home.

Bailly and Boulianne (1993) have interviewed producer service firms in two medium-sized French urban areas, Dijon and Grenoble. The respondents stressed proximity to clients as well as car accessibility for clients (though usually the service producers visit the clients) and for staff. The authors mention that public planning has influenced the location by providing well-equipped office centres, especially in Grenoble.

Hessels (1992) has made a survey of 737 business service establishments in the urban areas of Amsterdam, The Hague, Rotterdam, and Utrecht. Table 11.4 shows how many respondents considered various factors of location to be important. The most important factor, especially for suburban respondents, was car accessibility

Table 11.4. The importance of location factors among business services employing more than 4 people, in four large Dutch urban areas. *Source:* M. Hessels (1992), *Locational Dynamics of Business Services: An Intrametropolitan Study on the Randstad Holland.* Utrecht: Geografisch Instituut Rijksuniversiteit Utrecht. Reproduced by permission of the Faculty of Geographical Sciences Utrecht/Royal Dutch Geographical Society.

	Total			Urban		Suburban	
	%	Abs.	V	%	Abs.	%	Abs.
Accessibility-related:							
Accessibility by automobile	90.6	653	0.11*	87.6	346	94.2	307
Parking facilities	88.6	640	0.05	87.1	345	90.5	295
Accessibility to/for clients	86.1	621	0.03	85.1	337	87.4	284
Accessibility for employees	83.0	594	0.08*	80.3	318	86.3	276
Accessibility by public transport	64.7	466	0.04	66.3	264	62.7	202
Accessibility for suppliers	43.1	307	0.04	41.1	162	45.6	145
Proximity to railway station	35.6	253	0.02	36.5	143	34.5	110
Proximity to international airport	18.2	129	0.05	16.5	64	20.3	65
Proximity-related:							
Proximity to employees	19.4	138	0.12*	14.9	58	24.8	80
Proximity to city centre	16.1	114	0.25*	24.3	95	6.0	19
Proximity to clients	14.7	105	0.08*	17.3	68	11.5	37
Proximity other offices/activities	8.6	61	0.07	10.3	40	6.6	21
Proximity to suppliers	6.0	42	0.04	5.2	20	6.9	22
Accommodation-related:							
Prestigious accommodation	80.1	578	0.03	79.1	314	81.2	264
Telecommunication facilities	75.7	526	0.04	74.4	287	77.4	240
Low price	52.6	361	0.00	52.5	200	52.8	161
Expansion possibilities	50.8	363	0.01	50.5	199	51.1	164
Single use of accommodation	35.8	248	0.00	35.7	137	35.9	111
Renting the accommodation	31.5	205	0.06	28.8	104	34.8	101
Owning the accommodation	18.3	129	0.04	17.0	66	19.9	63
Visibility accommodation	8.3	59	0.08*	6.4	25	10.7	34
Environment-related:							
Prestigious environment	72.7	514	0.04	74.2	288	70.8	226
Personal safety	65.5	466	0.05	67.5	264	63.1	202
Proximity to shops	12.6	90	0.04	13.8	54	11.2	36
Proximity to cafés/restaurants	12.2	87	0.02	12.8	50	11.5	37

* Significant at $p \leq 0.05$.

and parking facilities for clients and employees, followed by prestigious premises, buildings with telecommunications, and a prestigious environment. Proximity to clients, suppliers and other activities was only considered important by a few respondents. Some 57 per cent of the establishments had moved, in most cases to suburban locations, and these were asked about push-and-pull factors. The reason for moving was in most cases lack of room (especially for the central city-leavers), with lack of accessibility as a secondary reason. New premises were chosen on the basis of good accessibility or good premises.

To summarize: three factors of intra-urban location of producer services turn up in most of the few empirical investigations available:

1   The need for car accessibility and parking facilities for both staff and clients. This is clearly a factor pulling towards suburban locations.
2   Prestige and attractiveness. This factor may pull towards both historical cores and high-amenity suburbs.
3   Sufficient room for expansion. This factor—which is given high priority by space-demanding activities—is primarily cited by firms that have moved. In other words, as long as there is room enough, producer service firms are not aware of it, but once it becomes a problem, it forms a strong push factor away from cores and inner cities.

Fourthly, for back offices, costs (rents and wages) pull towards suburbs. Though only investigated by two of the above-mentioned studies, there is ample evidence elsewhere.

In the empirical studies, intra-urban proximity to service users and information providers was only rarely mentioned as an important factor of location for producer service firms.

Thus, the majority of factors pull towards suburbanization. This fits well with the recent locational tendencies of producer service activities we have observed.

CONCLUSIONS

The intra-urban location of service activities has to be discussed separately for household and producer services.

Private and public household services tend generally—though no longer in detail—to locate in such a way that distance to the customers is minimized. They have followed the post-war suburbanization of the population, though with a time-lag.

Producer services were historically concentrated in the city cores, partly because of their high accessibility in the monopoly days of public transport, and partly because of the need for frequent face-to-face contact with their main clients and sources of information. Much of the theoretical literature maintains that due to the importance of interaction, and hence the need for proximity, between business services, financial activities, and corporate headquarters, this pattern of location is reinforced, except for back offices.

This notion is curiously out of touch with recent empirical research which finds that though there is still a concentration of business services in the urban cores, the prevailing tendency (not only for back offices) is now towards suburbanization. (There are exceptions, such as the growth of the Los Angeles CBD.) This trend corresponds well with surveys of locational factors which have found that business service firms primarily stress (car) accessibility, sufficient space (for expansion), and prestige/amenity. The two former factors pull towards suburbanization, the latter may in different cases pull either way. On the other hand, proximity to clients and business connections is rarely mentioned in empirical studies. But it must be emphasized that more studies are needed.

A theory that is to explain these observations must stress the importance of car transport and modern telecommunications, which have made it possible for producer services to locate in many places, provided that there are good roads, ample parking, and telecommunication infrastructures. The actual locations are then influenced by many factors, such as the prestige and amenities of various areas, their accessibility for the personnel of each firm, and the availability of offices with reasonable quality/price ratios.

Part IV

SERVICES IN THE ECONOMICALLY DEVELOPED WORLD

12 International Variation

The question to be examined in this chapter is whether the development of service activities is uniform in all economically developed countries. Can different paths be traced in different countries? To answer this question, a short comparative study of five selected Western countries will be carried out: the United States, Japan and West Germany are leading industrial producers with different societal structures, Sweden will represent the Scandinavian welfare state, and France is typical of continental West European countries. After that, the radically different development of services in the East-Central European countries will be discussed.

International comparisons and efforts to put together comparable data have been carried out by, *inter alia*, Fontaine (1987), Godbout (1993), Elfring (1988), Britton (1991), ECONAnalyse (1995), and Illeris (1991d), on whom this chapter relies.

THE GROWTH OF SERVICE ACTIVITIES IN FIVE WESTERN COUNTRIES

The evidence in Chapter 1 shows that the percentage of service activities as a share of total economic activity is growing everywhere in the Western world, whether measured in terms of service sector employment, service occupation employment, or service sector GDP at current prices (as regards GDP in constant prices, the increase in share is much more modest).

However, no less conspicuous are the differences in levels in service activity, as illustrated by Tables 1.1, 1.3, 1.4, and Figure 1.1. Among the five countries, the United States tops the list with over 70 per cent of employment (both in sectoral and occupational terms) and about 70 per cent of GDP in service activities. Sweden is a little lower, and France a little lower again, but still between 65 and 70 per cent. Japan and West Germany, on the other hand, still have less than 60 per cent of their employment and their GDP in the service sector. What is the background for these differences?

FRANCE

As already mentioned, France was selected as a fairly typical representative of continental Western Europe, a kind of standard reference country. In the figures and tables referred to, it generally has a middle-of-the-road position among the countries studied. One may notice, however, the rather steep increase in both service employment and service production. France is a major exporter of services, as shown in Chapter 13.

WEST GERMANY—THE COMPENSATION OF A SMALL SERVICE SECTOR

As already mentioned in Chapter 1, West Germany's service sector employment and production is clearly less than in most Western countries. On the other hand, there is no reason to believe that the supply of services should be inferior to that of other countries. How can this paradox be explained?

At least two sources of service provision seem to fill the gap. First, international trade in services, which is shown in Table 13.2. The table shows that while most economically developed countries are net exporters of services, West Germany and Japan are net importers. In other words, West Germany imports a good deal of its service provision (and pays through the export of goods). And it not only buys transport (e.g. from the Netherlands) and holidays (e.g. from Southern Europe), but also a considerable amount of business services.

The other West German source of service provision consists of producer services supplied internally in the user firms. Of course internal service production exists in all countries, as discussed in Chapter 2. But it seems to be relatively more important in West Germany than elsewhere. For instance, it is a normal part of German company culture to develop one's own software instead of buying it from the outside (Elfring 1988; Plougmann 1988; Tordoir 1993; Gruhler 1990; Schamp 1995). As shown by Table 6.3, among five EU countries West Germany had the lowest share of business services bought externally, and by far the highest share produced internally (Commission of the European Communities 1990).

This can also be illustrated by comparing service sector employment and service occupations employment, see Tables 1.1 and 1.3. In most countries, service occupations account for roughly the same share of total employment as does the service sector. West Germany, however, forms an exception. Here the share of service occupations is about 6 percentage points higher than the share of the service sector, indicating the large number of employees in other sectors occupied with service activities.

A third way of compensating for the small service sector is by internal production in households. This possibility will be discussed in connection with Japan.

JAPAN—A DUAL ECONOMY

Japan also has fairly low shares of service employment and service production. In order to analyse the reasons, we have to show the composition of the service employment. This has been done in Figure 12.1, in which the Singelmann classification of service activities (see Chapter 3) has been applied.

According to Figure 12.1, the very weak part of the Japanese service sector is social services (whether in private, non-profit or public ownership). Part of the

Personal services: Hotel, restaurant, entertainment, domestic services, repair

Social services: Government, health, education, welfare.

Producer services: Finance, insurance, business services.

Distribution: Wholesaling, retailing, transport, communications.

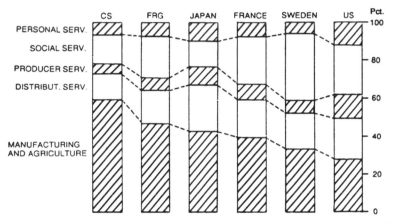

Figure 12.1. Service employment by Singelmann classes, six countries 1984. *Sources:* Elfring (1988) and Michalova and Fronkova (1989). Czechoslovak data for 1985.

explanation is that welfare services are provided internally by firms for their personnel (Elfring 1988). The main explanation, however, is probably to be found in the participation rates, which are shown in Table 12.1.

Table 12.1 shows that a relatively low proportion of Japanese women are gainfully employed, compared to the proportion of men. A good part of the social services (childcare, etc.), which in other countries are performed in the formal economy, takes place inside households. (In West Germany, where social service employment is also relatively weak, the same applies to some degree.)

Table 12.1. Participation rates, six countries 1993. *Source:* ILO Yearbook of Labour Statistics (1994).

	Economically active population over 14, as % of total population		
	Men	Women	Difference
Czech Republic (1991)	72.9	60.8	12.1
Finland	67.7	55.4	12.3
France	63.1	47.5	15.6
W. Germany (1992)	71.6	46.1	25.5
Japan	78.0	50.3	27.7
USA	71.5	55.7	15.8

Another part of the explanation of low service sector production in Japan, as revealed by Table 13.2, is the same as in West Germany: Japan is a net importer of services. In particular, Japan is a net importer of business services, patents and technological information (Saxonhouse 1985). In spite of all its efforts, Japan lags behind the United States as regards R&D.

On the other hand, Figure 12.1 shows that among the selected countries, Japan has the highest employment share in distribution and the second highest in personal services. This fact is connected with the low level of labour productivity. As discussed in Chapter 5, there are many problems involved in the measurement of productivity in service activities, and data should be interpreted with great caution. Still, the level of productivity is undoubtedly low in most of the Japanese service sector (Saxonhouse 1985). There is a marked bi-polarization between the large, internationally very competitive manufacturing corporations, and the many very small establishments— partly sheltered by legislation—with low remuneration and low productivity gains which characterize the service sector (Galibert & Le Dem 1986).

It should be stressed, however, that since the mid-1980s, this dual character of the Japanese economy has diminished. Female participation rates are increasing, and so is the production of services, the productivity in retailing and other areas.

SWEDEN—THE SCANDINAVIAN WELFARE STATE

Sweden, as a representative of the Nordic countries, scores above average in total service employment and production. The component which is responsible emerges clearly from Figure 12.1—the extremely well developed social services, which in Scandinavia are still mainly public. This is connected with the high female participation rate (for lack of Swedish data, Finland represents the Nordic countries in Table 12.1). Social services have to an extremely high degree been shifted from households and informal social networks to the formal economy. However, after two decades of rapid growth, the increase in public services has gradually slowed in the 1980s and 1990s. As everywhere in the Western world, people are not willing to accept further tax increases.

On the other hand, employment in personal services is low in Sweden. As shown by Scharpf (1985), there is a clear negative correlation between taxation and private service employment, and a clear positive correlation between wage differentials and private service employment. The situation of Sweden is the opposite to that of Japan and, as it will be shown, of the US: wages are relatively equal and taxes high in Sweden. This means that few people can afford to spend much on expensive personal services, and the high wage level of low-skilled labour forces retailing and personal service activities to rationalize and save personnel.

UNITED STATES—EXPANSION OF BOTH HIGH-GRADE AND LOW-GRADE SERVICES

As already mentioned, the United States stands out as the country in which the service sector forms the largest share of the economy. In the 1980s and 1990s, there has been considerable debate as to why the US has been able to create many more new jobs than Western Europe. Some of this question is false in the sense that it only reflects different demographic trajectories—the population of the US grows much faster than that of Western Europe. According to Plougmann (1988), this accounts for 35 per cent of the difference in absolute terms. The remaining, real difference is often explained by the American growth in low-skill, poorly paid service jobs, the so-called 'bad jobs' discussed in Chapter 7. Figure 12.1 shows that one of the subsectors in which the US has the highest share is personal services. Up to the mid-1980s, it seems likely that increases in labour productivity in US services were lower than in Western Europe, which was due to the increase in low-skill jobs (Galibert & Le Dem 1986; Cette et al 1993). (There are exceptions, for instance a detailed study by Gadrey, Noyelle and Stanback (1991) showed that the apparent low productivity growth in American food retailing compared to French was due to quality increases.) Correspondingly, wage and price developments were different in the service sector in the US and in (most of) Western Europe. In the US, wages have stagnated or even declined in real terms since the 1970s, while they have increased in Western Europe, and prices have followed them. For instance, Springer and Riddle (1987) show that women employed in US banks (mainly as tellers) have experienced considerably smaller salary increases than women in EU banks.

The large income differentials in the US contribute to the explanation of the high consumption of personal services. More people than in Sweden, for instance, can afford to buy a considerable amount of these services, and this gives rise to employment growth (Scharpf 1985; Barcet 1987).

However, these mechanisms only explain part of the employment growth in the US service sector. Figure 12.1 shows that in producer services, too, the US have a larger employment share than any other country, and Figure 12.2 indicates further strong growth in the corresponding occupations. There is no doubt about the extraordinary growth in sophisticated and well-paid information services, the 'symbolic analysts' of Reich (1991). These are the activities responsible for the substantial net export of services from the US, which are shown in Table 13.2, and which are exemplified in the Appendix. Several authors indicate that the high degree of division of labour and demanding local markets, the low degree of regulation of labour and product markets and the flexibility of US business service firms are the reasons for their international competitiveness (Noyelle & Stanback 1991; Bengtsson 1987; Quinn & Gagnon 1986; Porter 1990).

Recent studies indicate that the growth in high-grade services now prevails, even in absolute terms (McKinsey 1994). As shown also by Figure 12.2, 1980–90 data indicate that most of the growth in service occupations now takes place in professional, technical, administrative and managerial occupations—which earlier were leading only in percentage terms. However, compared to France, it is still in the growth in low-grade service jobs (clerical, sales and service occupations) that the US have the largest lead.

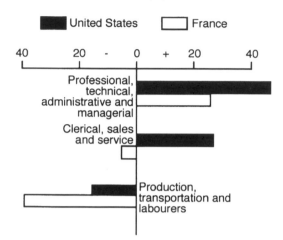

Figure 12.2. Employment growth by occupation in the US and France, 1980–1990. *Source:* Redrawn after *The Economist* 19.11.1994.

SERVICES IN EAST-CENTRAL EUROPE

Service activities in the former Communist countries of Eastern Europe still have a volume and a quality that is lower than in other advanced economies. There is reason to discuss and explain the particular characteristics of service development in these countries, focusing primarily on the East-Central European countries that were not incorporated in the Soviet Union. In Russia, the situation is still even more unclear.

The discussion is primarily based on seminar papers. There is little research and still fewer printed publications on services in East-Central Europe.

SERVICES UNDER COMMUNIST REGIMES

Basically, service supply before 1989 was miserable, the physical facilities were worn down, the technology outdated, the skills and wages of personnel were poor, productivity was low, and above all, production of household services was so limited that people had to spend a major part of their lives in queues. The state of producer services was even worse (Illeris 1991b). One of the consequences was a considerable black economy, which was necessary to make the economy function at all, but which was not able to make it function satisfactorily.

As an example, Figure 12.1 shows employment in the service sector of Czechoslovakia—excluding of course the black economy. It should be stressed that even more than in the West, service activities were internalized in the user sectors. Not only were external producer services almost non-existent, but also services for final consumption by the staff (childcare, health services, canteens and holiday accommodation) were mainly organized inside the large enterprises. The state of service activities may also be illustrated by the distribution of GDP, as shown earlier in Figure 1.3.

Figures 12.1 and 1.3 show that the service sector in East-Central Europe was relatively smaller than in the West. It was also smaller than in Western countries with a similar GDP per capita, and, according to historical data, smaller than it was in rich Western countries, when these were as poor as the East-Central European countries in the 1980s.

Figure 12.1 shows that the deficit, compared to the West, was most marked in producer services. The lack of development in this subsector could not be compensated for by internal activities in the user enterprises, nor by services obtained from the ministries or other centralized organizations. Banks and insurance companies were not mediators of capital movements. Civilian applied research and development was very underdeveloped. Consultancy and marketing were almost non-existent.

The only service subsector with a share of the total economic activity comparable to the West was transport. The transport system required substantial resources, due to the organization of manufacturing production in few, but gigantic, plants, and to the resulting long distances over which raw materials, intermediate and final products had to be transported. Thus the OECD (1991) notes that transport volumes in East-Central European countries were 0.5–2 tonne km per dollar of GDP, whereas the comparable figure for Western Europe is 0.2–0.5 tonne km per dollar of GDP.

The subsector of social services was considerably smaller in East-Central Europe than in the West. Most of this category consists of education, health and social services—in which the Communist countries had always boasted of their results. Some of them actually had improved the level of education considerably, compared to their poor starting points. But altogether, the use of resources was smaller than in the West, even if the need for social institutions was large, since the participation rate of women was close to that of men, see Table 12.1. Furthermore, East European researchers all stress that the quality of the services was poor, the physical facilities worn down, and the skills of the personnel mediocre. This may be connected with the wage structure, which is illustrated by Table 12.2.

The so-called 'unproductive services' (see below) constituted a low-wage sector, compared to blue-collar sectors like transport. They were, even more than in the West, dominated by women.

Trade, tourism, repair shops and personal services employed a much smaller share of the labour force than in the West. The state-owned system of retailing was kept at an absolute minimum; especially in rural districts and suburbs, the number of shops and other service outlets was extremely limited, and people had to travel far and to wait long in queues. In some East-Central European countries, small private enterprises were tolerated in these sectors, but in others (Czechoslovakia, Romania) they were not allowed. In return, barter trade, corruption and the black economy were widespread.

Table 12.2. Average monthly wages in Czechoslovakia 1987.
Source: based on Michalova and Fronkova (1990).

	Czechoslovak crowns
Total economy	2985
Material production	3006
Non-productive sector	2765
Highest service sectors:	
Transport	3487
Foreign trade	3376
Communications	3366
Lowest service sectors:	
Culture	2049
Research	2071
Social services	2298

However, state-produced services were cheap, in particular cultural services and public transport were heavily subsidized. But of course, services were standardized and not adapted to the individual preferences of the consumers.

WHY WERE SERVICES SO POOR?

In these economies, the Party and government decided everything of importance. Why did they decide that investments, employment, wages and prices should be at minimum levels in service activities, while as many resources as possible were devoted to material production, and in particular to heavy manufacturing (coal, steel, mechanical and chemical industries, etc.)?

The original reason is probably to be found in Marxist theory and its distinction between 'productive' and 'unproductive' activities (see Chapter 2). This notion was adopted in the early days of the Soviet Union and later transferred to the East-Central European countries. However, it is an over-simplification to explain the low priority of service activities by the ruling theory alone. Undoubtedly, other factors have played a role.

First, according to the theory, it was only in an initial stage with so-called extensive growth that the heavy basic industries should have priority. Later the growth should be 'intensive', consumer goods and quality should have higher priority. However, this stage never came—or, if after all service activities were expanding, it was only because pressure from the population made it necessary to produce at least some consumer goods and services. The causes of this conservatism are probably to be found in the hostility of the decision-makers towards innovation and in the vested interests of the heavy manufacturing sector (e.g. the Polish 'coal and steel lobby'). It may also have played a role that the powerful 'military-industrial complex' in the East focused on heavy material, while the parallel complex in the West from an early day focused on electronics.

Indeed, East-Central European researchers warn against the belief that the economy was rationally planned, though of course the image officially presented was one of scientifically based leadership. On the contrary, the researchers tell us that the decisions were usually the result of accidental pressures on a primitive and 'ignorance-based' leadership (Ghibutiu 1990; Ehrlich 1990; Ofer 1990). This is not least true for services, which are more difficult to standardize than goods production, and which complicate a command economy.

The lack of externalization of producer services may be explained by the substantial uncertainty connected with subcontracted inputs in a centrally planned economy. Very often, enterprises did not receive the planned inputs in due time. Quite sensibly, they tried to internalize the production of inputs as much as possible, even if quality suffered. This was especially true of service inputs, since the exchange of information was regarded with suspicion and often restricted.

Finally, it is possible that Communist parties—originally workers' parties—by setting the wages for service work at such low levels were seeking revenge on a part of the bourgeoisie which had been their enemy.

CONSEQUENCES OF THE POOR LEVEL OF SERVICES

The poor quantity and quality of household services meant, of course, a poor standard of living. Furthermore, the long queues absorbed a lot of leisure time. The queues also contributed to low productivity, since in many working places it was an accepted necessity that employees were absent for hours to shop or to queue up in some office.

The lack of business services may have been just as serious. The lack of innovative capacity, the hopeless organization of production, the bottlenecks in distribution, and the lack of adaptation of production to the needs of consumers were not only caused by the lack of a market, of cost consciousness, and of economic stimuli. Another essential cause was the lack of any apparatus to work on these questions—in other words, the lack of business services. The poor service level was not only a consequence, but also a cause of economic stagnation and low productivity. It was after Khrushchev's remark, that the Soviet Union would catch up with and overtake the United States, that the East European economies started to stagnate, relative to the West. It was precisely on this stage of economic development that business services became vitally important in the West.

East-Central European authors stress the lack of externalization as a decisive negative factor (Ghibutiu 1990; Miskinis 1990; Ehrlich 1990). The isolation, the lack of external impulses, the inbreeding have, in their opinion, been of crucial importance. Their conclusions must be kept in mind in the debate on externalization or internalization (Chapter 6).

CHANGES IN SERVICE PRODUCTION

Since the breakdown of the Communist regimes in 1989, the economic changes

Table 12.3. Share of service employment in East-Central European countries, 1970–1992 (%). *Source:* Ehrlich (1994).

	1970	1980	1985	1989	1990	1991	1992
Czechoslovakia	33.6	37.3	38.7	39.4	41.1	41.8	—
Hungary	30.4	36.6	37.8	41.7	43.9	45.7	49.1
Poland	27.5	30.7	32.8	35.6	36.9	37.5	39.3
Bulgaria	25.3	31.8	32.8	35.4	36.7	38.9	—
Romania	19.3	25.6	25.5	26.0	27.5	30.3	29.9

have, as is well known, been tremendous. Market economies were introduced, private and foreign firm creation allowed, and many state-owned activities gradually privatized. Developments have differed from country to country, but the following discussion will be limited to features found all over East-Central Europe.

It is still difficult to follow the economic processes through official statistics, which are in the middle of a change to Western definitions and concepts. They are unreliable, too, because of new methods of data collection (new taxation systems, etc.) and because there is still a large unregistered economy (in Hungary estimated at 25 per cent, see Kostecki 1994).

As regards the service sector, there is no doubt that as a whole it constitutes the most dynamic part of the economy, though it attracts less attention from governments and media than do the huge ailing manufacturing plants. For instance in Hungary, official data show that during the initial recession which followed the breakdown of the old system, the GDP of the service sector in 1992 was down to 96.9 of its 1989 level, while the economy as a whole was down to 81.2 per cent (Ehrlich 1994). Accordingly, its share of the total GDP has grown, for instance in Romania from 28.4 per cent in 1989 to 39.7 per cent in 1992 (in current prices, see Ghibutiu 1994). Table 12.3 shows service employment as a share of total employment in five countries during 1970–92.

More recent figures are available from Estonia, where the *Baltic Review* (spring/ summer 1995) reports that the service sector had 41 per cent of total employment in 1992, but 55 per cent in 1994. At any rate, the increasing share of service employment is clear. Given the recession, this need not mean an employment increase in absolute terms. For instance, in Romania and East Germany, reductions in service employment have occurred (Ghibutiu 1994; Gäbe 1995). The general impression is that this process has been accompanied by a gain in productivity. Developments have been different in different subsectors, however, see OECD (1991), Schneider (1993), Ehrlich (1994), Kostecki (1994), Scheuer (1994) and Gäbe (1995).

In retailing, repair, trucking, restaurants and personal services, the state enterprises were quickly privatized, and the internal household service activities of state enterprises were sold off. At the same time, new businesses were started at an almost explosive rate, in spite of the recession. There was a large unfulfilled demand, and entry costs and skill requirements were low. Pavements were filled with street vendors, and some businesses had a speculative character or were connected with crime. Gradually, retailing standards have increased, more regular shops have taken over, and Western chains have invested in retailing and ousted some of the entrepreneurs.

Business services also constituted a field of widespread entrepreneurship, some of the new enterprises being part-time outfits set up by people such as academics or public administrators. It has not been studied to what degree they now perform the same crucial functions as they do in the West. However, it is clear that demand has been especially strong for enterprises which could guide the new firms and foreign investors through the new type of regulations connected with privatization and taxation, i.e. lawyers and accountants. Knowledge of marketing, of management in a market economy and of environmental problems and repair of buildings has been demanded, too. It seems that many of the entrepreneurs had limited qualifications and have closed down again, while others have been drawn into the networks of Western firms who needed local partners or branch offices to enter these countries (RESER 1995). Because of low salaries coupled with satisfactory technical skills, exports may be possible in sectors like computer services, certain R&D types and so on.

Infrastructural services, especially telecommunications and banks which were in a poor state, are rapidly being improved. However, it takes time for banks to learn to function well in a totally new economic system. Public administration, education and social services which remain in public ownership have met severe problems. Governments cannot afford to increase salaries (which already were low) and cannot compete for qualified persons, and administrative attitudes and procedures are slow to change.

Geographically, the development of services is concentrated in the largest cities where the best markets and the most qualified persons already were, and where Western firms find it easiest to start. However, the Western regions of these countries are generally much more dynamic than the Eastern ones. This is due to their better contacts with the Western market economies and historical traditions of entrepreneurship, as well as to the current border trade which includes cheap repair and medical services for Western customers (Murphy 1992; Illeris 1991c).

CONCLUSION

Even this short survey clearly shows that service activities develop very differently in different parts of the Western world. The share of service activities in the total economies is increasing everywhere, but the levels and composition of the service activities are markedly different, and the factors which influence service development have very different emphases in different countries. Such factors as female participation rates, labour market mechanisms, taxation, public service production, regulation, income differentials, company culture and local markets influence the different roads towards the service society and, undoubtedly, more factors can be added.

In the East-Central European countries, after decades of underdevelopment under the Communist regimes, the service sectors now approach the shares of the total economies observed in Western countries on similar economic development levels. But the remaining public service sectors are in a poor shape. However, there are still private subsectors where needs are not met and, with the general economic growth now accelerating in these countries, there is no doubt that their service activities are in for further growth.

13   International Trade in Services

Among the many aspects of service activities ignored by research until recently, international trade was one of the most ignored. However, international negotiations on the liberalization of service trade started in the 1980s, as part of the negotiations on the Single European Market and as part of the Uruguay round GATT (eventually leading to the General Agreement on Trade in Services, GATS). Negotiators soon realized how little was known about these questions, and a number of studies were launched. The following discussion is largely based on their results and the monograph by Daniels (1993b).

Traditionally, services have been considered intra-national activities, hence the lack of research and statistical data on international trade in services. The first authors who took up the question felt that they had to argue why services might be traded at all. In this chapter, the approach will be the opposite; assuming that international trade in services is a normal activity and a way to expansion and specialization—though different from trade in goods—I shall first focus on the factors which explain why it is not larger than it is. Second, the modes by which these barriers are overcome will be discussed. Third, the resulting pattern of internationalization will be presented, and service trade policies briefly discussed.

BARRIERS TO INTERNATIONAL TRADE IN SERVICES

As discussed in Chapter 2, typical services are relations, which means that trade in services is of another character than trade in goods; there is no material product that is shipped (against payment) from the place of production to the place of consumption. Usually the producer and the user of services have to meet in order to create the relation. However, the establishment of these relations meets more barriers when they try to cross international frontiers than it does inside countries. Hence, international trade in services is relatively modest, compared to international trade in goods and to the importance of service activities within national economies. The barriers are of four kinds.

Physical distances and the costs involved in bridging them form the first kind of barriers. Of course, physical distances also constitute obstacles within countries, as discussed in Chapter 9. But distances between countries are usually longer (except between border regions), and cross-frontier transport and telecommunication facilities are often poorer than the intra-national networks. However, the general reduction of transport and communication costs, relative to other prices, as well as the EU's efforts to improve trans-frontier infrastructure, will favour increased international trade in services.

A second group are *institutional barriers*. Examples are customs duties, quantitative restrictions or total import prohibitions, technical requirements, restrictions on foreign ownership of establishments, qualification requirements, restrictions on the movement of staff and profits, preference for domestic suppliers in public procurement, and national monopolies (often held by public institutions). Thus, public services are rarely traded internationally, except a few produced by international organizations.

These barriers have undoubtedly contributed to keeping international trade in services modest, since they have effectively kept out foreign competition in many sectors which are reserved for national service producers and often for public monopolies, e.g. in education, health, railways, airlines, telecommunications, police, armed forces, and government. The GATS agreement and, more radically, the Single European Market aim at the reduction or abolition of these institutional barriers, and coincide with a general worldwide tendency towards deregulation. All these initiatives should increase international trade in services.

Cultural and language barriers constitute a third type of obstacle, usually much more important between than within countries, and more important for trade in services—being relations between human beings and connected with uncertainty—than for trade in goods. They are particularly important for verbal, media-based services (books, journals, software, etc.), unless they are written in a world language, are translated, or are dubbed (films, TV), while they are less important for very standardized or highly technical services. They are more important if the partners have little knowledge of languages and of the societal context of the use of services in other countries (which is often the case in small and medium enterprises) than if they have broad international qualifications.

These barriers cannot be removed quickly by government action. They can only be mitigated in the long run, for instance by increased teaching of languages and geography, cultural exchange programmes and similar educational methods. On the whole, cultural and language barriers do decline, but it is a slow process.

Finally, even apart from institutional and cultural barriers, there is *a range of barriers created by the complicated and risky nature of international trade itself*. It is necessary to organize transport, financing, insurance, translations, adaptation to different legislation and various formalities which are not required or are easier to organize within countries. (Incidentally, this means that there is a need for a number of intermediate services.) In some cases, risks of political instability or fluctuating exchange rates add to the obstacles. All these barriers may well be higher for the more untraditional export of services than for trade in goods. For instance, there are reports that banks may be reluctant to finance service exports (Århus Amt 1994).

DIRECT AND INDIRECT INTERNATIONAL TRADE

The many barriers to international trade in services have had the effect that services are not often exported in the simple way that goods are, but are sold via service establishments in the customer's country ('indirect trade'), and hence are not registered as international trade. Before discussing the volume and development of international trade in services, it will be necessary to survey the modes of trade thus available:

1 *Direct trade via visiting service producers.* This is the most traditional mode; staff from the exporting firm visit the customers and produce the service (at least partially) together with them. This is in many cases how firms start to export services (O'Farrell, Wood & Zheng 1994). Often a service firm simply follows a client, when the latter sets up a branch establishment abroad. In the case of transport services, the ship, plane or lorry must come to the customer or to the place where the cargo is.

2 *Direct trade where the customer travels to the service producer.* This is the case in tourism and sometimes in educational and health services when the student/ patient travels to a teaching institution or hospital abroad. Even sports and cultural events increasingly attract foreign visitors.

3 *Direct trade without meetings of service producers and users.* This is the case in the increasing amount of services which are delivered via telecommunications (including post). This mode is primarily used by standardized back office services which are produced in low-cost countries for customers in high-cost countries. But sophisticated services, e.g. information from databanks or television broadcasts, may also be transmitted via telecommunications, videos or disks. In the case of repair services, the object to be repaired may be transported to the service producer and back.

4 *Indirect trade via exporter-owned establishments in the customers' country*: branch offices, subsidiaries or majority-owned joint ventures. The division of tasks between the head office and the subsidiary may vary: the latter may be a mere sales office, or it may make customized modifications of standard services provided by head office. In other cases, branch offices may carry out most of the service production using procedures developed by the head office, or it may participate on equal footing in the operations of a transnational corporation (including exports to third countries). Even in household service activities such as retailing, internationalization via subsidiaries has become widespread in recent years.

The aim of setting up a branch office or acquiring a well-established local firm is usually to overcome the above-mentioned barriers to reach the customers. But it may also be important to reduce barriers to information inputs, to be present where e.g. new financial tendencies emerge (de Bandt 1995). Or the purpose may be, as it normally is in manufacturing, to reduce production costs; for instance by having an engineering office in a Third World or East European country where cheap but qualified staff can be recruited.

The Foreign Direct Investment (FDI) involved in this mode is highlighted in available statistical information (see below), whereas it is normally impossible to get data on the transactions between parent and branch establishments. The growing importance of this mode has made the right of establishment and of free personal movement crucial questions in the GATS negotiations. If movement of persons is prevented, direct and indirect trade in services withers away.

Multinational service corporations have grown rapidly in the 1980s and 1990s, for instance in retailing, insurance, accountancy and management consultancy, advertising, engineering, cleaning, and computer services (see examples in the Appendix). Banks also establish branch offices abroad, but seem largely to remain national enterprises.

5   *Indirect trade via independent partners.* Such partners may be agents, minority-owned joint ventures, franchisers or independent service producers. The purposes of cooperating with alliance partners are largely the same as with exporter-owned partners, and the value added in the user country may again be small (sales agents) or large (franchising hotels or restaurants). Networks with independent partners are cheaper to create, but of course the exporter has less control and must rely more on trust. Statistically, little is known about trade flows via this mode.

HOW IMPORTANT IS INTERNATIONAL TRADE IN SERVICES?

What is the pattern of internationalization resulting from these forces? *Few household services are traded*, though of course there are exceptions such as tourism and media services (books, journals, films, TV, videos, tapes, etc.). In other words, most private and public household services are shielded against international competition, which undoubtedly influences their productivity and wage levels. They form the 'in-person services' in the terminology of Reich (1991). However, in countries with legal or illegal immigration, many of these sectors are likely to be undertaken by immigrants who are willing to accept low remuneration (e.g. restaurants, retailing, bus driving, nursing, cleaning, etc.). Household services may also be traded indirectly.

On the other hand, *many producer services are able to overcome the barriers to international trade* (though some less sophisticated, proximity-demanding producer services are not). One group of rather simple, standardized services may be transmitted cheaply via telecommunications, for instance 'back office services', see examples in the Appendix. They belong, together with many goods, to what Reich calls routine production. Other producer services are so valuable that even high transport costs of staff do not matter. This group of service producers is the problem-identifying, problem-solving and strategy-brokering 'symbolic analysts' in Reich's terminology. In both of these markets, there is international competition with its risks and opportunities.

Data on international trade in services, to be found in balance of payments statistics, leave much to be desired, especially compared to the data on trade in goods. They are clearly incomplete—the world's registered imports are bigger than

Table 13.1. World trade in services 1980–1990. *Source:* IMF. Incomes from capital and work excluded.

	1980 (US$bn)	1990 (US$bn)	Of which % from industrialized countries	Growth factor 1980–90
Services	244	769	79	3.2
of which: transport	83	223	79	2.7
travel	60	237	77	4.0
other	82	255	82	3.1
Goods	1085	3265	73	3.0

registered exports—they do not include intra-firm trade, services embodied in goods cannot be distinguished, and in the financial sector payments for services cannot be distinguished from capital movements. Gadrey (1992a), from whom Table 13.1 has been borrowed, quotes a study according to which the under-evaluation of US service exports could be of the order of magnitude of one-third.

International trade, both in goods and services, shows higher growth rates than GDPs. The share of services in world trade increased slightly, according to these (questionable) data, from 18.4 per cent in 1980 to 19.1 per cent in 1990—the increase taking place after 1985. However, this increase may be due to increasing prices of services relative to goods (see discussion in Chapter 4).

As shown in the third column of Table 13.1, the industrialized countries are by far the most important service exporters, more dominant than in goods exports. But they are also the biggest service importers. The balance of world trade in commercial services (including labour and property income) of the largest economies is shown in Figure 13.1.

Besides the US, whose service exports are growing rapidly, most of the West European countries as well as the Mediterranean countries are net exporters of services. Elsewhere, Singapore is one of the few net exporters. Germany, Japan, most South East Asian countries, and Canada are net importers. The Third World countries are net service importers, too, and some of the imports (e.g. technical services) are paid for by Western governments and international organizations, as part of their development assistance.

The composition of service exports is very different from country to country. The US is strong in several business services and air transport, the UK in financial services and market research, France in tourism and engineering, the Mediterranean countries in tourism, Norway and Denmark in shipping, Finland in forestry-related services, and so on. Many factors—traditional qualifications as well as demanding and unregulated/unprotected domestic markets—may contribute to large exports (Porter 1990; Noyelle & Dutka 1986). In verbally based services, countries with world languages as mother tongues have an advantage, as witnessed by British publishing and Irish computer services.

Table 13.2 shows that in the 1979–88 period, the highest export growth rates

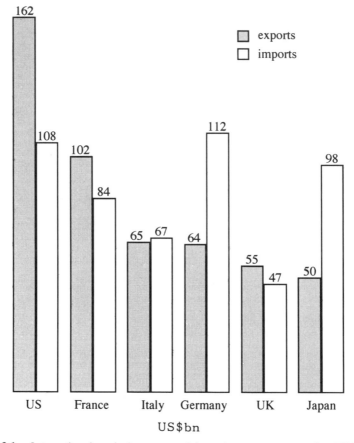

Figure 13.1. International trade in commercial services, seven countries 1992. *Source:* GATT.

among EC producer services (very broadly defined) were produced by activities based on telecommunications.

Foreign Direct Investments are not well documented, either. Table 13.3 shows stocks of outward FDI from the six largest economies.

FDI in services makes up a higher share of total FDI than the corresponding share of services in total international trade. FDI in services grows faster than direct trade in services, too. For instance, French FDIs in services grew in only five years (1984–85 to 1989–90) from 11 billion francs annually to 88, while service FDIs into France in the same period increased from 11 billion francs to 48 (Gadrey 1992a). Drennan (1992) reports that sales from US producer service branch offices abroad amount to twice as much as US producer services export directly. Indirect trade via independent partners probably grows at even higher rates (Rasmussen 1993), but no data exist to highlight this.

The US Office of Technology Assessment has estimated direct exports to

Table 13.2. Exports of producer services from EC12 countries, 1988. *Source:* J. Rasmussen (1993), Internationalisering af erhvervsservice, in N. Veggeland (ed.) *Norden utfordres—internationaliseringens mange regionale aspekter*, København: NordREFO, Table 1. Reproduced by permission of Jasper Rasmussen.

	1988 (ECUbn)	Annual growth 1979–88 (%)
Insurance	6	11
Bank services	8	16
Advertising	3	9
Business services	14	8
Construction	7	2
Communications	3	13
Film, TV	1	16
Commercial transactions	11	4
Incomes from patents	5	12
Other producer services	24	9
Producer services, total	82	8
Service exports, total	222	8
Goods exports, total	871	9

constitute 42 per cent of all service sales abroad in 1983 (Noyelle 1989). However, this estimate may be questioned.

SERVICE TRADE POLICIES

Some governments have conducted service export policies of a traditional, not to say mercantilistic, type, often combined with policies aimed at attracting firms from abroad. They have offered subsidies or very low regulation standards. Examples are banks in Luxembourg, shipping under convenience flags, and back offices in Ireland. Some West European governments have promoted the export of know-how about well-functioning public services, though so far with limited success.

Table 13.3. Foreign Direct Investment in services, six countries at the end of 1987. *Source:* Reproduced with permission from J. Gadrey (1992a) *L'Economie des Services*, Paris: La Découverte.

	US$bn	Share of total FDI (%)
USA	140	41
Japan	91	62
UK	65	39
W. Germany	39	48
France	22	39
Italy	17	54

More untraditional policies have been those already mentioned, which aim at breaking down barriers to mutual trade, such as the completion of the Single European Market and the GATS agreement. The background was a growing recognition that, in particular, increased competition among business services would improve their quality, and that again would promote the innovativeness and competitiveness of all economic activities. Societies as a whole benefit. It was this recognition that persuaded Third World countries to enter the GATS treaty which will open these countries for the import of business services. Accompanying policies focus on the conditions which are required for the good performance of business services and on such conditions for easy interaction between service producers and users as governments can influence, for instance transport and telecommunications infrastructure, education and research infrastructure, legal frameworks (taxation systems, protection of intellectual ownership, etc.), and other questions mentioned in connection with regional policies in Chapter 10.

CONCLUSION

Increased international trade and hence increased competition may be expected to strengthen the most competitive service producers and weaken the least competitive. Each producer and each country must try to find quality/price niches where they are competitive. In some cases, activities will be pulled towards the exporting country, in others towards the user country, or they may be split as in the case of insurance standardization and subsequent customization (Noyelle & Dutka 1986).

International trade in services is modest, compared to trade in goods, but growing. Its modest volume is due to the need for service producers and users to meet—hence distance barriers as well as cultural and language barriers play a big role. Institutional barriers have also been higher than for goods, but the GATS agreement and the completion of the Single European Market are now breaking them down. Services may be exported via telecommunications or embedded in printed and other media, but often exporters must visit the importing country, or customers must travel to the exporting country (e.g. tourists). To avoid these barriers, many exporters choose indirect exports via branch offices or acquire subsidiaries (foreign direct investments) in the importing countries, or via cooperation with independent partners in them. It is primarily transport services, tourist services and business services that are traded internationally. The economically developed countries are, with a few exceptions, net exporters, but the net importers have recognized the positive role of these services for their economic development.

Part V

CONCLUSIONS

14   The Service Society

As a way of concluding the discussions of this book, this chapter will attempt to describe, in a crude and simplified way, the 'service society' which is emerging in the economically advanced world, a society which is fundamentally different from the former industrial economy, and in which service activities play a crucial role.

THE SERVICE SOCIETY

It is of course impossible to prove in any traditional, positivist sense that a new type of society is emerging. The contemporary world is complicated, and it is easy to find exceptions to the trends on which I focus, even to find opposite trends. It is also possible to argue that the transformations taking place now are no more radical than those of many other periods—after all, societies are always changing. Only time will show who was right.

The exercise of describing a 'service society' has the character of constructing an 'ideal type'. It is a tool, a method to structure the innumerable and chaotic observations in such a way that hypotheses about processes and connections can be studied. Can they yield a consistent model or scenario of how society operates? If that is the case, there is some likelihood that the simplified picture is a reasonable model of the complicated real world. But its ability to be a scenario for the future should not be overestimated. At best, it is a synthesis of the most crucial processes and forces now operating, and may easily have omitted some which will become important tomorrow.

However, since the first ideas about fundamental societal changes in the direction of a service society were raised in the 1970s, more and more authors have followed suit, and during the last decade it has been widely accepted by researchers and to an increasing degree by the general public—with the consequence that it influences the decisions of governments, firms and people.

Different authors use different labels to denote more or less the same emerging society. I prefer to call it a 'service society', characterized by the dominant economic activity, and distinguishing it from earlier hunting, agricultural, and industrial societies (a more detailed discussion following below). Other labels such as the 'information' or 'knowledge' society focus less clearly on the difference between this and the former societies. Several authors talk about the 'post-industrial' society, but this is an unfortunate expression since manufacturing industries, just as agriculture, continue to be important economic activities. Finally, the 'post-Fordist economy' is a widespread term, focusing on the difference between the emerging society and 'Fordism' from the inter-war period to about 1970, with its particular characteristics of mass production, mass consumption, Keynesian regulation and so on.

The different terms reflect the fact that there are differences of opinion as regards the details of the emerging society and the weight that should be attached to each of these details. I think that the most interesting thing is that most authors largely agree on the main characteristics, and I shall only briefly mention a few of the most important authors and schools (a more detailed discussion is offered in Illeris 1994b). The sociologists Touraine (1967), Toffler (1970, 1980) and Bell (1973, discussed in Chapter 4) were the first to discover that fundamental economic changes were taking place. Porat (1977) focused on the consequences of the basic changes in information and communication technologies. Piore and Sabel (1984) focused on the decline of mass production and the growth of 'flexible specialization', while the French 'regulation school' focused on the consequences of the now declining Keynesian regulation. An admirable recent summary of the transitions, with a main focus on labour market and qualification issues, is offered by Reich (1991), further discussed in Chapter 7.

The first part of this chapter will include a brief survey of the most important aspects of the emerging service society, followed by a slightly more detailed discussion of the roles of household and producer service activities. In the second part, the locational and regional characteristics of service society will be summarized.

CHANGES IN PRODUCTION, MARKETS, ORGANIZATION AND QUALIFICATIONS

Table 14.1 attempts in a crude way to summarize the most important characteristics of industrial society (Fordist version) and service society, respectively. In the Fordist economy, the prevailing mode of production was mass production of long series of identical manufactured goods. Markets were homogeneous (mass consumption), usually within a nation state, where Keynesian regulations as well as the collective wage bargaining systems ensured stability and predictability. The assembly line produced economies of scale which minimized costs and prices. The capital deployed in the machines formed the decisive factor of production. Production was steered from the top of the hierarchy, and work was organized according to Taylorist and Fordist principles. Each worker monotonously performed the maximum number of a minimum of different operations and needed only a minimum of qualifications—the most important being obedience. Production was carried out by men, while women performed the reproduction work in the households. Firms merged into large corporations with a vertical integration of production chains.

Today the most important activity is the production of household and producer services. The modes of production have changed. Even if economies of scale still exist—only big corporations can establish R&D units—production series tend to

Table 14.1.   Before and after the transition to a service society

Industrial society	Service society
Mass production	Differentiated production
Long series of production	Short series of production
Standardization	Flexibility and complexity
Economies of scale	Economies of scope
Capital most important factor of production	Knowledge and creativity most important factors of production
Goods production most important function	Development, planning, management, marketing most important functions
Cost minimization	Quality maximization
Price competition	Product competition (quality, service, adaptation to customer needs)
Stable and homogeneous markets	Turbulent and segmented markets
National markets	International markets
Mass consumption	Individual consumption
Monotonous routine work	Automation
Standard qualifications	High and diversified qualifications
Job specialization	Job enrichment
Standardized labour market	Flexible employment
Hierarchical organization	Flat hierarchies, network organization
Vertical integration	Sub-contracting, externalization
Large corporations	Small and medium enterprises, divisionalization
Nation states	International cooperation, local and regional self-government
Division of labour among persons	Division of labour among firms

become short. On the other hand, economies of scope become more important. Competition parameters are quality, adaptation to the demand from different market segments, and service contents, rather than price. While routine operations are automated, the labour force is occupied in such operations as development, planning, management, and marketing. It must be stressed, however, that these producer services are complementary to goods production. The interaction between business services and industrial production becomes the driving force in the creation of wealth.

Production becomes increasingly complex: a hammer was simple to produce and to sell compared to a computer which must be accompanied by programs, instructions and error-finding before a buyer can use it. At the same time, production gets more flexible and easier to change. This is made possible by information technologies allowing the machine programs to be changed quickly. And it has been made necessary by the turbulence of markets. Improved transport and communication technologies allow markets to become international, but products must be adjusted to the special characteristics of different countries. Even national markets become increasingly segmented. Individual life-styles supplant mass consumption—it is no longer a question of 'keeping up with the Joneses', but of differentiating ourselves from them (Dale 1994). Wage bargaining has become local or individual, markets more unstable. Small enterprises become competitive through flexibility and adaptation to differentiated consumer demands. The sales of the 500 largest companies corresponded to 58 per cent of the US GDP in 1979, but declined to 37 per cent in 1993 (*The Economist*, 24.6.1995). They survive, however, by giving more independence to their divisions in order to avoid bureaucratic rigidity, or by disintegrating vertically.

To take an example, mentioned by Murray (1992). While the 'model T Ford' of the 1920s was produced in over 1 million completely identical copies each year, and production was closed down for 6 months when in 1927 it was supplanted by the 'model A', today's Toyota is produced in 45 000 variants as regards equipment, colour and fittings, and the computer system changes the production machines from one variant to the next one in fractions of a second.

Inside the individual firms, hierarchies tend to become flatter. Complex and flexible production cannot be commanded in detail from the top, but requires that individuals or groups make informed and responsible decisions at all levels of the firm. New technologies break the earlier information monopoly of management. Repetitive jobs are either threatened by competition from the Third World or automated, while the number of analytical, planning and decision-making jobs increases. There is a third class of jobs, 'in-person services', which cannot be automated and which are not exposed to international competition, employ many workers, but face financing difficulties. The knowledge, creativity and cooperative abilities of the staff become the most scarce and most important factors of production. As the Federal Reserve Bank of Dallas has expressed it: the industrial age required horsepower, while the information age requires brainpower. Increased and ever-updated skills are needed, and education and training systems enlarged. This has repercussions on production; the labour force demands more interesting work. A mode of production which needs all human resources tends (slowly) to reduce discrimination by gender.

The fundamental conflicts in the service society are different from those of the industrial society. Instead of traditional class antagonisms, we observe a polarization between a skilled majority on the labour market and an unskilled, more or less excluded minority. Instead of conflicts between the 'haves' and 'have-nots', we get conflicts between the 'knows' and 'know-nots' who risk either unemployment or low wages.

It is not easy to distinguish cause and effect in this complex web of societal changes. It may be fruitful to consider changing consumer attitudes and indivi-dualized demand as a primary cause, as does Vandermerwe (1993), and the technological change which allows flexible and differentiated production as a necessary (but not sufficient) condition.

THE ROLE OF SERVICES IN SERVICE SOCIETY

Why call this emerging new economy a 'service society'? For two reasons; the first one, stressed by Touraine and Bell who continued a line of thinking already suggested by Fisher (1935), is that *services form an increased share of final consumption*. As we grow richer, we use more education, health services, cultural, tourism and other leisure services, while our consumption of goods does not grow at the same rate. As mentioned in Chapter 4, this notion has been heavily criticized, but the conclusion of the debate is that it is basically correct, though the increase in services is hampered by slow productivity increases and rising relative prices, and though much of the increase has been in services—in many countries public services such as childcare—which confront great financing problems.

The second reason, which only came into focus in the 1980s (though it was anticipated by the geographer Gottmann as early as 1961) is that *the interaction between intermediate service producers (whether internal or external) and users is decisive for contemporary production of both goods and services*. In particular, business services have a crucial role, discussed in Chapter 6, of mediating between production and the ever more complex society and allowing an increased division of labour in the following ways (de Bandt 1991a):

1   The segmentation, internationalization and turbulence of markets require marketing services which not only distribute products but also gather, analyse and communicate information about demand back to producers.
2   R&D and design services are necessary in order to innovate products and adapt qualities to market demand as well as to innovate flexible production processes.
3   Increasing diversity of financing and raw material inputs requires specialist services.
4   A more complex regulatory framework must be dealt with by other service functions.
5   On the other hand, firms increasingly find it important to influence the outside world by means of public relation services.
6   The qualifications of human resources become essential, and recruitment, personnel management and upskilling services crucial.
7   Coordination of all these factors, from strategic planning to immediate preparation, requires increased (and decentralized) management services.

Another way to understand the increasing role of producer service activities is to see them as a result of the increasing division of labour between firms, sectors, and countries, and the derived increasing need for exchange of information, goods and persons.

Figures 14.1, 14.2 and 14.3 attempt, in an extremely simplified way, to illustrate the increasing division of labour from hunting and agricultural, through industrial to service society. Figure 14.1 depicts pre-industrial society in which households or at least local communities were largely self-sufficient.

Figure 14.2 illustrates the division of labour in industrial societies: a chain from primary production through manufacturing to distribution and consumption. Service activities are limited to trade and transport, a little bit of government regulation (increasing under Keynesianism), and some consumer services. We have all grown up with this image of the economy.

Figure 14.1. Subsistence society

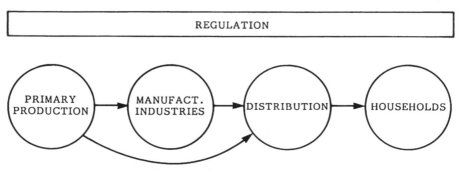

Figure 14.2. Industrial society

Figure 14.3 suggests an image of the far more complex society which is now emerging. Producer services—performed internally or bought externally—are necessary for the performance of producers. They are also responsible for innovation and dynamism and for the productivity gains that can be obtained in the total production system. Household services are important, too, not only for consumption, but also because the (re)production by means of education, health services and so on of a qualified, innovative and fit labour force is a *sine qua non* of economic activity.

However, it must be emphasized that transition from one type of society to another takes time. In many sectors and regions, pockets of industrial society still exist.

FORDISM IN EAST-CENTRAL EUROPE

The developments described here took place in the Western societies. It is obvious that in the East-Central European economies, the characteristics of industrial societies, and in particular the Fordist mode of production, were dominant before 1989. Here, industrial mass production in gigantic plants prevailed, with their hierarchical organization, their inflexibility, and their lack of quality and

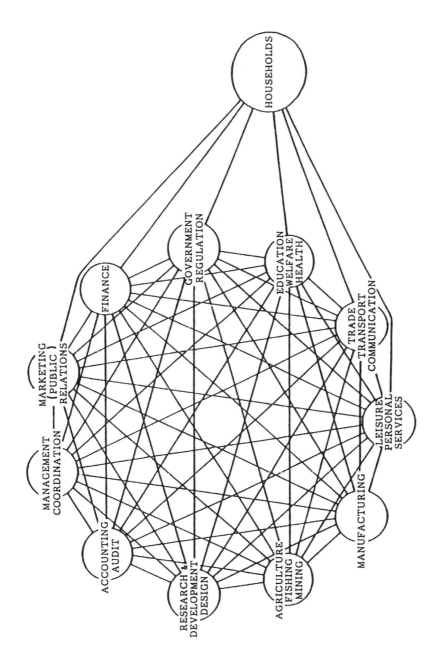

Figure 14.3. Service society

innovation. Service activities were deliberately minimized, and external producer services hardly existed. Stable mass consumption was secured in a way different from the West, by state monopoly.

The reasons are probably to be found in the early years of the Soviet regime, where Fordism was consciously copied as the most advanced system of the West, and Marx's views on the unproductive nature of service activities were interpreted as an ever-valid reason for neglecting them. But of course, the centralized system of production suited the general organization of society only too well. After World War II, this system was copied in the East-Central European countries.

On the whole, the performance of this system was not bad in the industrial phase. But while market competition made it possible for new modes of production to supplant Fordism in the West, no such mechanism existed in the East-Central European countries. The neglect of service activities, and in particular of producer services, was one of the main reasons for their stagnation and final breakdown. The pressure from vested interests in the Party, the administrative nomenklatura and the (military-)industrial complex has been an enormous conservative force. It is the irony of history that the Communists forgot Marx's elementary statement, that the superstructure of society must adapt to the basic productive forces.

Their legacy is a technically well-educated labour force with poor organizational and innovative skills. For the future of these countries, a crucial question is whether advanced producer services will be created and applied.

LOCATION OF SERVICES IN A SERVICE SOCIETY

How do service activities locate in the emerging service society? It is clear that traditional theories of location of household services, based on the minimization of distances between customers and supply (see Chapter 8), are no longer sufficient in a society where so many characteristics have changed, and where producer services have become an important sector.

Table 14.2 provides a summary of the conclusions of Chapters 9 and 10, as a step towards a revised theory. Their starting points are the societal changes discussed above.

The structural effect. The first hypothesis is concerned with the effect of the increasing share of service activities, in particular of high-quality services, in the economy. It states that service activities with high growth rates tend to be geographically concentrated in large metropolitan areas. Examples are business services. On the other hand, service activities with low growth rates tend to be more evenly spread—e.g. retailing. The effect of this structure is an increasing concentration of service activities in the major metropolitan areas.

Some authors stop their analysis at this point and conclude that the service society will be characterized by increasing geographical concentration, but that is clearly not warranted. It is necessary to look at the locational changes which may take place inside each service sector, too. In shift-share terminology, not only the

Table 14.2.   Changes in society, in service activities and in service location

Societal changes	Service activities concerned	Locational forces	Locational impact	New Locational role of service activities
Increasing share of high-quality services in total economy	All	Structural changes	Increased concentration of economic activities in big cities	
No major changes	Household services and some producer services	Proximity to customers remains important	Growing consumption, reduced economies of scale cause decentralization. Vice versa	Remain non-basic
Increased exchange of complicated information	Qualified information services	Need for face-to-face contacts. Growing agglomeration advantages	Increased concentration in big cities	May become indirectly basic
Improvements in communication and transport technologies	Qualified information services	Reduced travel time-costs and agglomeration advantages	Many locations become possible	Basic
	Routinized information services	Telecommunications relax need for proximity	Many locations become possible	Basic
Increased role of knowledge and creativity as factors of production	Information services	Human resources decisive (education, labour market, environment)	Individual qualities of localities become decisive	Some services become indirectly basic

share component, but also the shift component must be taken into consideration. The following paragraphs will discuss these shifts in service location.

Proximity to customers remains important. The second hypothesis is concerned with the large part of the service activities for which the societal changes do not seem to cause major revolutions. For these, the central place theory remains valid. Despite all modern technologies, it is still costly to overcome distance, especially if it has to be done frequently. So proximity to customers remains important for many service activities. If retailers need not locate quite as close to us as previously, now that we have private cars, they must still avoid being too far from us if they are to attract our custom. Proximity remains important wherever service production normally requires that service producer and service user are present at the same time and place.

Central place theory was developed with large numbers of ubiquitously distributed customers in mind, typically households. It may also be valid for producer services which supply a large number of firms with rather similar services, for instance simple accounting and audit services to retail shops and small manufacturing firms.

Central place theory has a static character, but of course the parameter values may change which means that a process of adaptation towards a new equilibrium of the central place system starts and contributes to the regional dynamics of services. For instance, a changed distribution of customers may cause such a process. The Danish regional shift of manufacturing firms and households out of the Copenhagen region during the last two decades has been followed by a redistribution of service activities. Furthermore, changing consumption patterns may trigger off a change in the location of services. When in the 1960s it was decided to expand public service activities in Scandinavia, this first took place in universities, specialized hospitals and similar institutions located in a few big cities. In the 1970s, however, the growth mainly took place in local welfare services and secondary education, spread over a large number of small towns. The rapidly growing market for computer services has allowed firms which supply them to find sufficient turnover in quite small local areas. The internal economies or diseconomies of scale in service firms may also change, causing the minimum threshold of customers to increase or decrease, which again means geographical concentration (retailing) or decentralization (mental care).

On the whole, the multiplier effect tends to increase. These services are still limited by the amount of basic economic activities in the area. But per unit of basic activities, the amount of non-basic service activities increases, creating new divisions of labour, new productivity growth, new employment, new incomes, and higher satisfaction of human needs.

Increased need for face-to-face contacts. The third hypothesis concerns the increasing exchange of complicated information which is inherent in the growing importance of external and internal business service activities and their interaction with service users. Personal contacts and face-to-face meetings between these actors often seem to remain necessary. Business travel and, especially, the lost working time of highly salaried staff are costly. Thus proximity remains an important advantage. We are here talking of information services which are used by relatively few firms and institutions, not forming a ubiquitous market. Hence, this factor pulls service producers and users toward agglomeration in big cities. Examples are business services such as management consultants.

Medium-sized cities can offer similar advantages of agglomeration if they specialize within one economic sector in such a way that firms can find all necessary contacts locally. This is the rationale behind such specialized industrial districts as the textile area of Prato in Tuscany.

Relaxation of proximity constraints. The fourth hypothesis is based on the revolutionary development in telecommunication and information technology, as well as on the important improvements in long-distance personal travel by means of cars, aeroplanes and high-speed trains. These changes have led to the question of whether the traditional need for service activities to locate close to their customers will disappear. The answer will be different for different types of services.

As regards qualified service activities, it has already been mentioned that face-to-face meetings remain necessary in many cases. But meetings between distant partners have become much easier and cheaper, thanks to developments in personal transport. Even though travel costs have not disappeared, they have been reduced, especially in terms of lost working time, and may have become insignificant compared to the value of the services produced. Distances still matter, but they are 'shrinking'. Consequently, some authors (Toffler 1980; Planque 1983) argue that agglomeration advantages are decreasing. The handicaps of peripheral locations diminish, 'there is everywhere' as Pascal (1987) says. A few meetings plus contact via telecommunications now seems to be a combination that may reduce agglomeration advantages more radically than imagined only a few years ago.

For routinized information services, there is no doubt that the increasing possibilities of transmitting data by relatively cheap telecommunications have reduced the friction of distance. Increasingly complicated information can be transmitted, provided of course that the necessary infrastructure is present. This fact has allowed many service activities to locate independently of their customers, for instance 'back offices'.

There is a clear conflict between the third and the fourth hypothesis. In the emerging service society, there are both forces which increase and those which reduce advantages of agglomeration, forces which pull towards a more concentrated pattern of location and forces which relax these pulls. It is possible to talk of a race between these forces, where in different cases different forces may gain and lose. This notion may contribute to an understanding of the different patterns of service location observed in the Western world over the last decades.

If we return to the fourth hypothesis, however, the decreasing need for proximity between these types of service producers and service users does not mean that service producers can operate equally well everywhere. It means only that other factors of location become decisive. Many locations become possible, but they are not equally good, several factors constitute local conditions that differ from place to place. There are differences in the cost levels of labour and premises, and in some places costs may partly be covered by regional policy subsidies or local economic policies. For back offices, the minimization of costs is often decisive, though certain requirements of labour qualifications must also be met. There are also differences from place to place in equipment and infrastructure. There are variations in the quality of local markets which mean that they form unequally good bases for later remote market development. And so forth.

The supply of qualified persons. The fifth hypothesis is that, as a consequence of the increasing role of knowledge and creativity as factors of service production, the availability of good human resources is the most important local condition for qualified service activities that do not need to locate close to their customers. This of course means that the traditional notion, that the man must come to the job, is reversed. These activities must come to the man or, put in another way, firms which locate where qualified staff prefer to be have a competitive advantage.

As regards residential preferences, big cities have several advantages: that is where most educational institutions are, ensuring the supply of young candidates. The large labour markets increase the job opportunities of persons with specialized qualifications, who often have spouses with equally specialized qualifications. And many people appreciate the big cities with their cultural services, professional milieux and other advantages. But clearly some other regions, too, are able to attract people because of their physical and social environments: old university towns, attractive landscapes and townscapes, the sunbelts of southern France, Germany and the United States, places where professional milieux and cultural services have also been created.

THE ROLE OF SERVICE ACTIVITIES IN REGIONAL DEVELOPMENT

The last column of Table 14.2 suggests some answers to the question of the role of service activities in regional economic development in the emerging service society.

To some degree, the traditional economic base model remains valid. Many household services as well as simple, ubiquitous producer services keep a passive, non-basic role; they have to locate in the proximity of their customers. They must play a secondary role in a regional development policy, but possible opportunities to accelerate the multiplier effects of the basic economic activities should be seized.

For more advanced producer services that need to be close to their customers, but are not found everywhere, the question is more intricate. Do they passively follow the location of their customers, as stated by the economic base model? Or have their services become so important for the competitiveness of their clients that their presence is now a necessary condition for the location of the latter? In other words, have they, although indirectly, become the true economic base of their area? Already in 1955, Blumenfeld claimed that this was the case. To the degree that he is right, regional development policies should support the location of such producer service activities.

Producer services which are no longer required to locate close to their customers, and which sell their services all over the country and even internationally, clearly contribute to the economic base of their region. Such service activities—whether low-skill 'back offices' or high-skill individualized service producers—should obviously be targets of regional development policies.

Finally, a number of household services contribute to the supply of human resources in their area and thus indirectly to its economic development. Educational services are an obvious example. But also cultural, leisure and other services which contribute to attract qualified people from elsewhere come into this category. In recent years, several towns and regions have adopted development policies that include measures to make the environment, in a broad sense, attractive.

In sum, in the emerging service society, some producer services directly contribute to the economic development of the regions in which they are located, through regional exports. Other producer services and some household services do so indirectly, by supplying necessary services and qualified personnel, or by attracting such personnel, and in these ways improve the competitiveness of the region's directly basic firms. Still other service activities, especially many household services, retain passive roles in regional development.

15 Important Conclusions and Further Questions

The purpose of this brief chapter is twofold. First, to accentuate the most interesting findings of the book. And second, to emphasize important questions to which we still have no or only weakly documented answers, and on which further research must have high priority. On the other hand, the chapter will not repeat all findings, since each chapter is concluded with a brief summary.

UNEXPECTED FINDINGS

Some of the findings of this book are insufficiently known to a broader public which still tends to perceive economic activities as more or less identical with manufacturing. For instance the finding that in the Western world, most production and most employment are now found in service activities. And that services are not derived activities, but are important for total economic development, together with other activities, in regions as well as in whole societies.

For academics working on services, these findings are trivial. For this target group, I shall stress the following findings which are more unexpected or at least not sufficiently accepted. However, at present some of them are not well documented, but rather have the character of hypotheses.

1   75–80 per cent of the costs of consumer goods typically represent service inputs (R&D, production planning, administration, marketing, distribution, etc.), while only 20–25 per cent represent raw materials and physical production.

2   The results of many services are not well defined 'products' that can be measured and reproduced. Hence valid measurement of productivity is impossible and instead, evaluation of effects should be undertaken. There is no well-defined market, sellers and buyers act in a state of uncertainty.

3   The share of household consumption that is spent on services increases slowly when measured at constant prices. The growth of service consumption is probably hampered by low productivity increases, and certainly by relative price increases. As regards public services, the taxpayers have to pay more, only to receive a constant volume and quality of services.

4   When firms choose between internal production of services and external purchases, the dominant theory—that the choice depends on a comparison of

transaction costs—must be rejected. The choice is primarily decided on the basis of the user firm's own capacities, and there is more often complementarity than substitution between internal and external services.

5   Theories of deskilling of labour and dual labour markets rarely apply in service activities. The personnel must be perceived more relevantly as the main resource than as a cost.

6   Improvements in transport and telecommunications seem to relax the traditional necessity of proximity between service producers and service users, especially for producer services which now on average sell a third of their services in other regions.

7   The location of most advanced business services in big cities should, according to much theoretical literature, be explained by the need for proximity to sources of information inputs. But empirical investigations seem to show that this is a factor of only secondary importance.

8   In the situation of locational freedom thus created for many business services, the possibility of recruiting skilled staff becomes a decisive factor of location. Hence it is important for cities and regions to offer education and to attract qualified people.

9   Traditionally, service activities had only a passive role in regional economic development. Now many producer services acquire a directly basic function through their ability to export to other regions. It seems that other service activities acquire an indirectly basic role as local input-providers to exporting firms, or as activities which educate or attract the necessary skilled personnel.

10 Inside city regions, a clear suburbanization of service activities is now taking place in the Western world. Many producer services are leaving city centres, since proximity to customers or information sources no longer determines their location. Car accessibility and sufficient space seem to have become the most important factors.

A RESEARCH AGENDA

As mentioned before, some of these findings have only the status of insufficiently documented hypotheses, and other questions remain unanswered. The work on this survey has, within the research field which it covers, pointed to the following questions as being the most urgent ones to explore:

1   Do service activities contribute to the creation of wealth—assuming that this concept can be given a clear meaning?

2   What determines the prices of services?

3   How does innovation take place in service activities?

4   Can household services be organized and financed in such a way as to offer substantially increased employment for—especially unskilled—labour and satisfy unmet service needs?

5   How are business services concretely applied by the users, and what are their detailed effects?
6   What skills do personnel in different types of service activities use, and what changes take place in skill needs?
7   What are the consequences for different groups of the population in different geographical areas of the way in which household services are currently supplied?
8   More studies of location factors are needed, both in inter- and intra-urban contexts, and especially for household services and public services.
9   How important is it for different types of producer service users that there is a local supply of various services? How do improved transport and telecommunications modify the need for proximity?
10 How do services—in particular business services—contribute to the economic transformation in the formerly service-lacking East-Central Europe?

Beside the research needs, increased understanding of services will depend on a better supply of statistical data on all their aspects, not least their geographical distribution.

Appendix   Case Studies

This appendix presents case studies of three business service sectors. They are intended to serve as examples of most of the characteristics of advanced business services. The criterion of selection was the author's own research experience.

ENGINEERING CONSULTANTS

Engineering consultants offer advice to and design engineering projects for clients, as well as supervise the execution of projects. Two groups of projects may be distinguished (though not totally distinct): first, manufacturing product and process projects for industrial clients. And second (and generally more important), construction projects, either for private construction firms, developers or users, or for public authorities. The latter type of activity has in recent decades diversified into transport, energy, environment and similar projects and plans.

DEVELOPMENT OF THE SECTOR

The sector has grown considerably in recent decades. In Denmark for instance, employment increased by 56 per cent from 1980 to 1990 (Erhvervsfremmestyrelsen 1994). However, demand fluctuates according to business cycles and investment rates, especially the demand from the construction sector. The long-term trend is an expansion of energy and environmental services, while the demand for other services does not grow much.

Competition with alternative suppliers of similar services—including internal service production in the user organizations—influences the sector, too. In particular, manufacturing industries get only a minor part of the technical advice they need from engineering consultants. Advice (not invoiced separately) is also offered by machine suppliers and customers, from research institutes, in many countries from government-supported technological service agencies, and from the users' own engineers. In Denmark, Larsen (1992) has estimated that advice given in connection with machine and product purchases accounts for nine-tenths and independent advice only for one tenth of the external advice received by manufacturing firms. And the independent advice is primarily connected with peripheral problems (e.g. of internal environment), while the core or strategic problems of the users usually are dealt with by other sources of advice.

For small and medium-sized manufacturing enterprises, technical consulting may in reality develop into all-round consulting, including advice on management, organizational, financial, marketing and other issues. Since the owners/managers of the user firms typically have a technical background and communicate best with technically educated partners, engineers are in the position to be such generalist 'house-consultants'. This is a major part of the activities of government-supported technical service agencies in Denmark (Illeris & Rasmussen 1992; Illeris 1994a).

Compared to engineering services to the manufacturing industry, engineering services in construction, transport, energy and environment undoubtedly account for a larger share of the technical services used by these sectors, though the share varies from country to country. In some countries, construction firms often prepare the projects themselves, while in other countries (e.g. Denmark) independent consultants are normally commissioned to perform this work. If the clients are public authorities or developers, they may also prepare the projects internally. But smaller clients who do not often demand construction projects cannot possibly themselves employ staff for that.

Altogether, engineering is one of the most externalized of business services: an EU survey reproduced in Table 6.3 shows that 56 per cent of engineering and related services are of exclusively external origin, 14 per cent exclusively internal, while 30 per cent are mixed. Most clients of engineering consultants are manufacturing firms, governments or parastatal companies—a market structure different from that of most business service sectors. Thus, in 71 American engineering and architectural firms interviewed, Beyers and Lindahl (1994a) found that 29 per cent of sales went to manufacturing firms, 7 per cent to construction firms, 24 per cent to transport, telecommunication and utility firms, and 27 per cent to government institutions at various levels.

STRUCTURE

Engineering consultants span an array of types. Some are very small, one-man or even part-time firms which have low costs and are able to prepare simple projects and offer general advice, primarily for local clients. At the other extreme are large, transnational corporations which are able to offer all the specialized knowledge that complicated projects require and to finance the development of new methods as well as the establishment of branch offices in many regions and countries. In addition, engineering consultants often cooperate with partners in the preparation of projects, both in order to offer all the specialized knowledge required (clients often prefer to deal with only one firm which may then subcontract parts of the task), and in order to serve more geographical markets (RESER 1995).

Civil engineers and other persons with at least three years of university-level education constituted half of the total staff of engineering consultant firms in Denmark in 1990 (Maskell 1993), technical assistants and administrative staff most of the rest. The routine tasks in design have largely been taken over by computers.

RELATIONS WITH CLIENTS AND LOCATION OF ENGINEERING
CONSULTANTS

The bulk of the work of engineering consultants, namely the design of projects based
on technical calculations, is normally done in the firms' own offices, with relatively
little contact with the clients. Nevertheless, most engineering consultants depend to
a high degree on proximity to clients. This is due to the initial and final stages of the
relation. First, engineering consultants have to establish frequent contacts with
potential clients in order to be informed about possible future tasks and negotiate
contracts with them, and hence have to locate in their vicinity. In particular, public
authorities have had a strong preference for firms with a local address, though EU
rules about tender now limit such local mono- or oligopolies. Second, industrial
engineering consultants often have to work in close contact with the production
facilities. Third, engineering consultants often supervise the execution of projects,
which makes frequent visits to the construction sites necessary (RESER 1995).

Broad advice-giving ('house consultancy') requires an intimate and long-lasting
knowledge of the client firms, as well as cultural familiarity. A small provincial
firm is simply not likely to communicate well with a theoretically trained
consultant arriving from the capital without any knowledge of the firm and the
context in which it operates. The high frequency of this type of relations also makes
it imperative to minimize travelling costs. Hence, proximity to clients is important.

This is confirmed by the evidence in Chapter 8 as well as Table 6.3 which show
that technical services more than other business services are bought in the clients'
own region, and that they consider proximity very important.

On the other hand, highly specialized advice may be so valuable to the client that
the costs of even long distance travel become insignificant. 'I need advice from the
best specialist, and it does not matter if I have to fly him in from the opposite side
of the globe' is a typical client's statement. Consulting firms which offer this type
of services may locate more independently of the clients. Other factors of location,
for instance the recruitment and preferences of qualified staff, then become
important (Illeris & Rasmussen 1992; Illeris 1994a).

The locational pattern of engineering consultants may be illustrated by
employment in technical services in France, Figure A.1. The total locational
pattern of engineering consultants is characterized by a high degree of concentration in big metropolitan areas. In the French case, the Paris region has more than
40 per cent of the country's employment. This must primarily be explained by the
large size of the local market, especially for high-quality services, and as a
secondary factor, by the large supply of qualified personnel. In particular,
headquarters of large engineering corporations are located in big city regions.
Beside the factors mentioned above, accessibility to international contacts also
plays a role for them. But they typically supplement the headquarters with a
network of local offices which serve local markets with less specialized services
and call in experts from headquarters when needed. Small engineering consultants
are located all over the country.

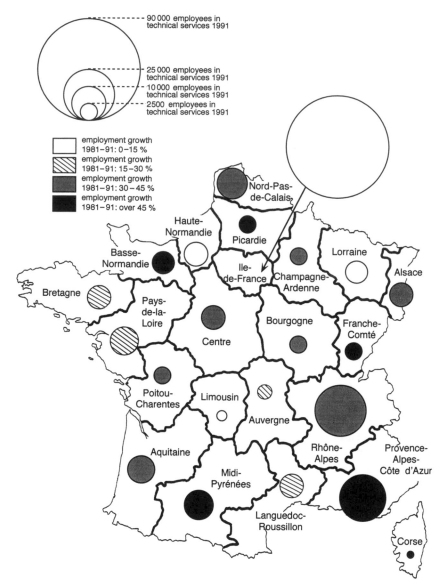

Figure A.1. Employees in technical services in France, 1981–1991. *Source:* Drawn on the basis of data in Gäbe and Strambach (coord.) (1993).

However, as Figure A.1 shows in the case of France, a regional decentralization may occur. This is primarily due to growing demand, which means that more local markets pass the threshold of offering sufficient turnover for engineering consultants. Probably, the most specialized engineering services tend to remain in the large city regions. But since such services may be produced far from the clients, they may also locate elsewhere. The large consulting firms report that provincial offices sometimes develop specialized services which may be used by the headquarters or even sold abroad (Rasmussen 1992). In Canada, Calgary has developed into a specialized engineering consultant centre, also serving bigger cities (Michalak & Fairbairn 1988). Léo and Philippe (1991) note a concentration of industrial consultants in Brittany.

The intra-urban location of engineering consultants seems to be relatively free from constraint, according to RESER (1995). They need not be very close to their customers, who anyway are spread all over the urban regions. Rather, car accessibility for staff, costs of premises, and easy access to an international airport play a role. In the Copenhagen region, only 5 per cent of the sector's employment is in the city centre, while the bulk is in the Northern, prestigious suburbs where most of the staff live (Maskell 1993).

INTERNATIONALIZATION

Compared to other services, engineering services are relatively often exported. American engineering consultants are great exporters (Porter 1990), and so are the French. Danish engineering consultants export 35 per cent of their turnover (Schaumburg-Müller 1987; Erhvervsfremmestyrelsen 1994). The reason for the substantial exports is that the technical character of the services makes them fairly universally applicable and reduces cultural barriers. However, engineers have often failed to consider the different socio-economic and cultural contexts in which their projects should operate. It also becomes more and more important to combine the technical advice with optimal organizational structures. Transnational engineering firms now increasingly employ staff with social science training to remedy this, and employ 'locals' in the user countries.

Another factor conducive to internationalization is the large demand for technical infrastructure, energy and environment projects in the Third World and in Eastern Europe. Exports into these parts of the world are often funded by Western governments or international organizations.

On the other hand, the preference of governments for local suppliers has hampered international trade between Western countries. Only with the completion of the Single European Market have these barriers now been reduced inside Western Europe.

The frequent need for proximity between engineering consultants and their clients is true not only within countries, but also between countries. Hence, direct exports are limited, and engineering firms tend to invest in branch offices abroad or cooperate with local partners in the user country (RESER 1995). In the EU, engineering consultants increasingly establish cooperation networks, partly in order to improve information gathering about future tasks, partly to supplement their special skills, and partly because the EU often requires contractors from more than one member country to cooperate.

Offices abroad are largely staffed with 'locals' who have better contact networks,

who know the local language, legislation and culture, and who in the Third World
and Eastern Europe get lower salaries than Westerners (while their technical
qualifications are high, at least in Eastern Europe). The leaders, however, may
come from the firm's headquarters in order to transfer its technical methods and
company culture (RESER 1995).

COMPUTER SERVICES

Computer service firms constitute a heterogeneous group of service activities
connected with the use of computers, all established since 1960 and most since
1980. The activities may roughly be classified into the following types (Noyelle
1990d; Moulaert, Martinelli & Djellal 1991; Illeris & Jakobsen 1991):

A   The production of packaged standard software, sold in large quantities,
    especially for personal computers.
B   The production of customized software.
C   The integration of software (and hardware) in customized systems (with the
    required adaptations for individual use).
D   Training, installation, error location and correction, maintenance and updating
    of computer systems, often combined with trade in hardware and software to
    form 'complete computer solutions'.
E   Data processing, including programming, adaptations and data entry.

A sixth class might be data-banks. However, they have not been studied in
connection with other computer services and will not be discussed here.

The first and last class are relatively well defined (though not always
distinguished in statistical classifications). The three classes in the middle often
overlap, and all include consulting activities.

It must be emphasized that many firms perform more than one of these activities.
And it should be stressed that identical activities are also carried out by hardware
producers, by other service producers (management consultants, accounting firms,
etc.), and in user organizations. Hence the number of people working in computer
service occupations is considerably larger than those working in the sector of
computer services. For instance in Sweden, in 1990 the former number was 66,000,
while the latter was 29,000 (Lundmark 1994).

DEVELOPMENT AND STRUCTURE OF COMPUTER SERVICES

In its short life, the sector has not only grown rapidly, but has also been through
radical changes (Gentle & Howells 1994). All the crucial changes happened first in
the United States and soon spread all over the globe.

In the early life of computers, specialized skills—obtained by people with very
different backgrounds—were required to handle them. Large user firms and
institutions established internal computer departments, while other users became

the customers of specialized data processing firms (sometimes set up by user organizations, e.g. banks). Typically, the services were simple calculations used in large numbers, such as bookkeeping.

Programming had originally been intimately linked with hardware production. Software was tied to specific makes of hardware. But in 1969, American anti-trust authorities forced the largest producer (IBM) to set up its software production as a separate unit, which gave birth to a new type of service firm providing independent software.

The introduction of personal computers in about 1980 and the subsequent acceleration in the number of computer users revolutionized the sector. First, it gave rise to the hierarchy of software production mentioned above, from standard packages to various kinds of specialized and customized additions and adaptations. Some of the niches are extremely specialized, while others are rather less skill-demanding. Together with new firms, many firms invading these fields evolved out of firms in neighbouring sectors.

Second, the rapidly increasing user friendliness of hardware and software as well as the increasing qualifications of the users meant that the tasks earlier handled by specialist departments or firms could be (re-)internalized by the user groups and persons (Rallet 1994). The growth of the data processing subsector with its large mainframe computers decelerated, and it specialized in the performance of simple 'back office' operations at lowest possible cost. They might be called the 'Fordist' relics in a 'Post-fordist' world (concepts discussed in Chapter 14). But the ever-increasing technical possibilities of rationalization, e.g. of substituting data entry by optical reading or direct data transmission from the source, tended to reduce employment in this subsector. On the other hand, the tasks of adapting computer software to the increasing variety of user needs now became the central activity, and cooperation with users became crucial (Noyelle 1990c). Software turnover now tends to surpass hardware turnover (Gentle & Howells 1994).

The interaction between service producers and users is reflected in Table 6.3, according to which 55 per cent are produced as combined ex- and internal services—more than in any other branch of business services—while the rest is equally split between the two origins (however, internal services are difficult to define).

However, traditions vary from subsector to subsector and from phase to phase. Firms with a technical origin tend to work less with users than firms with a consultant origin. The phases of analysis and of implementation require more interaction than the development stage (Moulaert, Martinelli & Djellal 1991).

The recent growth of the sector may be illustrated by the following data (it should be kept in mind that there are numerous delimitation problems and frequent changes in the balance between external and internal production). In the UK, an increase of employment by 169 per cent from 1981 to 1991 (Wood 1993b). In Sweden, by 233 per cent from 1980 to 1990 (Lundmark 1994). In France (including a minor group of management consultancy employees), by 221 per cent from 1981 to 1991 (Moulaert & Gallouj 1995).

The markets for external computer service firms are found in all sectors. For instance, in Sweden in 1990, 29 per cent of sales were to the manufacturing sector, 51 per cent to private service firms, 16 per cent to public authorities, and 4 per cent abroad (Lundmark 1994).

In the above classification of computer service activities, the fast-growing subsectors A–D require high and increasing qualifications—A–C even very high— while the more modestly growing data-processing subsector is less demanding, but still requires good schooling and social qualifications (stability, precision, carefulness). In Sweden, 55 per cent of those employed in the sector in 1990 had university education (Lundmark 1994). In Denmark, Illeris and Jakobsen (1991) found percentages from under 33 in data processing to 50–80 in types B–C.

Computer service firms often cooperate in networks, in order to supplement their skills with others, to improve their information gathering, or to exploit geographically distant markets (see later) (RESER 1995).

RELATIONS WITH USERS AND LOCATION OF COMPUTER SERVICE FIRMS

The different types of computer service activities show different locational patterns, depending on different factors. The production of packaged standard software takes place independently of users, and can be located more or less anywhere, provided that qualified staff can be recruited. A few American firms dominate this activity; according to Haug (1991) 70 per cent of the incomes of American software firms derive from packaged software. The software firms concentrate in a few geographical clusters: Silicon Valley and Orange County in California, Seattle (with the world's largest firm, Microsoft), and route 128 west of Boston.

The production of customized software and systems requires intensive face-to-face contacts with users, especially in the planning and implementation stages. Hence many firms are found near major user concentrations, e.g. the aeroplane industry in Toulouse (Swyngedouw, Lemattre & Wells 1992) or the military complex near the M4 motorway west of London (Hall et al 1987). However, the value of the services is very high, and travelling costs are insignificant compared to the need for high quality in each particular case (Illeris & Jakobsen 1991). Hence location does not depend heavily on proximity to clients, or on proximity to information sources (Haug 1991; RESER 1995), but more on the possibility of recruiting qualified staff. Metropolitan areas with large labour markets and interesting professional milieux are such places, e.g. New York (Noyelle & Peace 1988), especially if they have an attractive environment (e.g. Amsterdam, see de Jong & Lambooy 1984). However, sunbelt locations such as California may also be attractive (Haug 1991), and it is possible to perform well in quite odd places (Illeris 1994a). It should be noted that Western firms increasingly buy programming from subcontractors in low-wage countries with highly qualified experts, e.g. India, Ireland, Israel, increasingly Eastern Europe, and Singapore (Noyelle 1990d)—this last exports packaged software as well.

1980   1990

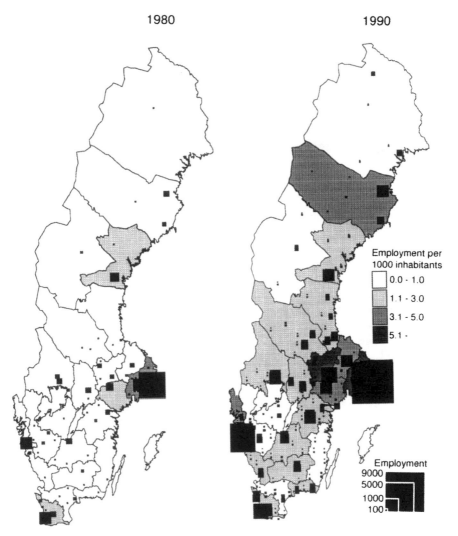

Employment per
1000 inhabitants

| 0.0 - 1.0 |
| 1.1 - 3.0 |
| 3.1 - 5.0 |
| 5.1 - |

Employment
9000
5000
1000
100

Figure A.2. Employment in computer services in Sweden 1980 and 1990. *Source:* Reproduced from M. Lundmark (1994), *Databranschen i Sverige*, Stockholm, ERU, by permission of ERU.

The production of mixed computer services to less demanding clients (type D) depends heavily on proximity to users. Not only is it necessary to know user needs intimately in order to provide individual solutions for them, but it also requires that installation takes place on the client's hardware, and that the service firm can come to their assistance at very short notice in case of problems (Illeris & Jakobsen 1991). The rapid growth of demand for these services has therefore led to the establishment of independent computer service firms as well as branch offices of big firms all over Western countries, in medium-sized and even quite small towns—see Figure A.2.

Finally, data processing has followed a particular locational logic, based on reliable and cheap transmission of standardized input and output data via telecommunications to locations far from the users ('back offices'). These activities have shifted from big Western cities towards low-cost locations where the necessary staff—mainly female—with good general qualifications can be recruited. In the early 1980s, shifts from central cities into suburbs or peripheral regions were widespread (Nelson 1986). Later however, further shifts took place, especially from the United States to English-speaking areas such as the Caribbean, the Philippines and Ireland. While the former two countries largely undertake data entry operations, more sophisticated operations on journal subscriptions, insurance damage claims and so on are handled in Ireland where wages are higher. Political stability and government subsidies play a role in the choice of locations. Western airlines have located reservation services in India, China and Barbados. But, as already mentioned, employment in these activities is insecure (Wilson 1993, 1994; Richardson 1994).

Thus, the total pattern of locational development in computer service activities is the result of complex and sometimes contradictory forces. In the most sophisticated end of the range of services, recruitment concerns dominate, on the medium level proximity to customers, at the lower end cost minimization. Large firms operate in several fields and develop networks of branch offices in order to meet all their requirements. Compared to other business services, customers buy a medium share of their computer services in their own region (Chapter 8, Table 6.3).

As a whole, computer service employment is strongly concentrated in major city regions. Recent changes may be illustrated by the following examples:

1 In the United Kingdom, the share of the South East increased from 56.0 per cent in 1981 to 57.3 per cent in 1987, but then declined to 55.7 per cent in 1991, the decentralization primarily benefiting other southern regions (Wood 1993b).
2 In Sweden, the share of the county of Stockholm declined from 54.4 per cent in 1980 to 45.2 per cent in 1990, primarily to the benefit of medium-sized towns in many regions (Lundmark 1994—see Figure A.2).
3 In Denmark, the share of the Copenhagen region declined from 65 per cent in 1981 to 61 per cent in 1987, then increased to 62 per cent in 1992.
4 In France, where the two statistical classes covering computer services also include a (smaller) group of management consultancy employment, the share of the Ile-de-France region (with Paris) kept a constant 57.5 per cent from 1981 to 1991 (calculated from Moulaert & Gallouj 1995).

While there is growth in computer service employment everywhere, in some cases metropolitan concentration has increased, in other cases decentralization into regional markets has dominated, in still other cases the shifts are into amenity-rich regions.

Intra-regionally, there seems to be a general shift from metropolitan centres to peripheries. This may be illustrated by British data. The share of London in total South East employment declined from 57 per cent in 1981 to 41 per cent in 1991 (Wood 1993b). In the Copenhagen region, the two central municipalities had 54 per cent of the employment (by place of work) in 1982, but only 30 per cent in 1992. In the four large Dutch metropolitan areas, 54 per cent of the computer service establishments were in the suburbs in 1989, more than in any other business service sector (Hessels 1992). According to Hessels, accessibility was the most important factor of location.

INTERNATIONALIZATION

Internationalization of computer services is considerable—for instance 15 per cent of Danish turnover consists of exports (Erhvervsfremmestyrelsen 1994). Markets are worldwide, depending on the purchasing power of the different countries. Internationalization partly depends on telecommunications, and will be favoured by future infrastructural progress such as the so-called 'electronic highways'.

However, internationalization takes different forms. Standard packaged software is exported directly, provided that it is translated. Other software is exported, too, and altogether American firms had 60 per cent of the 1988 world software market (Haug 1991). But as mentioned before, programming tasks are increasingly subcontracted to qualified producers in cheaper countries, for instance Israel, India, or South East Asia. It should be noted that national legislation and regulation (e.g. on taxes) sometimes constrain internationalization. In the GATS negotiations, the US argued for liberalization, but even a country like India foresaw export opportunities.

Customized services have to be developed in close contact with the users, and internationalization takes the form of setting up branch offices (staffed with 'locals') or cooperation with local partners in the user country (RESER 1995).

Back office services, finally, are exported via telecommunications from low-cost countries with well-educated and English-speaking labour forces (Caribbean, South East Asia, Ireland, etc.). But the employment thus created may be threatened by further rationalizations.

MANAGEMENT CONSULTANTS

Management consultants offer analyses and advice to clients concerning management problems. The typical composition of the services of the sector in the late 1980s was as follows: 15 per cent administrative and organizational issues; 5 per cent general strategy; 15 per cent production problems; 15–25 per cent human resources, recruitment and training (increasing); 5 per cent marketing strategy; 5–10 per cent economic and financial questions; 25–30 per cent computer issues (increasing) (Tordoir 1992). Keeble and Schwalbach (1995) present a table covering eight West European countries, from which the median values indicate about 25 per cent corporate strategy and organization, 15 per cent financial and administrative systems, 15 per cent human resources, 10 per cent production management, 10 per cent marketing and communication, and 10 per cent information technology—but the variations between countries are large. In the fields of recruitment (head-hunting) and staff development, consultants traditionally do not stop at advice, but work far into the implementation stages. The limits of the sector are far from well defined, and management consultants overlap with several other sectors, e.g. computer services, accounting and auditing, even banking.

It is a small sector; Keeble and Schwalbach (1995) estimate 200 000 consultants worldwide, in Western Europe alone, 100 000 consultants (plus 50 000 supporting staff).

DEVELOPMENT OF THE SECTOR

Born in the United States, management consultancy was in its early days—before World War II—influenced by Taylor's engineer-orientated 'scientific management'. After World War II, it spread into Western Europe. American firms were in 1988 still estimated to cover half of the world market, and West European firms to cover another third (Keeble & Schwalbach 1995). Just as with the managers of the user firms, it cannot now be said to have one unified philosophy—a variety of approaches exist side by side.

Management consultancy has shown high growth rates in recent decades where the use of such services has spread from large corporations to smaller firms and government agencies. In Denmark, for instance, employment has almost trebled from 1980 to 1990 (Erhvervsfremmestyrelsen 1994). The reasons for growth are those discussed in Chapter 6: the increasing internal complexity of firms and the increasing complexity and uncertainty of the surrounding world. Decisions must take into account both the former, best known by the internal staff, and the latter, often better understood by external consultants. Competitiveness is gained by not only reacting to changing conditions, but also by foreseeing them, preventing risks, and making strategies to benefit from new opportunities (Gadrey 1992b).

However, the sector is more sensitive to business cycles than most service activities (Aharoni 1993), and the recession of the early 1990s set it back considerably. Undoubtedly, the years of rapid growth in a sector where fees are high had attracted a number of less qualified consultants who did not survive. Entry costs into the sector are low, but so are exit costs. It now seems that the sector is recovering.

Management consultancy is a sector where competition between internal and external provision is sharp, while at the same time complementarity is a condition *sine qua non*—the services of the external consultant must nearly always be absorbed and applied by the staff of the client. Table 6.3 shows roughly one third external, one third mixed, and one third internal production—but of course, the latter is difficult to delimit. The reasons for users to choose external consultants are to obtain specialized knowledge and know-how which they do not possess themselves, to have problems approached with fresh eyes, to acquire neutral assessments, to expand resources in peak periods, and to keep costs down (Poulfeldt 1990; Beyers & Lindahl 1994a; Aharoni 1993). Of course, consultants are sometimes hired to legitimize decisions already made. There is clear evidence that clients get better and better qualified, and demand higher quality services from consultants (Noyelle 1990c; Tordoir 1993; Manenti 1993).

Management consultants compete on the basis of expertise, creativity, adaptation to the needs of clients, personal contact networks, and reputation (Noyelle 1990c; Tordoir 1993; Keeble et al 1992; Beyers & Lindahl 1994a). The importance of contacts and reputation reflects the fact that in this sector, it is very difficult to know in advance what one buys. In Bryson, Wood and Keeble's study (1993), 53 per cent of all contracts were with former clients, and 17 per cent were obtained via references from former clients, while Aharoni (1993) mentions that about 80 per cent of the total turnover in the United States is repeat business. In order to supplement their skills, management consultants often cooperate in networks (RESER 1995).

Clients are spread over many sectors. Beyers and Lindahl (1994a) found in 51 interviews in the United States that 6 per cent of turnover was from industries such as agriculture, 29 per cent from the secondary sector, 14 per cent from governments, 39 per cent from areas such as transport, and 12 per cent from other service firms. In Europe, public authorities have been important clients in recent years—buying 40 per cent of the total 1989 turnover in the Netherlands, according to Tordoir (1992). The counterparts of management consultants are top- or medium-level managers in the client organizations (Tordoir 1993).

STRUCTURE OF THE SECTOR

Large international corporations play a prominent role in management consultancy, most of them developed out of American accountancy firms. They charge high fees and primarily serve large clients. But there is also a multitude of medium and small enterprises—as already mentioned, entry costs are low. According to Aharoni (1993), the average establishment in the US had 6–7 employees in 1991.

Management consulting firms depend to an extremely high degree on the skills of their staff. They have to strike a balance between, on the one hand, the pull towards standardization of methods in order to promise clients a well-defined product, and to reap economies of scale; and, on the other hand, the necessity to motivate staff by allowing them to develop their individual capacities. Hence, most large firms are in reality rather loose conglomerates of individual consultants, according to Tordoir (1992). Personnel turnover is high and a constant menace to the firms. Possibly the strong position of staff is reflected by the high fees in this sector.

The qualifications of the staff are extremely different in this young, ill-defined sector with weak interest organizations. There is a sharp distinction between persons responsible for consultancy contracts ('consultants') and support staff. The former typically have an education at university level. They typically constitute two-thirds of the total staff of consultancy firms (Keeble & Schwalbach 1995; RESER 1995). Furthermore, consultancy firms often employ freelancers for special tasks. Studies of entrepreneurs in the sector in the UK (Keeble et al 1992) and the US (Beyers & Lindahl 1994a) show that they usually have experience from other jobs in the sector or in client firms, while Aharoni (1993) writes that personnel increasingly is recruited directly from universities and business schools.

RELATIONS WITH CLIENTS AND LOCATION OF MANAGEMENT CONSULTANTS

The analytical and advice-giving work of typical management consultants requires very close and frequent face-to-face contacts with the clients, in order to discuss problems, to obtain an impression of the functioning of the organization, and for access to documents. As a consultant said: We work *with* them, not *for* them. Hence, management consultants spend most of their time at the clients' premises, according to RESER (1995), up to 60–90 per cent.

Still, it is not absolutely necessary for management consultants to locate close to their clients, since the high value of the services makes travelling costs, even lost working time, relatively unimportant. Management consultants often have considerable turnover outside their local area (80 per cent came from more than 20 miles away, according to Keeble et al 1992). According to Table 6.3, a lower percentage of management consultancy (59 per cent) was bought in the client's region than of any other business service. And proximity to this service was considered unimportant by a higher percentage of users (58 per cent) than for any other business service. This finding is confirmed by the data in Chapter 8 on the geographical distribution of supply and demand for management consultants. Actually, consultants do travel extensively (RESER 1995).

A factor which often pulls more strongly towards proximity to the clients is the need for cultural closeness. In particular, consultants must usually come from the same country, in order to be able to assess problems and possible solutions. Consultants who specialize in computer problems, training, or recruitment spend less time at the clients' premises.

Management consultants have high requirements for information. They must know about new methods, possibilities of new contracts, and relevant processes in the business world. This often leads to the establishment of information networks (RESER 1995); in particular, headhunters have to maintain extensive contacts in order to know about job candidates. The need for information also draws management consultants towards location in dense professional milieux (RESER 1995).

A third important factor of location is the need to recruit qualified staff members—the decisive resource of consultancy firms.

As a result, management consultants are very concentrated in big city regions, where most clients are—and in particular their top managements—where the information milieu is most dense, and where it is easiest to recruit the best qualified staff. Apart from that, many big management consultant firms have networks of branch offices in major provincial cities, in order to serve regional markets.

Statistical data on the location of management consultants are very scarce, due to the lack of a clear definition of the sector. French data from various statistical classes indicate a very high degree of concentration in the Paris region (60–70 per cent of total national employment). But in the 1980s, growth rates in the Paris region were below average (Moulaert & Gallouj 1995).

The intra-urban pattern of location in the four large Dutch metropolitan areas in 1989 is highlighted by Hessels (1992). He finds that management consultants are relatively more concentrated in the central municipalities than most business services. However, according to his survey, this is not in order to be close to clients—the most frequently cited factors of location are accessibility and prestige.

The performance of management consultants does not seem to be very sensitive to their intra-regional location and, anyway, consultants often travel from their residences to their clients' premises, while they visit their offices less often (RESER 1995).

INTERNATIONALIZATION

Management consultants often go international, in order to serve multinational clients abroad, and in order to expand. More than other business service activities, they are able to export directly. At least 45 per cent of the international turnover of American firms in 1983 was direct exports (Noyelle 1989), which confirms the relatively low importance of proximity to clients. But of course, in many cases they buy up local firms or establish branch offices, in order to serve new markets in a way that is adapted to local conditions, cultures and languages. The branch offices primarily employ local staff and have a high degree of independence, but are provided with standards and methods by the corporation (Sundbo 1992; Rasmussen 1992).

The trends toward market economies in the Third World and even more in Eastern Europe have opened important new markets for Western management consultants.

Bibliography

Aasbrenn, K. (1987), *Tiltaksarbeid på servicesektoren*. Oslo: Kommunaldepartementet.

Abler, R. (1977), The Telephone and the Evolution of the American Metropolitan System, pp. 318–341 in I. de Sola (ed.), *The Social Impact of the Telephone*. Cambridge, Mass.: MIT Press.

Aharoni, Y. (1993), *Management Consulting: A Survey of the Industry and Its Largest Firms*. New York: United Nations.

Aksoy, A. & Marshall, J. N. (1992), The Changing Corporate Head Office and its Spatial Implications. *Regional Studies*, **26**, 2, 149–162.

Allen, J. & Henry, N. (1995), Fragments of Industry and Employment: Contract Service Firms and Contemporary Restructuring, pp. 149–166 in C. Hadjimachalis & D. Sadler (eds), *Europe at the Margins*. Chichester: John Wiley.

Andersen, O. W. (1988), *Elementer til en 'ny-institutionalistisk' kritik af deindustrialiseringsdebatten*. Roskilde: Samfundsøkonomi og Planlægning.

Andersen, O. W. (1991), Production de services, organisation et croissance de la productivité: Une nouvelle approche institutionelle, pp. 241–256 in J. de Bandt (dir), *Les services, productivité et prix*. Paris: Economica.

Andersson, Å. E. (1985), *Kreativitet—Storstadens framtid: En bok om Stockholm*. Stockholm: Prisma/Regionplanekontoret.

Appelbaum, E. & Albin, P. (1990), Shifts in Employment, Occupational Structure, and Educational Attainment, pp. 31–66 in T. Noyelle (ed.), *Skills, Wages, and Productivity in the Service Sector*. Boulder, Col.: Westview.

Archambault, E. (1987), The Family and the Dynamics of Personal Services. *The Service Industries Journal*, **7**, 4, 46–55.

Århus Amt (1994), *Servicefagenes eksport*. Århus.

Aydalot, P. & Camagni, R. (1986), Tertiarisation et développement des métropoles: un modèle de simulation du développement régional. *Revue d'Economie et Urbaine Régionale*, **2**, 171–186.

Bailly, A. S. (1994), Evolution des systèmes de production et localisations des activités de service: 25 ans au service des services, pp. 109–120 in J. Bonamy & N. May (dir), *Services et mutations urbaines: Questionnements et perspectives*. Paris: Anthropos/Economica.

Bailly, A. S. & Boulianne, L.-M. (1993), *Services et aménagement urbain: Le cas des villes moyennes*. Paper, 3rd Annual RESER Conference, Siracusa.

Bailly, A. S. & Maillat, D. (1988), *Le secteur tertiaire en question: Activités de service, développement économique et spatial*. Genève: Editions régionales européennes.

Bannon, M. J., Brassil, D. & Murphy, C. (1994), *Job Creation in the Services Sector*. Dublin: Service Industries Research Centre, University College.

Barcet, A. (1986), *Les services dans le système productif—vers une typologie de la production des services*. Lyons: Economie et Humanisme.

Barcet, A. (1987), *La montée des services: Vers une économie de la servuction*. Lyons: Université Lumière.

Barcet, A. (1988), The Development of Tertiary Services in the Economy, Labour Market and Employment. *The Service Industries Journal*, **8**, 1, 39–48.

Barcet, A. (1991), Production and Service Supply Structure, pp. 59–69 in P. W. Daniels & F. Moulaert (eds), *The Changing Geography of Advanced Producer Services*. London:

Belhaven.

Barcet, A. & Bonamy, J. (1990), *Les services. Revue d'Economie Industrielle*, **52**, 99–115.

Barcet, A. & Bonamy, J. (1994a), Qualité et qualification des services, pp. 153–174 in J. de Bandt & J. Gadrey (dir), *Relations de service, marchés de services*. Paris: CNRS.

Barcet, A. & Bonamy, J. (1994b), *Internalisation versus externalisation: Valeur et dynamique de l'offre*. Paper, 4th Annual RESER Conference, Barcelona.

Barcet, A., Bonamy, J. & Mayère, A. (1983), *Economie des services aux entreprises: Approche empirique et théorique*. Lyon: Economie et Humanisme.

Baró, E. & Soy, A. (1989), Business Services and Urban Development: The Case of Barcelona Conurbation, pp. 195–224 in *Papers de Seminari 32*. Barcelona: Centre d'Estudis de Planificació.

Barras, R. (1990), Interactive Innovation in Financial and Business Services: The Vanguard of the Service Revolution. *Research Policy*, **19**, 215–237.

Baumol, W. J. (1967), Macroeconomics of Unbalanced Growth: the Anatomy of Urban Crisis. *The American Economic Review*, **LVII**, 3, 415–426.

Baumol, W. J., Blackman, S. A. B. & Wolff, E. N. (1985), Unbalanced Growth Revisited: Asymptotic Stagnancy and New Evidence. *American Economic Review*, **75**, 4, 806–817.

Baumol, W. J., Blackman, S. A. B. & Wolff, E. N. (1988), *Productivity and American Leadership: The Long View*. Cambridge, Mass.: MIT Press.

Beaverstock, J. V. (1990), New International Labour Markets: The Case of Professional and Managerial Labour Migration within Large Chartered Accountancy Firms. *Area*, **22**, 151–158.

Begg, I. G. & Cameron, G. C. (1988), High Technology Location and the Urban Areas of Great Britain. *Urban Studies*, **25**, 361–379.

Bell, D. (1973), *The Coming of the Post-Industrial Society*. New York: Basic Books.

Bengtsson, J. (1987), L'évolution des ressources humaines dans le secteur des services. *Economie et Humanisme*, **295**, 9–13.

Beniger, J. R. (1986), *The Control Revolution: Technological and Economic Origins of the Information Society*. Cambridge, Mass.: Harvard University Press.

Bertrand, O. (1988), Qualité et hétérogénéité des emplois de service. *Formations—Emploi*, **23**, 19–29.

Bertrand, O. & Noyelle, T. (1988), Employment and Skills in Financial Services: A Comparison of Banks and Insurance Companies in Five OECD Countries. *The Service Industries Journal*, **8**, 1, 7–18.

Bertrand, O. & Noyelle, T. (1989), *Le changement technologique et la formation des compétences dans les services*. Paris: OECD (mimeo).

Beyers, W. B. (1989), Speed, Information Exchange, and Spatial Structure, pp. 3–18 in H. Ernste & C. Jaeger (eds), *Information Society and Spatial Structure*. London: Belhaven.

Beyers, W. B. (1994), *Producer Services in Urban and Rural Areas: Contrasts in Competitiveness, Trade, and Development*. Paper, 41st North American Regional Science Meetings, Niagara Falls.

Beyers, W. B., Alvine, M. J. & Johnsen, E. G. (1985), *The Service Economy: Export of Services in the Central Puget Sound Region*. Seattle: Central Puget Sound Economic Development District.

Beyers, W. B. & Lindahl, D. P. (1994a), *Competitive Advantage and Information Technologies in the Producer Services*. Paper, Association of American Geographers Meetings, San Francisco. (A revised version is forthcoming in *Papers in Regional Science* under the title 'Explaining the Demand for Producer Services: Is Cost-Driven Externalization the Major Factor?')

Beyers, W. B. & Lindahl, D. P. (1994b), *On the Dynamics of Producer Service Markets: Externalisation, Internalisation, and Innovation Processes*. Paper, Symposium on Externalisation/Internalisation, Roskilde.

Beyers, W. B. & Lindahl, D. P. (forthcoming), Paper Pushers and Data Apes: The Growth and Location of Business Services in the American Economy. *L'Espace Géographique*.

Birley, S. & Westhead, P. (1994), New Producer Services Businesses: Are They Any Different from New Manufacturing Ventures. *The Service Industries Journal*, **14**, 4, 455–481.

Block, F. & Burns, G. (1988), Productivity as a Social Problem: The Uses and Misuses of Social Indicators. *American Sociological Review*, **51**, 767–780.

Blumenfeld, H. (1955), The Economic Base of the Metropolis: Critical Remarks on the 'Basic-Nonbasic' Concept. *Journal of the American Institute of Planners*, **21**, 4, 114–132.

Bonamy, J. (1988), Business Services and the Transformation of the Production System: Towards the Emergence of a Service Economy, pp. 10–37 in O. W. Andersen, J. S. Pedersen & J. Sundbo (red), *Service- og erhvervsudvikling*. Roskilde: Samfundsøkonomi og planlægning.

Bonamy, J. & Mayère, A. (1987), Logiques des activités de service et inscription spatiale, pp. 59–183 in D. Barbier de Reulle et al: *Mutations des services et dynamiques urbaines*. Lyons: Economie et Humanisme.

Bonke, J. (1988), *Husholdninger og husholdningsproduktion—socioøkonomiske forklaringer på efterspørgslen efter varer til husholdningsproduktion og alternativ service*. København: Københavns Universitet, Økonomisk Institut.

Bonnet, J. (1991), Les services dans le développement régional: Le cas de la région Rhône-Alpes, pp. 47–63 in *Services, Espace et réseaux*. Milano: RESER.

Borum, F. (1987), *Beyond Taylorism: The IT-Specialists and the Deskilling Hypothesis*. Copenhagen: Institute of Organization and Industrial Sociology, Copenhagen School of Economics.

Boulianne, L.-M. (1991), Types de services et types de territoires: Questions à partir des territoires non-métropolitains, pp. 37–46 in *Services, espace et réseaux*. Milano: RESER.

Braverman, H. (1974), *Labor and Monopoly Capital*. New York: Monthly Review Press.

Bressand, A. & Nicolaïdis, K. (1988), Les services au coeur de l'économie relationelle. *Revue d'Economie Industrielle*, **43**, 141–163.

Britton, S. (1990), The Role of Services in Production. *Progress in Human Geography*, **14**, 4, 529–546.

Britton, S. (1991), Services and National Accumulation. *International Journal of Urban and Regional Research*, **15**, 3, 415–431.

Browne, L. E. (1986), Taking In Each Other's Laundry—the Service Economy. *New England Economic Review*, July/Aug., 20–31.

Browning, H. C. & Singelmann, J. (1975), *The Emergence of a Service Society*. Springfield: National Technical Information Service.

Bryson, J., Wood, P. A. & Keeble, D. (1993), Business Networks, Small Firm Flexibility, and Regional Development in UK Business Services. *Entrepreneurship and Regional Development*, **5**, 265–277.

Buursink, J. (1985), *De dienstensector in Nederland*. Assen: van Gorcum.

Cappellin, R. (1988), Transaction Costs and Urban Agglomeration. *Revue d'Economie Régionale et Urbaine*, **2**, 261–278.

Cappellin, R. (1989), The Diffusion of Producer Services in the Urban System. *Revue d'Economie Régionale et Urbaine*, **4**, 641–661.

Castells, M. (1989), *The Informational City*. Oxford: Blackwell.

Cavola, L. & Martinelli, F. (1995), The Regional Distribution of Advanced Producer Services in the Italian Space Economy, pp. 223–240 in F. Moulaert & F. Tödtling (eds), The Geography of Advanced Producer Services in Europe. *Progress in Planning*, **43**, 2–3.

Cette, G. et al (1993), Nouveaux emplois de services. *Futuribles*, **176**, 51–55.

Christaller, W. (1933), *Die zentralen Orte in Süddeutschland*. Jena: Gustav Fischer.

Christensen, P. R. (1994), De nordiske virksomheders internationalisering, pp. 164–197 in L. Lindmark et al, *Småföretagens internationalisering—en nordisk jämförande studie*.

Stockholm: NordREFO.

Christopherson, S. (1989), Flexibility in the US Service Economy and the Emerging Spatial Division of Labour. *Transactions of the Institute of British Geographers*, **14**, 2, 131–143.

Christopherson, S. & Noyelle, T. (1992), The US Path toward Flexibility and Productivity: The Re-making of the US Labour Market in the 1980s, pp. 163–178 in H. Ernste & V. Meier (eds), *Regional Development and Contemporary Industrial Response*. London: Belhaven.

Clark, C. (1940), *The Conditions of Economic Progress*. London: Macmillan.

Coase, R. (1937), The Nature of the Firm. *Economica*, **4**, 386–405.

Coffey, W. J. (1990), Panacea or Problem? The Role of Services and High Technology in Regional Development. *Revue d'Economie Régionale et Urbaine*, **5**, 715–729.

Coffey, W. J. & Bailly, A. S. (1990), Service Activities and the Evolution of Productive Systems: An International Comparison. *Environment and Planning A*, **22**, 1607–1620.

Coffey, W. J. & Bailly, A. S. (1991), Producer Services and Flexible Production: An Exploratory Analysis. *Growth and Change*, **22**, 4, 95–117.

Coffey, W. J. & Bailly, A. S. (1992), Producer Services and Systems of Flexible Production. *Urban Studies*, **29**, 6, 857–868.

Coffey, W. J. & McRae, J. J. (1990), *Service Industries in Regional Development*. Montreal: Institute for Research on Public Policy.

Coffey, W. J. & Polèse, M. (1987), Intrafirm Trade in Business Services: Implications for the Location of Office-Based Activities. *Papers, Regional Science Association*, **62**, 71–80.

Coffey, W. J. & Polèse, M. (1989), Producer Services and Regional Development: A Policy-Oriented Perspective. *Papers, Regional Science Association*, **67**, 13–27.

Coffey, W. J. & Polèse, M. (1990), *The Trade and Location of Producer Services*. Paper, North American Regional Science Association Meetings, Boston.

Cohen, S. C. & Zysman, J. (1987), *Manufacturing Matters: The Myth of the Post-industrial Economy*. New York: Basic Books.

Commission of the European Communities (1990), *Business Services in the European Community: Situation and Role*. Brussels.

Commission of the European Communities (1993), *White Paper: Growth, Competitiveness and Employment: The Challenges and Ways Forward into the 21st Century*. Luxemburg.

Cronberg, T. (1987), *Det tekniske spillerum i hverdagen*. København: Nyt fra samfundsvidenskaberne.

Cuadrado Roura, J. R. (1990), Services and New Information Technologies—Producer Services, pp. 195–226 in R. Cappellin & P. Nijkamp (eds), *The Spatial Context of Technological Development*. Aldershot: Avebury.

Dahlström, M. (1993), *Service Production: Uneven Development and Local Solutions in Swedish Child Care*. Uppsala: Kulturgeografiska Institutionen.

Dale, B. (1994), *Service og samfunn i endring*. Trondheim: Geografisk Institutt.

Daniels, P. W. (1985), *Service Location: A Geographical Appraisal*. London: Methuen.

Daniels, P. W. (1987), *Supply and Demand for Intermediate Services.: An Exploratory Study of Firms on Merseyside*. Lampeter: St David's College/University of Liverpool.

Daniels, P. W. (1988), Competition, Diversification, Internationalization and the Location of Business Services in Britain. *Revue d'Economie Industrielle*, **43**, 49–69.

Daniels, P. W. (1989), Moving Out of Metropolitan Economic Crisis: The Role of Tertiary Industries, pp. 63–76 in *Papers de Seminari*, 32. Barcelona: Centre d'Estudis de Planifació.

Daniels, P. W. (1991a), Do Producer Services Matter? pp. 7–19 in *Services, Espace et réseaux*. Milano: RESER.

Daniels, P. W. (1991b), Service Sector Restructuring and Metropolitan Development: Processes and Prospects, pp. 1–25 in P. W. Daniels (ed.), *Services and Metropolitan Development*. London: Routledge.

Daniels, P. W. (1993a), *Spatial and Sectoral Specialization of Producer Services: Implications for the UK in the 1990s*. Paper, 3rd Annual RESER Conference, Siracusa.

Daniels, P. W. (1993b), *Service Industries in the World Economy*. Oxford: Blackwell.

Daniels, P. W. (1995), The Locational Geography of Advanced Producer Services Firms in the United Kingdom, pp. 123–138 in F. Moulaert & F. Tödtling (eds), The Geography of Advanced Producer Services in Europe. *Progress in Planning*, **43**, 2–3.

de Bandt, J. (1988), Le débat sur la productivité dans les services: Des problèmes mal posés. *Revue d'Economie Industrielle*, **43**, 179–195.

de Bandt, J. (1991a), L'Economie de service, pp. 39–49 in J. de Bandt (dir), *Les services: Productivité et prix*. Paris: Economica.

de Bandt, J. (1991b), Les paradoxes de la productivité dans les activités de service, pp. 51–73 in J. de Bandt (dir), *Les services: Productivité et prix*. Paris: Economica.

de Bandt, J. (1991c), La productivité telle qu'on la mesure, pp. 115–135 in J. de Bandt (dir), *Les services: Productivité et prix*. Paris: Economica.

de Bandt, J. (1994a), La notion de marché est-elle transposable dans le domaine des services informationnels aux entreprises? pp. 217–240 in J. de Bandt & J. Gadrey (dir), *Relations de service, marchés de services*. Paris: CNRS.

de Bandt, J. (1994b), De l'économie des biens à l'économie des services: La production de richesses dans et par les services, pp. 309–338 in J. de Bandt & J. Gadrey (dir), *Relations de service, marchés de services*. Paris: CNRS.

de Bandt, J. (1995), *Services aux entreprises*. Paris: Economica.

de Jong, M. W. (1990), *Innovation in the Producer Services*. Paper, Progress Seminar on the Service Economy, Geneva.

de Jong, M. W. & Lambooy, J. G. (1984), *De informatica-sector centraal: Perspectieven voor de Amsterdamse binnenstad*. Amsterdam: Economisch-geografisch Instituut.

de Jong, M. W., Machielse, K. & de Ruijter, P. A. (1992), Producer Services and Flexible Networks in the Netherlands, pp. 147–162 in H. Ernste & V. Meier (eds), *Regional Development and Contemporary Industrial Response*. London: Belhaven.

Delaunay, J.-C. & Gadrey, J. (1987), *Les enjeux de la société de service*. Paris: Presses de la Fondation Nationale des Sciences Politiques. Partially translated in 1992 as *Services in Economic Thought: Three Centuries of Debate*. Dordrecht: Kluwer.

Delgado, A. P. (1991), *Small Manufacturing Firms and Producer Services: Linkages and Regional Impacts*. Paper, 31st European Regional Science Congress, Lisbon.

Department of the Taoiseach (1993), *Report of the Task Force on Jobs in Services*. Dublin: The Stationery Office.

Dicken, P. (1992), *Global Shift*. 2nd edn. London: Chapman.

Dowall, D. E. (1987), Back Offices and San Francisco's Office Development Growth Cap. *Cities*, **4**, 2, 119–127.

Drennan, M. P. (1989), Information Intensive Activities in Metropolitan Areas of the United States of America. *Environment and Planning A*, **21**, 1603–1618.

Drennan, M. P. (1992), Gateway Cities: The Metropolitan Sources of United States Producer Services Exports. *Urban Studies*, **29**, 217–235.

Ecalle, F. (1987), Croissance de l'emploi dans les services: L'exemple américain. *Futuribles*, **110**, 49–69.

Ecalle, F. (1989), *L'Economie des services*. Paris: Presses Universitaires de France.

ECONAnalyse (1995), Tusen blomster: Lønn, skatt og sysselsetting i ni industriland, Del 1, bilag 7 til Kommissionen om fremtidens erhvervs- og beskæftigelsesmuligheder, *Velstand og velfærd*. København: Erhvervsministeriet.

Edvardsson, B., Fureh, T. & Karlsson, C. (1987), *Medelstora städer och privata producenttjänster*. Karlstad: Centrum för Tjänsteforskning.

Ehrlich, E. (1990), *Study on the Present State and Future Development Tendencies of Hungarian Infrastructure and Services*. Paper, Progress Seminar on the Service Economy,

Geneva.
Ehrlich, E. (1994), International Tendencies: Infrastructure and Services in Hungary, pp. 7–53 in G. Csáki (ed.), *Transition—Infrastructure*. Budapest: Institute for World Economics.
Eiglier, P. & Langeard, E. (1987), *Servuction: Le marketing des services*. Paris: McGraw-Hill.
Elfring, T. (1988), *Service Employment in Advanced Economies: A Comparative Analysis of its Implications for Economic Growth*. Aldershot: Avebury.
Elfring, T. & Kloosterman, R. C. (1990), *The Dutch 'Job Machine': The Fast Growth of Low-Wage Jobs in Services 1979–1986*. Paper, Progress Seminar on the Service Economy.
Eliasson, G. (1990). The Knowledge-Based Information Economy, pp. 9–87 in G. Eliasson et al, *The Knowledge-Based Information Economy*. Stockholm: IUI/Almqvist & Wiksell.
Ellger, C. (1988), *Informationssektor und räumliche Entwicklung—dargestellt am Beispiel Baden-Württembergs*. Tübingen: Geographisches Institut der Universität.
Ellger, C. (1995), *Planning Christallerian Landscapes: The Current Renaissance of Central Place Studies in East Germany*. Paper, 5th Annual RESER Conference, Aix-en-Provence.
Engel, C. (1857), Die Produktions- und Consumptionsverhältnisse des Königreiches Sachsen. *Zeitschrift des statistischen Bureaus des königlichen sächsischen Ministerium des Innern*.
Erhvervsfremmestyrelsen (1994), *Serviceydelser—en erhvervsøkonomisk analyse*. København.
Esparza, A. (1992), Small Manufacturing Firm Business Service Externalization in the Chicago Metropolitan Region. *Urban Geography*, **13**, 68–86.
Fich, C. (1990), *Erhvervsservice i større byer*. Lyngby: Institut for Veje, Trafik og Byplan.
Finansministeriet (1992), *Vejen til fuld beskæftigelse*. København.
Fisher, A. G. B. (1935), *The Clash of Progress and Security*. London: Macmillan.
Fontaine, C. (1987), *L'Expansion des services: Un quart de siècle en France et dans le monde développé, I–III*. Paris: Rexervices.
Fourastié, J. (1949), *Le grand espoir du XXe siècle*. Paris: Presses Universitaires de France.
Fournier, S. F. & Axelsson, S. (1993), The Shift from Manufacturing to Services in Sweden. *Urban Studies*, **30**, 2, 285–298.
Gäbe, W. (1995), The Significance of Advanced Producer Services in the New German Länder, pp. 173–184 in F. Moulaert & F. Tödtling (eds), The Geography of Advanced Producer Services in Europe. *Progress in Planning*, **43**, 2–3.
Gäbe, W. & Strambach, S. (coord.) (1993), *Employment in Business Related Services: An Inter-Country Comparison of Germany, the United Kingdom, and France*. Stuttgart: Geographisches Institut Universität Stuttgart.
Gadrey, J. (1986a), *Société de services ou de self-services? Examen du cas français*. Lille: Johns Hopkins European Center for Regional Planning and Research.
Gadrey, J. (1986b), *Productivité et évaluation des services: La construction sociale du produit*. Lille: Université de Lille I.
Gadrey, J. (1987), Sur 'l'effet d'éponge' et le 'nouveau dualisme' des services. *Cahiers Lillois d'Economie et de Sociologie*, **9**, 73–85.
Gadrey, J. (1988a), Rethinking Output of Services. *The Service Industries Journal*, **8**, 1, 67–76.
Gadrey, J. (1988b), Productivité, Output médiat et immédiat des activités de services: Les difficultés d'un transfert des concepts, pp. 113–141 in O. Giarini & J. R. Roulet (dir), *L'Europe face à la nouvelle économie de service*. Paris: Presses Universitaires de France.
Gadrey, J. (1988c), Des facteurs de croissance des services aux rapports sociaux de service. *Revue d'Economie Industrielle*, **43**, 34–48.
Gadrey, J. (1991a), L'Insoutenable légèreté des analyses de productivité dans les services, pp. 137–151 in J. de Bandt (dir), Les services: *Productivité et prix*. Paris: Economica.

Gadrey, J. (1991b), Les systèmes d'emploi tertiaires: De la segmentation flexible aux approches typologiques, pp. 137–163 in J. Gadrey & N. Gadrey (dir), *La gestion des ressources humaines dans les services et le commerce*. Paris: L'Harmattan.

Gadrey, J. (1992a), *L'Economie des services*. Paris: La Découverte.

Gadrey, J. (1992b), Complexité et incertitude au coeur du besoin de services de conseil, pp. 157–175 in J. Gadrey et al, *Manager le conseil*. Paris: Ediscience international.

Gadrey, J. (1992c), Manager le recours aux consultants: Equilibre, complémentarité, interaction, pp. 177–193 in J. Gadrey et al, *Manager le conseil*. Paris: Ediscience international.

Gadrey, J. (1994a), Les relations de service dans le secteur marchand, pp. 23–41 in J. de Bandt & J. Gadrey (dir), *Relations de service, marchés de services*. Paris: CNRS.

Gadrey, J. (1994b), Relations, contrats et conventions de service, pp. 123–151 in J. de Bandt & J. Gadrey (dir), *Relations de service, marchés de services*. Paris: CNRS.

Gadrey, J. (1994c), Relations de service et relations d'assurance dans la géographie des services, pp. 121–140 in J. Bonamy & N. May (dir), *Services et mutations urbaines: Questionnements et perspectives*. Paris: Anthropos/Economica

Gadrey, J. & de Bandt, J. (1994), Introduction: De l'économie des services à l'économie des relations de services, pp. 1–7 in J. de Bandt & J. Gadrey (dir), *Relations de service, marchés de services*. Paris: CNRS.

Gadrey, J. & Gadrey, N. (dir) (1991), *La gestion des ressources humaines dans les services et le commerce*. Paris: L'Harmattan.

Gadrey, J. & Gallouj, C. (1988), *Enquête régionale sur les sociétés de services aux entreprises*. Lille: Chambre Régionale de Commerce et d'Industrie Nord-Pas-de-Calais.

Gadrey, J., Noyelle, T. & Stanback, T. (1991), *La productivité dans les services aux Etats-Unis et en France, I-II*. Lille: Université de Lille I.

Galibert, A. & Le Dem, J. (1986), Les services au secours de l'emploi? Une analyse comparée des évolutions en France, en Allemagne, aux Etats-Unis et au Japon. *Economie prospective Internationale*, **28**, 5–35.

Gallouj, C. (1993), *Les enjeux et dynamiques du développement des marchés régionaux de services aux entreprises: Le cas de la région Nord-Pas-de-Calais*. Lille: Université des Sciences et Technologies de Lille.

Gallouj, C. (1995), *Le commerce interrégional des services aux entreprises: Une revue de la littérature*. Lille: LAST-CLERSE.

Gentle, C. & Howells, J. (1994), The Computer Services Industry: Restructuring for a Single European Market. *Tijdscrift voor Economische en Sociale Geografie*, **85**, 4, 311–321.

Gershuny, J. (1978), *After Industrial Society: The Emerging Self-service Economy*. London & Basingstoke: Macmillan.

Gershuny, J. (1986), Employment and the Service Economy. In *The Emergence of the Service Economy*. Services World Economy Series.

Gershuny, J. & Miles, I. (1983), *The New Service Economy: The Transformation of Employment in Industrial Societies*. London: Frances Pinter.

Ghibutiu, A. (1990), *The Reassessment of Services in the Romanian Economy: A Prerequisite of its Future Development and Integration in Europe*. Paper, Seminar on the Role of Services in the Socio-Economic Transformation, Budapest.

Ghibutiu, A. (1994), *Business Services as Instruments of Economic Development in Central and Eastern Europe: The Case of Romania*. Paper, Progress Seminar on the Service Economy, Prague.

Giarini, O. (1988), Les nouvelles conditions du progrès économique: De la rigidité de l'offre à l'économie de service. *Revue d'Economie Industrielle*, **43**, 196–205.

Giarini, O. & Roulet, J. R. (1988), La relance des activités productives par l'économie de service. In O. Giarini & J. R. Roulet (dir), *L'Europe face à la nouvelle économie de service*. Paris: Presses Universitaires de France.

Giarini, O. & Stahel, W. R. (1989), *The Limits to Certainty: Facing Risks in the New Service Economy*. Dordrecht: Kluwer.

Gillespie, A. E. & Green. A. E. (1987), The Changing Geography of Producer Services Employment in Britain. *Regional Studies*, **21**, 5, 397–411.

Gillis, W. R. (1987), Can Service-Producing Industries Provide a Catalyst for Regional Economic Growth? *Economic Development Quarterly*, **1**, 249–256.

Gilly, J.-P. (1990), *Sociétés de services, production de technologies et développement urbain: Le cas des activités spatiales à Toulouse*. Paper, European Regional Science Congress, Istanbul.

Glasmeier, A. & Borchard, G. (1989), From Branch Plants to Back Offices: Prospects for Rural Services Growth. *Environment and Planning A*, **21**, 1565–1584.

Glasmeier, A. & Howland, M. (1994), Service-Led Rural Development: Definitions, Theories, and Empirical Evidence. *International Regional Science Review*, **16**, 1–2, 197–229.

Godbout, T. M. (1993), Employment Change and Sectoral Distribution in 10 Countries. *Monthly Labor Review*, **116**, Oct., 3–20.

Goddard, J. B. (1975), *Office Location in Urban and Regional Development*. Oxford: Oxford University Press.

Goddard, J. B. & Morris, D. (1976), The Communications Factor in Office Decentralization. *Progress in Planning*, **6**, 1–80.

Goe, W. R. (1990), Producer Services, Trade and the Social Division of Labour. *Regional Studies*, **24**, 4, 327–342.

Goe, W. R. (1991), The Growth of Producer Service Industries: Sorting Through the Externalization Debate. *Growth and Change*, **22**, 4, 118–141.

Gottmann, J. (1961), *Megalopolis: The Urbanized Northeastern Seaboard of the United States*. New York: Twentieth Century Fund.

Green, M. J. (1985), The Development of Market Services in the European Communities, the United States and Japan. *European Economy*, **25**, 69–96.

Greffe, X., Arnaud, G. & Leprince, F. (1990), *Nouvelles demandes, nouveaux services*. Paris: La documentation française.

Grönroos, C. (1990), *Service Management and Marketing*. Boston: Lexington.

Groshen, E. L. (1987), Can Services be a Source of Export-Led Growth? Evidence from the Fourth District. *Economic Review*, Federal Reserve Bank of Cleveland, 3rd quarter, p. 2–15.

Gruhler, W. (1990), *Dienstleistungsbestimmter Strukturwandel in deutschen Industrie-unternehmen*. Köln: Deutscher Instituts-Verlag.

Hall, P., Breheny, M., McQuaid, R. & Hart, D. (1987), *Western Sunrise: The Genesis and Growth of Britain's Major High Technology Corridor*. London: Allen & Unwin.

Hansen, N. (1990), Do Producer Services Induce Regional Economic Development? *Journal of Regional Science*, **30**, 4, 465–476.

Hansen, N. (1994), The Strategic Role of Producer Services in Regional Development. *International Regional Science Review*, **16**, 1–2, 187–195.

Harrington, J. W., Macpherson, A. D. & Lombard, J. R. (1991), Interregional Trade in Producer Services: Review and Synthesis. *Growth and Change*, **22**, 4, 75–94.

Haug, P. (1991), Regional Formation of High-technology Service Industries: The Software Industry in Washington State. *Environment and Planning A*, **23**, 869–884.

Hepworth, M. (1989), *Geography of the Information Economy*. London: Belhaven.

Hessels, M. (1992), *Locational Dynamics of Business Services: An Intrametropolitan Study on the Randstad Holland*. Utrecht: Geografisch Instituut Rijksuniversiteit Utrecht.

Hill, T. P. (1977), On Goods and Services. *Review of Income and Wealth*, **23**, 315–338.

Hirschhorn, L. (1988), The Post-Industrial Economy: Labour, Skills, and the New Mode of Production. *The Service Industries Journal*, **8**, 1, 19–38.

Hjalager, A.-M. (1986), *Lokal erhvervspolitik i informationssamfundet.* Århus: Nellemann.
Holloway, S. R. & Wheeler, J. O. (1991), Corporate Headquarters Relocation and Changes in Metropolitan Corporate Dominance, 1980–1987. *Economic Geography*, **67**, 1, 54–74.
Hutton, T. & Ley, D. (1987), Location, Linkages, and Labor: The Downtown Complex of Corporate Activities in a Medium Size City, Vancouver British Columbia. *Economic Geography*, **63**, 2, 126–141.
Illeris, S. (1972), *Lokaliseringen af liberale erhverv og erhvervsservice.* København: Landsplanudvalgets sekretariat.
Illeris, S. (1985), How to Analyse the Role of Services in Regional Development, pp. 1–22 in M. J. Bannon & S. Ward (eds), *Services and the New Economy: Implications for National and Regional Development.* Dublin: Regional Studies Association.
Illeris, S. (1989a), Producer Services: The Key Factor for Future Economic Development? *Entrepreneurship and Regional Development*, **1**, 267–274.
Illeris, S. (1989b), Service Activities and Regional Development in Western Europe, pp. 131–144 in L. S. Bourne et al (eds), *The Changing Geography of Urban Systems.* Pamplona: Universidad de Navarra.
Illeris, S. (1989c), Formal Employment and Informal Work in Household Services. *The Service Industries Journal*, **9**, 1, 94–109.
Illeris, S. (1989d), Produktivitet i privat og offentlig service, pp. 106–118 in S. Illeris & C. Boll (red), *Borgeren og det offentlige.* København: AKF.
Illeris, S. (1989e), *Services and Regions in Europe.* Aldershot: Avebury.
Illeris, S. (1990), Local and Distant Service Provision, pp. 127–152 in S. Illeris & L. Jakobsen (eds), *Networks and Regional Development.* Copenhagen: NordREFO.
Illeris, S. (1991a), Location of Services in a Service Society, pp. 91–107 in P. W. Daniels & F. Moulaert (eds), *The Changing Geography of Advanced Producer Services.* London: Belhaven.
Illeris, S. (1991b), Serviceproduktionen i Østeuropa—eller manglen på samme. *Nordisk Samhällsgeografisk Tidskrift*, **13**, 37–43.
Illeris, S. (1991c), *Ungarn under forvandling: Udviklingsmuligheder for små virksomheder i Tolna amt.* Roskilde: Institut for Geografi, Samfundsanalyse og Datalogi.
Illeris, S. (1991d), The Many Roads Towards a Service Society. *Norsk Geografisk Tidsskrift*, **45**, 1, 1–10.
Illeris, S. (1991e), Små, eksporterende industrivirksomheder i Jyllands udkantamter, pp. 90–105 in N. Veggeland (red), *Småforetaket—økonomiens nye motor.* København: NordREFO.
Illeris, S. (1994a), Proximity between Service Producers and Service Users. *Tijdschrift voor Economische en Sociale Geografie*, **85**, 4, 294–302.
Illeris, S. (1994b), *Essays on Regional Development in Europe.* Roskilde: Department of Geography and International Development Studies.
Illeris, S. & Jakobsen, L. (1991), Computer Services and the Urban System. A Case Study in Denmark, pp. 39–45 in D. Pumain, T. Saint-Julien & H. van der Haegen (eds), *Cities in Movement.* Leuven: Katholijke Universiteit.
Illeris, S., Kongstad, P. & Larsen, F. (1966), Servicecentre i Midtjylland og teori for servicecentre. *Geografisk Tidsskrift*, **65**, 27–47.
Illeris, S. & Rasmussen, J. (1992), *Regionalisering af teknologisk service: En evaluering af Industriministeriets initiativ.* Roskilde: Institut for Geografi, Samfunds-analyse og Datalogi.
Illeris, S. & Sjøholt, P. (1994), *The Regional Distribution of Producer Services in the EC and the Nordic Countries.* Roskilde: Department of Geography and International Development Studies.
Illeris, S. & Sjøholt, P. (1995), The Nordic Countries: High Quality Services in a Low Density Environment, pp. 205–221 in F. Moulaert & F. Tödtling (eds), The Geography of

Advanced Producer Service in Europe. *Progress in Planning*, **43**, 2–3.
Jaeger, C. & Dürrenberger, G. (1991), Services and Counterurbanization: The Case of Central Europe, pp. 107–128 in P. W. Daniels (ed.), *Services and Metropolitan Development: International Perspectives*. London: Routledge.
Jönsson, B. (1986), *Tillverkningsindustrins inköp av uppdragstjänster år 1985*. Stockholm: Statens Industriverk.
Kaldor, N. (1966), *The Causes of the Slow Rate of Growth in the United Kingdom*. Cambridge: Cambridge University Press.
Keeble, D., Bryson, J. & Wood, P. A. (1991), Small firms, Business Services Growth and Regional Development in the UK: Some Empirical Findings. *Regional Studies*, **25**, 5, 439–457.
Keeble, D., Bryson, J. & Wood, P. A. (1992), Entrepreneurship and Flexibility in Business Services: The Rise of Small Management Consultancy and Market Research Firms in the UK. Ch. 4 in K. Caley et al (eds), *Small Enterprise Development*. London: Chapman.
Keeble, D. & Schwalbach, J. (1995), *Management Consultancy in Europe*. Cambridge: ESRC Centre for Business Research.
Kellerman, A. (1993), *Telecommunications and Geography*. London: Belhaven.
Kelly, D. (1995), The Quantity and Quality of Service Sector Job Gains. *The Service Economy*, **12**, 2, 12–14.
Kirn, T. (1987), Growth and Change in the Service Sector of the US: A Spatial Perspective. *Annals of the Association of American Geographers*, **77**, 3, 353–372.
Kostecki, M. M. (1994), *Service Economies in Eastern Europe: A Framework for Inquiry*. Paper, Conference on Service Economies in Eastern Europe, Neuchâtel.
Kristensen, N. B. (1989), *Empirisk belysning af servicesektorens udvikling i Danmark siden 1966*. København: Danmarks Statistik.
Kristiansen, S. (1992), Personlige bostedspreferanser som bestemmende lokaliserings-faktor for kunnskapsbasert tjenesteyting, pp. 33–53 in S. Illeris & P. Sjøholt (red), *Internationalisering af service og regional udvikling i Norden*. København: NordREFO.
Kutay, A. (1986), Optimum Office Location and the Comparative Statistics of Information Economies. *Regional Studies*, **20**, 6, 551–564.
Kutscher, R. E. (1988), Growth of Services Employment in the United States, pp. 47–75 in B. R. Guile & J. B. Quinn (eds), *Technology in Services*. Washington: National Academy Press.
Lambooy, J. G. (1989), Coûts transactionnels et informationnels: La croissance des services aux entreprises, pp. 93–104 in F. Moulaert (ed.), *La production des services et sa géographie*. Lille: Université de Lille I.
Lambooy, J. G. & Tordoir, P. P. (1986), Professional Services and Regional Development: A Conceptual Approach, pp. 50–76 in S. Illeris (ed.), *Seminar on the Present and Future Role of Services in Regional Development*. Brussels: Commission of the European Communities.
Lamonde, P. & Martineau, Y. (1992), *Désindustrialisation et restructuration économique: Montréal et les autres grandes métropoles nord-américaines, 1971–1991*. Montréal: Institut National de la Recherche Scientifique—Urbanisation.
Larsen, J. N. (1992), Teknisk rådgivning—eksempel på samspillet mellem industri og service? pp. 83–104 in S. Illeris & P. Sjøholt (red), *Internationalisering af service og regional udvikling i Norden*. København: NordREFO.
Lensink, E. (1989), *Intermediaire diensten in landelijke gebieden: Een economisch-geografisch onderzoek in een rurale omgeving*. Nijmegen: Faculteit der beleidsweten-schappen.
Léo, P.-Y. & Philippe, J. (1991), Networks and Producer Services: Local Markets and Global Development, pp. 305–324 in P. W. Daniels (ed.), *Services and Metropolitan Development: International Perspectives*. London: Routledge.

Littek, W., Heisig, U. & Gondek, H.-D. (1991), Dienstleistungsarbeit, Angestellten-soziologie: Alte und neue Themen. In W. Littek, U. Heisig & H. D. Gondek (Hg), *Dienstleistungsarbeit*. Berlin: Sigma.

Lundmark, M. (1994), *Databranschen i Sverige—framväxt och lokalisering*. Stockholm: ERU.

Lyons, D. I. (1994), Changing Patterns of Corporate Headquarter Influence, 1974–89. *Environment and Planning A*, **26**, 733–747.

Machlup, F. (1962), *The Production and Distribution of Knowledge in the United States*. Princeton, NJ: Princeton University Press.

Maciejewicz, J. & Monkiewicz, J. (1989), Changing Role of Services in the Socialist Countries of Eastern Europe. *The Service Industries Journal*, **9**, 3, 384–398.

Madsen, P. T. (1989), *Servicesektoren og dens produktivitetsudvikling I–II*. Aalborg: Aalborg Universitetscenter.

Maillat, D. (1990), *Producer Services and Territorial Production Systems*. Neuchâtel: Université de Neuchâtel.

Malecki, E. J. (1987), The R&D Location Decision of the Firm and 'Creative' Regions: A Survey. *Technovation*, **6**, 205–222.

Malecki, E. J. & Bradbury, S. L. (1990), *Locational Decision-Making of R&D Facilities and Professional Labor*. Paper, North American Regional Science Meetings, Boston.

Manenti, Y. (1993), *Tension entre logiques artisanales et industrielles dans les petites entreprises de conseil en management*. Paper, 3rd Annual RESER Conference, Siracusa.

Marshall, J. N. (1989), Private Services in an Era of Change. *Geoforum*, **20**, 3, 365–379.

Marshall, J. N. (1990), The Dynamics of Producer Services, pp. 167–193 in R. Cappellin & P. Nijkamp (eds), *The Spatial Context of Technological Development*. Aldershot: Avebury.

Marshall, J. N. (1994), Business Reorganisation and the Development of Corporate Services in Metropolitan Areas. *Geographical Journal*, **160**, 41–49.

Marshall, J. N. et al (1988), *Service and Uneven Development*. Oxford: Oxford University Press.

Marshall, J. N. & Bachtler, J. (1987), Services and Regional Policy. *Regional Studies*, **21**, 5, 471–475.

Marshall, J. N. & Jaeger, C. (1990), Service Activities and Uneven Spatial Development in Britain and its European Partners: Determinist Fallacies and New Options. *Environment and Planning A*, **22**, 10, 1337–1354.

Marshall, J. N. & Raybould, S. (1993), New Corporate Structures and the Evolving Geography of White Collar Work. *Tijdschrift voor Economische en Sociale Geografie*, **84**, 5, 362–377.

Marshall J. N. & Wood, P. A. (1992), The Role of Services in Urban and Regional Development: Recent Debates and New Directory. *Environment and Planning A*, **24**, 1255–1270.

Marshall, J. N. & Wood, P. A. (1995), *Services and Space: Key Aspects of Urban and Regional Development*. Harlow: Longman.

Martinelli, F. (1989a), Productive Organization and Service Demand in Italian Textile and Clothing 'Districts': A Case Study, pp. 275–322 in *Services and Development Potential: The Indian Context*. United Nations.

Martinelli, F. (1989b), Business Services, Innovation and Regional Policy: Consideration of the Case of Southern Italy, pp. 10–26 in L. Albrechts et al (eds), *Regional Policy at the Crossroads*. London: Jessica Kingsley.

Martinelli, F. (1991a), A Demand-Orientated Approach to Understanding Producer Services, pp. 15–29 in P. W. Daniels & F. Moulaert (eds), *The Changing Geography of Advanced Producer Services*. London: Belhaven.

Martinelli, F. (1991b), Producer Services' Location and Regional Development, pp. 70–90 in

P. W. Daniels & F. Moulaert (eds), *The Changing Geography of Advanced Producer Services*. London: Belhaven.

Martinelli, F. (1991c), Branch Plants and Services Underdevelopment in Peripheral Regions: The Case of Southern Italy, pp. 151–176 in P. W. Daniels & F. Moulaert (eds), *The Changing Geography of Advanced Producer Services*. London: Belhaven.

Maskell, P. (1987), *Danmarks fremtidige erhvervs-og samfundsmæssige udvikling: Ændringer inden for servicesektoren*. København: Teknologinævnet.

Maskell, P. (1993), *Liberale erhverv i Hovedstadsregionen og deres betydning for ejendomsmarkedet*. Frederiksberg: Samfundslitteratur.

Massey, D. (1979), In What Sense a Regional Problem? *Regional Studies*, **13**, 233–243.

Massey, D., Quintas, P. & Wield, D. (1992), *High Tech Fantasies: Science Parks in Society*. London: Routledge.

May, N. (1994a), Service, espace et main d'oeuvre: Division spatiale du travail et marchés de l'emploi, pp. 55–77 in J. Bonamy & N. May (dir), *Services et mutations urbaines: Questionnements et perspectives*. Paris: Anthropos/Economica.

May, N. (1994b), Développement des services et transformations des configurations urbaines, pp. 79–92 in J. Bonamy & N. May (dir), *Services et mutations urbaines: Questionnements et perspectives*. Paris: Anthropos/Economica.

Mayère, A. (1988), *Information et système productif*. Lyons: Université Lumière.

Mayère, A. & Vinot, F. (1991), *Offre de services et dynamiques urbaines en Rhône-Alpes*. Lyons: INSEE Rhône-Alpes/Economie et Humanisme/CEDES.

Mayère, A. & Vinot, F. (1993), Firm Structures and Production Networks in Intellectual Services. *The Service Industries Journal*, **13**, 2, 76–90.

McKinsey Global Institute (1994), *Employment Performance*. Washington, DC.

Michalak, W. Z. & Fairbairn, K. J. (1988), Producer Services in Peripheral Economy. *Canadian Journal of Regional Science*, **11**, 3, 353–372.

Michalova, V. & Fronkova, V. (1990), *Economic Growth and Development in Services in Czechoslovakia: Past and Future*. Paper, Progress Seminar on the Service Economy, Geneva.

Miles, I. (1993), Services in the New Industrial Economy. *Futures*, July/Aug., 653–672.

Miskinis, A. (1990), *Services in Centralized Economies*. Paper, Progress Seminar on the Service Economy, Geneva.

Monnoyer, M.-C. (1993), Consultancy Companies and Their Regional Plants. *The Service Industries Journal*, **13**, 2, 107–117.

Moss, M. L. (1987), Telecommunications, World Cities, and Urban Policy. *Urban Studies*, **24**, 534–546.

Moulaert, F. & Gallouj, C. (1995), Advanced Producer Services in the French Space Economy: Decentralization at the Highest Level, pp. 139–154 in F. Moulaert & F. Tödtling (eds), The Geography of Advanced Producer Services in Europe. *Progress in Planning*, **43**, 2–3.

Moulaert, F., Martinelli, F. & Djellal, F. (1991), The Functional and Spatial Division of Labor of Information Technology Consultancy Firms in Europe, pp. 118–134 in P. W. Daniels & F. Moulaert (eds), *The Changing Geography of Advanced Producer Services*. London: Belhaven.

Moulaert, F., Tödtling, F. & Schamp, E. W. (1995), The Role of Transnational Corporations, pp. 107–122 in F. Moulaert & F. Tödtling (eds), The Geography of Advanced Producer Services in Europe. *Progress in Planning*, **43**, 2–3.

Moyart, L. (1995), *Place des services généraux aux entreprises dans le développement urbain*. Paper, 5th Annual RESER Conference, Aix-en-Provence.

Murphy, A. B. (1992), Western Investment in East Central Europe. *The Professional Geographer*, **44**, 3, 249–259.

Murray, R. (1992), Flexible Specialisation and Development Strategy: The Relevance for

Eastern Europe, pp. 197–218 in H. Ernste & V. Meier (eds), *Regional Development and Contemporary Industrial Response*. London: Belhaven.

Nelson, K. (1986), Labor Demand, Labor Supply and the Suburbanization of Low-Wage Office Work, pp. 149–171 in A. Scott & M. Storper (eds), *Production, Work, Territory*. London: Allen & Unwin.

Nielsen, B. & Sørensen, P. M. (1987), Den regionale udvikling—specielt indenfor erhvervsservice, pp. 63–79 in J. S. Pedersen & J. Sundbo (red), *Service—et spil om fremtid*. Frederiksberg: Samfundslitteratur.

Normann, R. (1984), *Service Management*. Chichester: John Wiley.

Noyelle, T. (1989), Business Services and the Uruguay Round: Negotiations on Trade in Services, pp. 309–363 in *Trade in Services*. New York: United Nations.

Noyelle, T. (ed.) (1990a), *Skills, Wages, and Productivity in the Service Sector*. Boulder, Col.: Westview Press.

Noyelle, T. (1990b), Toward a New Labor Market Segmentation, pp. 212–224 in T. Noyelle (ed.), *Skills, Wages, and Productivity in the Service Sector*. Boulder, Col: Westview Press.

Noyelle, T. (1990c), Business Services: Accounting, Management Consulting, and Computer Software, pp. 122–159 in T. Noyelle (ed.), *Skills, Wages, and Productivity in the Service Sector*. Boulder, Col: Westview Press.

Noyelle, T. (1990d), *Computer Software and Computer Services in India, Singapore, the Philippines, Hong Kong, and the Republic of Korea*. New York: Columbia University, Conservation of Human Resources.

Noyelle, T. (1991), Know-how, organisation et formation dans les services: Quelques hypothèses sur les facteurs de compétitivité des firmes américaines, pp. 203–219 in J. Gadrey & N. Gadrey (dir), *La gestion des ressources humaines dans les services et le commerce*. Paris: L'Harmattan.

Noyelle, T. (1994), Services et mutations urbaines aux Etats-Unis, pp. 210–238 in J. Bonamy & N. May (dir), *Services et mutations urbaines: Questionnements et perspectives*. Paris: Anthropos/Economica.

Noyelle, T. & Dutka, A. B. (1986), The Economics of the World Market for Business Services: Implications for Negotiations on Trade in Services, pp. 57–95 in *Barriers to International Trade in Professional Services*. Chicago: The University of Chicago.

Noyelle, T. & Peace, P. (1988), *The Information Industries: New York's New Export Base*. New York: Columbia University, Conservation of Human Resources.

Noyelle, T. & Stanback, T. M. (1984), *The Economic Transformation of American Cities*. Totowa NJ: Roman & Allanheld.

Noyelle, T. & Stanback, T. M. (1991), La productivité dans les services: Une mesure valable des performances économiques? pp. 77–107 in J. de Bandt (dir), *Les services: Productivité et prix*. Paris: Economica.

Nusbaumer, J. A. E. (1987), *The Service Economy: Lever to Growth*. Boston: Kluwer.

Ochel, W. & Wegner, M. (1987), *Service Economies of Europe: Opportunities for Growth*. London: Pinter.

OECD (1989), *The Improvement of Services to Industries as an Instrument of Regional Policy*. Paris.

OECD (1991), *Services in Central and Eastern European Countries*. Paris.

O'Farrell, P. N., Hitchens, D. M. & Moffat, L. A. R. (1993), The Competitiveness of Business Services and Regional Development: Evidence from Scotland and the South East of England. *Urban Studies*, **30**, 10, 1629–1652.

O'Farrell, P. N. & Moffat, L. A. R. (1995), Business Services and Their Impact on Client Performance: An Exploratory Interregional Analysis. *Regional Studies*, **29**, 2, 111–134.

O'Farrell, P. N., Moffat, L. A. R. & Hitchens, D. M. (1993), Manufacturing Demand for Business Services in a Core and Peripheral Region: A Process of Vertical Disintegration? *Regional Studies*, **27**, 5, 385–400.

O'Farrell, P. N., Wood, P. A. & Zheng, J. (1994), *Internationalisation of Business Services: Some Preliminary Evidence*. Paper, 4th Annual RESER Conference, Barcelona.

Ofer, G. (1990), *The Service Sector in Soviet Economic Reforms: Does Convergence Finally Arrive?* Paper, The Hebrew University, Jerusalem.

OhUallacháin, B. & Reid, N. (1991), The Location and Growth of Business and Professional Services in American Metropolitan Areas, 1976–1986. *Annals of the Association of American Geographers*, **81**, 2, 254–270.

Olivry, D. (1986), *Services to the Manufacturing Sector: A Long Term Investigation*. Brussels: Commission of the European Communities.

Ott, M. (1987), The Growing Share of Services in the US Economy: Degeneration or Evolution? *Review*, Federal Reserve Bank of St Louis, June/July, 5–22.

Pascal, A. (1987), The Vanishing City. *Urban Studies*, **24**, 597–603.

Patton, W. K. & Markusen, A. (1991), The Perils of Overstating Service Sector Growth Potential. *Economic Development Quarterly*, **5**, 3, 197–212.

Pedersen, P. O. (1986), *Business Service Strategies: The Case of the Provincial Centre of Esbjerg*. Brussels: Commission of the European Communities.

Perry, M. (1990), Business Service Specialization and Regional Economic Change. *Regional Studies*, **24**, 3, 195–209.

Perry, M. (1991), The Capacity of Producer Services to Generate Regional Economic Growth: Some Evidence from a Peripheral Metropolitan Economy. *Environment and Planning A*, **23**, 1331–1347.

Perry, M. (1992), Flexible Production, Externalisation and the Interpretation of Business Service Growth. *The Service Industries Journal*, **12**, 1, 1–16.

Petit, P. (1985), Les services: Un secteur abrité dans la crise, pp. 21–58 in J. de Bandt (dir), *Les services dans les sociétés industrielles*. Paris: Economica.

Petit, P. (1986), *Slow Growth and the Service Economy*. London: Frances Pinter.

Philippe, J. & Léo, P.-Y. (1993), La dynamique mercapolitaine: Une stratégie de développement pour les métropoles régionales. *Revue d'Economie Régionale et Urbaine*, **1**, 121–139.

Philippe, J. & Monnoyer, M.-C. (1989), Gestion de l'espace et développement des services aux entreprises. *Revue d'Economie Régionale et Urbaine*, **4**, 671–684.

Pinch, S. P. (1989), The Restructuring Thesis and the Study of Public Services. *Environment and Planning A*, **21**, 905–926.

Piore, M. J. & Sabel, C. (1984), *The Second Industrial Divide*. New York: Basic Books.

Planque, B. (1983), Une nouvelle organisation spatiale du développement, pp. 5–26 in B. Planque (coord.), *Le développement décentralisé*. Paris: Litec.

Planque, B. (1984), Télématique et réorganisation spatiale de l'industrie, pp. 25–38 in *Régions et politique industrielle*. Paris: Economica.

Plougmann, P. (1988), *Serviceerhverv og arbejdsmarkedspolitik i Norden i 1990erne*. København: Institut for Trafik-, Turist- og Regionaløkonomi.

Plougmann, P. (1994), Forbrugerservice og beskæftigelsesforventninger, pp. 49–85 in J. Sundbo & J. N. Larsen (red), *Forbrugsservice og vækst*. Frederiksberg: Samfundslitteratur.

Porat, M. U. (1977), *The Information Economy: Definition and Measurement*. Washington, DC: US Department of Commerce.

Porter, M. (1990), *The Competitive Advantage of Nations*. London: Macmillan.

Porterfield, S. L. & Pulver, G. C. (1991), Exports, Impacts, and Locations of Services Producers. *International Regional Science Review*, **14**, 1, 41–59.

Poulfeldt, F. (1990), *Profil af managementkonsulentbranchen i Danmark anno 1990*. København: Foreningen af Managementkonsulenter.

Pousette, T. & Lindberg, T. (1990), Services in Production and Production of Services in Swedish Manufacturing, pp. 117–133 in G. Eliasson et al, *The Knowledge-Based*

Information Economy. Stockholm: IUI/Almqvist & Wiksell.

Prosche, F. (1993), *Vers une Europe post-industrielle?* Paris: Economica.

Pye, R. (1979), Office Location: The Role of Communications and Technology, pp. 237–275 in P. W. Daniels (ed.), *Spatial Patterns of Office Growth and Location.* Chichester: John Wiley.

Quinn, J. B. (1988), Technology in Services: Past Myths and Future Challenges, pp. 16–46 in B. R. Guile & J. B. Quinn (eds), *Technology in Services: Policies for Growth, Trade, and Employment.* Washington, DC: National Academy Press.

Quinn, J. B. & Gagnon, G. (1986), Will Services Follow Manufacturing into Decline? *Harvard Business Review*, Nov./Dec., p. 95–103.

Quinn, J. B. & Doorley, T. L. (1988), Key Policy Issues Posed by Services, pp. 211–234 in B. R. Guile & J. B. Quinn (eds), *Technology in Services: Policies for Growth, Trade, and Employment.* Washington, DC: National Academy Press.

Quinn, J. B., Doorley, T. L. & Paquette, P. (1990), Beyond Products: Service-Based Strategy. *Harvard Business Review*, March/Apr., p. 58–67.

Rallet, A. (1994), *Réseaux de télécommunication, localisation des activités information- nelles et hiérarchie urbaine.* Paper, Colloque villes, entreprises et société à la veille du XXIe siècle, Lille.

Rappoport, P. (1987), Inflation in the Service Sector. *Quarterly Review*, Federal Reserve Bank New York, Winter, p. 35–45.

Rasmussen, J. (1992), Miljøservicesektoren i Storkøbenhavn, pp. 188–202 in S. Illeris & P. Sjøholt (red), *Internationalisering af service og regional udvikling i Norden.* København: NordREFO.

Rasmussen, J. (1993), Internationalisering af erhvervsservice—udfordring for erhvervspolitikken, pp. 113–128 in N. Veggeland (red), *Norden utfordres—internasjonal- iseringens mange regionale aspekter.* København: NordREFO.

Reich, R. B. (1991), *The Work of Nations.* New York: Vintage.

Rekkavik, J. & Spillum, P. (1990), *Tjenesteyting for næringslivet på ensidige industristeder.* Bergen: Norges Handelshøyskole.

RESER (1995), *Consultancy Services Networks in Europe.* Aix-en-Provence: Serdeco.

Richardson, R. (1994), *Teleservice Cities? Second Wave Back Offices and Employment in European Cities*, Paper, Colloque villes, entreprises et société à la veille du XXIe siècle, Lille.

Riddle, D. I. (1986), *Service-led Growth: The Role of the Service Sector in World Development.* New York: Praeger.

Ruyssen, O. (1987a), *L'Europe des services—un virage à réussir.* Bruxelles: Commission des Communautés Européennes.

Ruyssen, O. (1987b), *Services, technologies avancées et régions.* Bruxelles: Commission des Communautés Européennes.

Ruyssen, O. (1987c), The New Deal in Services: A Challenge for Europe. *The Service Industries Journal*, **7**, 4, 99–109.

Savage, M., Dickens, P. & Fielding, T. (1988), Some Social and Political Implications of the Contemporary Fragmentation of the 'Service Class' in Britain. *International Journal of Urban and Regional Research*, **12**, 3, 455–476.

Saxonhouse, G. R. (1985), Services in the Japanese Economy, pp. 53–83 in R. P. Inman (ed.), *Managing the Service Economy: Prospects and Problems.* Cambridge: Cambridge University Press.

Sayer, A. & Walker, R. (1992), *The New Social Economy: Reworking the Division of Labor.* Oxford: Blackwell.

Schamp, E. W. (1987), Business Services for Manufacturers: Demand Behaviour by Enterprises in Lower Saxony, pp. 270–291 in F. E. I. Hamilton (ed.), *Industrial Change in Advanced Economies.* London: Wolfeboro.

Schamp, E. W. (1995), The Geography of Advanced Producer Services in a Goods Exporting Economy: The Case of West Germany, pp. 155–172 in F. Moulaert & F. Tödtling (eds), The Geography of Advanced Producer Services in Europe. *Progress in Planning*, 43, 2–3.

Scharpf, F. W. (1985), *Strukturen der post-industriellen Gesellschaft, oder: Verschwindet die Massenarbeitslosigkeit in der Dienstleistungs- und Informations-ökonomie?* Berlin: Wissenschaftszentrum Berlin.

Schaumburg-Müller, H. (1987), *Small, Highly developed Countries' Specialization in Service Export: The Example of Denmark and Engineering Services.* Paper, Progress Seminar on the Service Economy, Geneva.

Scheuer, M. (1994), *Specific Business Services in Central Europe.* Paper, Conference Service Economies in Eastern Europe—Opportunities for Trade and Investments, Neuchâtel.

Schneider, O. (1993), The Problems of the Development of the Service Sector in Czechoslovakia, *The Service Industries Journal*, 13, 2, 132–143.

Selstad, T. (1987), Forretningsmessig tjenesteyting—motoren i den regionale utvikling, pp. 6–16 in Kommunal- og Arbeidsdepartementet, *Tiltaks- og utviklingsprogram for privat tjenesteytende virksomhet i distriktene, III.* Oslo.

Selstad, T. (1989), Informasjonsrevolusjonen i geografisk perspektiv, pp. 30–47 in T. Selstad & P. Sjøholt (red), *Søkelys på det tjenesteytende samfunn.* Bergen: Nærings-økonomisk Institutt.

Selstad, T. & Hagen, S. E. (1991), *Servicenæringer til besvær.* Lillehammer: Østlandsforskning.

Selstad, T. & Lie, T. (1987), *Innlands-Norge på vei mot kunnskapssamfunnet?* Lillehammer: Østlandsforskning.

Selya, R. M. (1994), Taiwan as a Service Economy. *Geoforum*, 25, 3, 305–322.

Senn, L. (1989), Développement économique et demande de services aux entreprises, pp. 143–164 in *Papers de Seminari 32*, Barcelona: Centre d'Estudis de Planificació.

Sheets, R. G., Nord, S. & Phelps, J. J. (1987), *The Impact of Service Industries on Underemployment in Metropolitan Economies.* Lexington, Mass.: Health & Co.

Shelp, R. (1981), *Beyond Industrialization: Ascendancy of the Global Service Economy.* New York: Praeger.

Silver, H. (1987), Only So Many Hours a Day: Time Constraints, Labor Pools, and Demand for Consumer Services. *The Service Industries Journal*, 7, 4, 26–45.

Siniscalco, D. (1989), Defining and Measuring Output and Productivity in the Service Sector, pp. 38–58 in H. Giersch (ed.), *Services in World Economic Growth.* Tübingen: J. B. Moor.

Sjøholt, P. (1990), Producer Services: A New Panacea for Marginal Regions? pp. 259–275 in L. Lundqvist & L. O. Persson (red), *Nätverk i Norden.* Stockholm: Allmänna Förlaget.

Sjøholt, P. (1992a), *Producer Services and Their Labour Market: A Geographical Interpretation and Differentiation.* Paper, 2nd Annual RESER Conference, Portsmouth.

Sjøholt, P. (1992b), Norsk eksport av tekniske rådgivningstjenester: Bakgrunn og noen vekstfaktorer, pp. 168–187 in S. Illeris & P. Sjøholt (red), *Internationalisering af service og regional udvikling i Norden.* København: NordREFO.

Sjøholt, P. (1993), The Dynamics of Services as an Agent of Regional Change and Development: The Case of Scandinavia. *The Service Industries Journal*, 12, 2, 36–50.

Sjøholt, P. (1994), The Role of Producer Services in Industrial and Regional Development: The Nordic Case. *European Urban and Regional Studies*, 1, 2, 115–129.

Skodvin, O.-J. (1987), *Tenesteyting og sysselsetting i Grenland.* Oslo: Universitetet i Oslo.

Skolka, J. (1976), The Substitution of Self-Service Activities for Marketed Services. *The Review of Income and Wealth*, 4, 297–304.

Skolka, J. (1989), Eigenleistungen, Zeit und Unabhängigkeit. *Wirtschaft und Gesellschaft*, 15, 4, 563–583.

Sofianou, Z. (1994), Anatomy of the Canadian Recession. *The Service Economy*, 8, 2, 13–17.

Springer, B. & Riddle, D. I. (1987), Women in Service Industries: European Communities— United States Comparisons. *Policy Studies Review*, Winter, p. 77–94.

Stabler, J. C. & Howe, E. C. (1988), Service Exports and Regional Growth in the Postindustrial Era. *Journal of Regional Science*, **28**, 3, 303–316.

Stabler, J. C. & Howe, E. C. (1992), Services, Trade, and Regional Structural Change in Canada 1974–1984. *Review of Urban and Regional Development Studies*.

Stambøl, L. S. (1988), *Tjenesteyting og sysselsetting på Romerike*. Oslo: Universitetet i Oslo.

Stanback, T. M. & Noyelle, T. (1990), Productivity in Services: A Valid Measure of Economic Performance? pp. 187–211 in T. Noyelle (ed.), *Skills, Wages, and Productivity in the Service Sector*. Boulder, Col: Westview.

Statens Industriverk (1986), *Tjänster inom industrin*. Stockholm.

Statens Industriverk (1989), *Privat tjänstesektor*. Stockholm: Allmänna Förlaget.

Strambach, S. (1994), Knowledge-Intensive Business Services in the Rhine–Neckar Area. *Tijdschrift voor Economische en Sociale Geografie*, **85**, 4, 354–365.

Strassmann, P. A. (1985), *Information Pay-Off: The Transformation of Work in the Electronic Age*. New York: The Free Press.

Sundbo, J. (1992), Drivkræfter bag servicevirksomheders internationalisering: Kulturbarrierer som internationaliseringsfaktor, pp. 203–225 in S. Illeris & P. Sjøholt (red), *Internationalisering af service og regional udvikling i Norden*. København: NordREFO.

Sundbo, J. (1994), Udviklingsmuligheder for service rettet mod private husholdninger, pp. 33–47 in J. Sundbo & J. N. Larsen (red), *Forbrugsservice og vækst*. Frederiksberg: Samfundslitteratur.

Swyngedouw, E., Lemattre, M. & Wells, P. (1992), The Regional Patterns of Computing and Communications Industries in the UK and France, pp. 79–128 in P. Cooke et al, *Towards Global Localization: The Computing and Telecommunications Industries in Britain and France*. London: University College London Press.

Thorngren, B. (1970), How do Contact Systems Affect Regional Development? *Environment and Planning*, **2**, p. 409–427.

Thwaites, A. & Alderman, N. (1990), The Location of Industrial R&D: Retrospect and Prospect, pp. 17–42 in R. Cappellin & P. Nijkamp (eds), *The Spatial Context of Technological Development*. Aldershot: Avebury.

Toffler, A. (1970), *Future Shock*. London: Bodley Head.

Toffler, A. (1980), *The Third Wave*. London: Collins.

Tordoir, P. P. (1991), Advanced Office Activities in the Randstad-Holland Metropolitan Region: Location, Complex Formation and International Orientation, pp. 226–244 in P. W. Daniels (ed.), *Services and Metropolitan Development*. London: Routledge.

Tordoir, P. P. (1992), Le conseil en management: Structure du secteur, concurrence et stratégies, pp. 29–47 in J. Gadrey et al, *Manager le conseil*. Paris: Ediscience International.

Tordoir, P. P. (1993), *The Professional Knowledge Economy*. Amsterdam: University of Amsterdam.

Tordoir, P. P. (1994), Transactions of Professional Business Services and Spatial Systems. *Tijdschrift voor Economische en Sociale Geografie*, **85**, 4, 322–332.

Törnqvist, G. (1970), *Contact Systems and Regional Development*. Lund: Gleerup.

Touraine, A. (1967), *La société post-industrielle*. Paris: Denoël.

Townsend, A. (1991), Services and Local Economic Development. *Area*, **23**, 4, 309–317.

Townsend, A. & Macdonald, K. (1994), *Sales of Business Services from a European City*. Paper, 4th Annual RESER Conference, Barcelona.

Urry, J. (1992), The Service Economy and the Politics of Place. In A. Scott & M. Storper (eds), *Pathways to Industrialisation and Regional Development*. London: Routledge.

Vandermerwe, S. (1993), *From Tin Soldiers to Russian Dolls: Creating Added Value*

Through Services. Oxford: Butterworth-Heinemann.

van Dinteren, J. H. J. (1989), *Zakelijke diensten in middelgrote steden*. Amsterdam: Koninklijke Nederlands Aardrijkskundig Genootschap.

van Dinteren, J. H. J. & Meuwissen, J. A. M. (1994), Business Services in the Core Area of the European Union. *Tijdschrift voor Economische en Sociale Geografir*, **85**, 4, 366–370.

Walker, R. A. (1985), Is There a Service Economy? The Changing Capitalist Division of Labor. *Science & Society*, **XLIX**, 42–83.

Warf, B. (1991), The Internationalization of New York Services, pp. 245–264 in P. W. Daniels (ed.), *Services and Metropolitan Development*. London: Routledge.

Webber, M. M. (1964), The Urban Place and the Nonplace Urban Realm, pp. 79–153 in M. M. Webber et al, *Explorations into Urban Future*. Philadelphia: University of Pennsylvania Press.

Williamson, O. (1985), *The Economic Institutions of Capitalism*. New York: The Free Press.

Wilson, M. (1993), The Office Farther Back: Business Services, Productivity, and the Offshore Back Office. In P. Harker (ed.), *The Service Quality and Productivity Challenge*. Dordrecht: Kluwer.

Wilson, M. (1994), *Offshore Relations and Producer Services: The Irish Back Office*. Paper, Michigan State University.

Wood, P. A. (1989), *The Single European Market and Producer Services Location in the United Kingdom*, Portsmouth: Portsmouth Polytechnic.

Wood, P. A. (1993a), *Regional Patterns of Business Service Externalisation in the UK: An Expert Labour Approach*. Paper: 3rd Annual RESER Conference, Siracusa.

Wood, P. A. (1993b), *Implications for Employment Policy of the Growth of Business Services in the UK during the 1980s and 1990s*. London: University College.

Wood, P. A. (1994), *Consultant Use and the Management of Change: Insight into Expertise*. Paper, 4th Annual RESER Conference, Barcelona.

Wood, P. A., Bryson, J. & Keeble, D. (1993), Regional Patterns of Small Firm Development in the Business Services: Evidence from the United Kingdom. *Environment and Planning A*, **25**, 677–700.

Index